International Socialism 144

Autumn 2014

Contributors

Talat Ahmed is lecturer in South Asian History at the University of Edinburgh. She is the author of *Literature and Politics in the Age of Nationalism: the Progressive Episode in South Asia, 1932-56*, and contributor to *Say it Loud: Marxism and the Fight Against Racism*.

Des Barrow is a a Geography teacher and member of the SWP in Hackney.

Adrian Budd teaches politics at London South Bank University, where he is UCU branch secretary. He is the author of *Class, States and International Relations: A Critical Appraisal of Robert Cox and Neo-Gramscian Theory*

Kevin Corr is a retired school teacher and member of Newham SWP.

Mark Dunk is a full-time print worker and Unite member living in London.

Martin Empson is the author of *Land and Labour: Marxism, Ecology and Human History*.

Rob Ferguson is a teacher and activist in East London, and a member of Newham SWP. He undertook research on the Russian labour movement in the 1990s.

Nicola Ginsburgh is a postgraduate student at the University of Leeds and an SWP member.

Elizabeth Humphrys is completing a PhD in the Department of Political Economy, University of Sydney. Her research is on the relationship between neoliberalism and the Australian Labor Party-trade union social contact of 1983 to 1996. Her research blog is An Integral State (http://anintegralstate.net/).

Gareth Jenkins used to teach English literature at the University of Greenwich until he retired. He has recently contributed a piece on multiculturalism to *Race, Racism and Social Work: Contemporary Issues and Debates*, edited by Michael Lavalette and Laura Penketh (Policy Press, 2014). He is a member of the SWP in Hackney.

Charlie Kimber is the national secretary of the Socialist Workers Party. He recently visited South Africa.

Keir McKechnie is a member of the SWP in Glasgow. He is the author of the pamphlet *Yes to Independence—No to Nationalism* and is the chair of Stop the War Coalition Scotland.

John Newsinger is a member of Brighton SWP and author of *The Blood Never Dried: A People's History of the British Empire* and *Orwell's Politics*.

Tony Phillips is a long standing member of the SWP based in Walthamstow in London and is a Unison trade union branch secretary working in the fire service.

Xanthe Rose is a postgraduate student and a member of the SWP.

Sabby Sagall is chair of Camden Palestine Solidarity Campaign and author of *Final Solutions: Human Nature, Capitalism and Genocide*.

Miriam Scharf is a teacher and activist in Newham, East London.

David Szuster is a member of Glasgow SWP and a part-time customer service assistant.

Tad Tietze is a public hospital psychiatrist working in Sydney. He co-runs the politics blog Left Flank (http://left-flank.org/) and co-edited (with Elizabeth Humphrys and Guy Rundle) *On Utøya: Anders Breivik, Right Terror, Racism and Europe*.

Andreas Ytterstad is Associate Professor at the Institute for Journalism and Media Studies, Oslo and Akershus University College of Applied Sciences and deputy leader of Concerned Scientists Norway.

Scotland: the genie is out of the bottle

Keir McKechnie

The British ruling class wheezed a huge collective sigh of relief at the Scottish independence referendum result. The No camp secured victory with 55 percent of the vote and the Yes side polled 45 percent. 97 percent of the electorate registered to vote and the turn-out was an incredible 86 percent, the highest in any election in the history of Britain.

The queen may well have "purred down the phone" to David Cameron at the result but that does not alter the fact that it was a close call for the British establishment. It is no exaggeration to say that the British state and the capitalist class it represents were truly panic stricken as the Yes campaign built up serious momentum in the final days before the ballot on 18 September. The No campaign managed to lose a massive lead of 22 points from last year to winning by only 10 percentage points. In numerical terms there were 2 million No voters and 1.6 million Yes voters. The British state came within 200,000 votes of its own dissolution and the end of the 307 year old Union as we know it.

All the reactionary forces of the British establishment and beyond were marshalled in the final phase of the campaign to avoid the impending disaster with the dirty tricks division of the ruling class going into overdrive. An avalanche of propaganda including blackmail, lies and scaremongering were showered upon the people of Scotland. Threats that an economic and social Armageddon would be the result of a Yes vote were the order of the day. Deutsche Bank made a panic intervention in the last week of the campaign promising another Great Depression as a consequence of independence. Project Fear as it became known mobilised the BBC, the bankers, the big supermarket chains, the bosses' organisation the CBI and an unholy pro-austerity alliance of the Tories, the Lib Dems and the Labour Party to bombard people with threats to their jobs, pensions and living standards.

Yet on their own these scare tactics were not enough to guarantee victory for the Unionist parties. The rapid and growing momentum of the grassroots Yes movement forced Cameron, Nick Clegg and Ed Miliband three days before the referendum vote to make their desperate historic "vow" of more "devo max" powers for the Scottish Parliament if voters rejected independence. The devo max option of more fiscal autonomy and tax-raising powers for the Scottish Parliament, while remaining part of the UK, had in 2012 been ruled out as an option on the ballot paper by an over-confident Cameron, when he and Scottish first minister Alex Salmond signed the Edinburgh Agreement that set the referendum timetable in motion. The pro-Union Better Together campaign's contempt for democracy was best illustrated by the fact that this "pledge" for more powers was not even discussed in the House of Commons with elected members of parliament, nor in the Welsh or Northern Ireland assemblies. Indeed, there was no discussion of the proposals with members of their own parties. Hundreds of thousands of Scots had cast their postal votes weeks before the "vow" had been conjured up by the three stooges of Westminster.

Within hours of securing the No vote and following the resignation of Salmond as first minister both Cameron and Miliband began backpedalling on their "devo max" promises. The cross-party consensus on more powers is now coming under severe strain as arguments break out as to what, how and when to deliver more home rule or more federalist powers to Scotland within Britain. Miliband's immediate response after the result was that the timetable proposed by former prime minister Gordon Brown was unrealistic. He proposed to kick the issue of more powers for the Scottish Parliament into the long grass by setting up a constitutional convention that will report its findings in autumn 2015—six months after the UK general election next May.

This is an untenable position for Labour in Scotland. Brown, Better Together leader Alistair Darling and a host of other senior Scottish Labour figures are demanding that Labour and the other pro-Union parties deliver on these promises by turning them into new legislation at Westminster by March 2015. As Labour former First Minister Henry McLeish put it in an article in the *Daily Record* there is a danger of Labour dying out in Scotland if it refuses to listen to its traditional working class supporters who voted Yes: "We can't ignore this. It's happening in solid areas of the old red Clydeside and Dundee... We need full autonomy from UK labour".[1] Brown has been reduced to appealing to Scots to petition the Unionist party leaders to honour their "vow".

Cameron's position is now shaped by pressures from his right inside the Tory party and outside from the UK Independence Party (UKIP). He is pushing to reframe the constitutional issues under the banner of what is variously called the "English question" or the "West Lothian question". This means that any new constitutional powers for Scotland would have to be part of a wider constitutional rearrangement giving more powers to English MPs at the expense of Scottish MPs' right to vote on "English" matters. Cameron put it like this shortly after the result: "We have heard the voice of Scotland and now the millions of voices of England must be heard... The question of English votes for English laws—the so called West Lothian question—requires a decisive answer".[2] In other words, the Tories will make every effort to ensure that the Labour Party is weakened at Westminster by excluding Scottish MPs from voting on "English matters" while ensuring that any extra powers for the Scottish Parliament are extremely limited.

Salmond was quick to remark that the Better Together campaign had "tricked" Scottish voters with the promise of more powers: "I think people in Scotland will be astonished and outraged, particularly those who voted No on this prospectus. There is doubt in Cameron's mind about carrying his own backbenchers, therefore a reluctance to have a Commons vote".[3]

Part of the political fallout from the referendum is the creation of a significant level of constitutional upheaval and political instability at the British level. The issue is also creating serious tensions and disagreements inside the wider UK Labour Party. John Denham, a senior Labour figure and Miliband ally, has argued that the impact of offering more powers to Scotland is that "English Labour needs its own voice in this process, unrestrained by Labour from other parts of the union." Frank Field, MP for Birkenhead near Liverpool, argues that "promises to Scotland ensure that the 'English' question will dominate May's general election. Voters will demand from all English candidates whether they support English home rule and if they support giving an additional £1,500 a year, for ever, for every person living in Scotland... Voters will demand 'yes' to the first question and 'no' to the second".[4]

1:    Philip, 2014.
2:    Wintour, 2014.
3:    *Herald*, 2014.
4:    Grice and Wright, 2014.

Labour saves the Union and reaps the whirlwind

The Labour Party have good reason to be petrified at what the future holds for them in Scotland. It is undeniable that their intervention played a major and decisive part in "saving" the Union. In the last days before the vote over 100 Labour MPs descended on Scotland to argue that the austerity Union should continue. Gordon Brown was happy to pedal lies that the National Health Service was safe with the Union. Douglas Alexander was quite happy to share platforms with Scottish Tory leader Ruth Davidson espousing the benefits of defending the status quo and rejecting the need for change. The Respect MP George Galloway, who also shared a platform with Davidson, mistakenly provided much needed left wing cover for the No camp by focusing on the dangers of Scottish nationalism. At the same time he "forgot" completely to raise the issue of British nationalism, with its bloody imperialist legacy from Ireland to Iraq, its ugly chauvinism and its anti-immigrant hysteria as the greatest danger facing the working class.

Sections of the trade union bureaucracy in unions such as the shop workers' union USDAW, the Communication Workers Union and the GMB contributed to confusing and disorienting many good trade unionists by adopting an official No position. They argued that what was at stake was the unity of the working class North and South of the border. Only a No vote could guarantee protection of the gains achieved by the British labour movement over the last hundred years or so. Other sections of the left in Scotland represented by the Red Paper Collective fell into the same trap of confusing the unity of the working class with the unity of the British state. Importantly, however, the Scottish TUC and the largest unions Unison and Unite remained officially neutral on the referendum—a reflection of how far we are from the days when Labour could rely on automatic support from such quarters.

The working class votes Yes

Nevertheless, despite the full weight of the Labour Party machine and sections of the trade union bureaucracy getting behind the No camp, hundreds of thousands of traditional Labour voters and trade unionists were convincingly won over to the Yes side. Many prominent trade union activists, chairs of local trades councils and prominent Labour Party members like Bob Thomson who set up Labour Supporters for Independence switched sides and campaigned for a Yes vote. These include the chairs of both Glasgow and Edinburgh trades councils and prominent labour activists including Unite political officer Pat Rafferty and Stephen Smellie, Deputy Convenor of Unison in Scotland.

These forces played their part in ensuring that an amazing 37 percent of Labour voters at the last Scottish general election in 2011 voted for independence in the referendum. This represents a political earthquake for Labour and an intensification of the process of decomposition in the party's support that has already been developing over the last two decades. Labour's resilience and ability to bounce back are well known but there is no question that they will be severely tested at the general election in 2015 and in the Scottish elections in May 2016.

The Labour Party lost the argument with working class voters in its traditional urban strongholds. Indeed, the Yes vote across Scotland was predominantly a working class vote and was concentrated in the big cities. Contrary to the myths circulated by the No campaign and some on the left, the Yes campaign was not characterised by a narrow Scottish nationalism or anti-English sentiment. On the contrary, it was primarily a movement of hope that was motivated by a strong desire to end austerity, poverty, inequality and war.

Tory businessman Lord Ashcroft's post-referendum poll highlighted that the two most important issues for Yes voters were the economy and defending the National Health Service. Decades of bitterness and alienation have accumulated from an economic and political system that millions of people understand is piling on austerity and misery. At the same time the institutions of the British state—parliament, the Bank of England, the BBC, the police, the army and so on are defending the interests of big business and other powerful elites against those of the majority of the working class.[5]

The Yes vote was a verdict on neoliberal Britain: 1.6 million people rejected the Union and, for a large majority of those, it was a rejection of it in favour of a different kind of society. In this sense it is important to stress that workers in England and Wales share the same anger and opposition to austerity and the corruption consensus in Westminster politics. The difference in Scotland at this juncture is that this anger and hope for real change has found its political voice through the referendum campaign and has culminated in the birth of a new and radical social movement for change with real roots inside the working class.

The breakdown of voting patterns clearly demonstrates the direction of travel. The areas of highest unemployment and social deprivation voted yes.
- In Dundee the Yes vote was at its highest with 57.3 percent.
- In Glasgow it was 53.5 percent.
- In North Lanarkshire the Yes vote was 51.1 percent.

5: Ashcroft, 2014.

- In Inverclyde, the big former shipbuilding and manufacturing centre, the No camp held on to a win by only 86 votes.

A closer look at the Glasgow result is instructive in establishing the general pattern in those cities voting Yes and as corroboration that the vote was also a clear judgement on the Labour Party. In the eight parliamentary constituencies the Yes side won in all of them.

- Anniesland—Yes majority of 742
- Cathcart—Yes majority of 2,811
- Maryhill—Yes majority of 5,985
- Kelvin—Yes majority of 1,337
- Southside—Yes majority of 2,412
- Pollok—Yes majority of 3,851
- Provan—Yes majority of 6,171
- Shettleston—Yes majority of 1,226

The pattern is essentially the same across Scotland. Poor areas voted Yes and richer areas voted No. In Edinburgh, where the No side won by a majority of 60 percent to 40 percent, key working class areas like Craigmillar and Leith voted Yes.

As *Financial Times* journalists John Burn-Murdoch and Aleksandra Wisniewska point out, "the No vote tended to fall as the proportion of people receiving unemployment or disability related benefit rose, supporting the narrative that perceived social injustice was one of the driving forces behind the Yes vote." It is also worth noting that turnout was lower in those areas with the highest levels of deprivation. As the *Financial Times* observed: "Glasgow, where employment deprivation is the highest of all Scottish districts, saw the lowest turnout of 75 percent. It was 10 percentage points below the figure for the whole of Scotland".[6] In the wealthier areas surrounding Glasgow the turnout was at 90 percent. In Dundee it was 79 percent (7 percent below the national average). Generally speaking, Scotland's highest earning regions voted No and the turnouts were extremely high. According to the *Financial Times*: "Lord Ashcroft's poll has respondents from the top social grade split 60:40 in favour of a No—the biggest margin across all groups."

The SNP indy lite strategy versus class politics

There is another area worth exploring in terms of voting patterns, as it highlights that Alex Salmond and the strategy of the Scottish National Party (SNP) of promoting "independence lite" throughout the campaign—keeping the monarchy and the Bank of England, remaining in NATO and cutting

---

6:   Burn-Murdoch and Wisniewska, 2014.

corporation taxes for businesses—actually cost the Yes campaign support among workers. This strategy not only failed to convince the middle classes to vote Yes but fed into much of the cynicism and scepticism among workers about the SNP only being interested in supporting big business at the expense of ordinary people. As I argued in a *Socialist Worker* pamphlet in October 2012, "What is desperately lacking in the SNP and the official Yes campaign is any inspiring vision of an independent Scotland leading the fight for serious wealth redistribution to tackle the deep-seated economic and social problems facing ordinary people."

For example, in Stirling—a seat held by the SNP in the Scottish Parliament—the No camp won by a margin of 60 to 40. The Falkirk area also rejected independence by 53 percent to 47 percent despite having SNP MSPs and Dennis Canavan, the chair of the Yes campaign, being based there. Angus, which has an SNP MP and MSPs also voted No by 53 percent. In Aberdeen, a city dominated by the SNP at Holyrood, the No camp won by a large majority of 59 percent to 41 percent. In Perth and Kinross, where two of Salmond's most senior ministers, John Swinney and Roseanna Cunningham, are MSPs, the result was a 60:40 split in favour of No.

One of the main lessons to draw from the referendum is that the SNP strategy of lowering expectations and emphasising that very little would fundamentally change in an independent Scotland did not appeal to working class people. In fact, it helped to alienate the working class vote because it consciously refused to focus on class arguments around defending the NHS, ending zero-hours contracts, renationalising the railways, the oil industry and so on. This lack of willingness to put forward the class arguments actually opened the door to the Unionist parties and allowed them to portray themselves as the defenders of working class interests.

It was not until he was convincingly beaten by Alistair Darling in the first big televised debate that Salmond shifted the focus in the second debate from the currency and the European Union towards defending the NHS, opposing privatisation of public services, defence of the welfare state, ending zero-hours contracts and opposing foreign wars. There was an immediate boost towards Yes once clear class arguments were injected into the campaign. It was at this point that Old Labour supporters started to change sides in favour of independence. It is important to underline that it was the growth and inspiring dynamism of a new radical left movement—in the form of the Radical Independence Campaign (RIC), the Hope Over Fear meetings with socialist Tommy Sheridan addressing huge working class audiences of up to 25,000 people and other groups like Women For Independence and the National Collective—that galvanised the working class and mobilised the movement that pushed the SNP and the official Yes campaign to the left and took us so close to victory.

The SNP's failure to put class centre stage and to take a clear side with the working class against the ruling class gets to the heart of the limitations of Scottish nationalism (or any nationalist movement for that matter). The notion that the fundamental antagonism between labour and capital at the centre of capitalist relations of production can be resolved or wished away by uniting the working class with the ruling class in the shared "national interest" inevitably fails to camouflage the real class divisions in capitalist society.

The SNP under Salmond's skilful and astute leadership have been masters at presenting the left face of nationalism in order to present themselves as a "social democratic" left alternative to labour. It was these efforts to position the SNP to the left of Labour through policies like scrapping tuition fees, introducing free prescription charges, defending the Scottish NHS from privatisation and opposition to Trident that catapulted the SNP into office first as a minority administration in 2007 and then to victory with a historic landslide over Labour in the 2011 Scottish election.

However, the right face of nationalism always re-emerges and sides with the ruling class as it is forced to choose sides in the conflict between labour and capital. From 2007 onwards the SNP has implemented cuts to business rates while simultaneously pushing through 2 percent "efficiency savings" to local council budgets which has led to job losses and attacks on pay and conditions across the public sector.

The SNP administration passed on UK government budget cuts to local councils across Scotland. When faced with the choice of refusing to implement cuts or "devolving the axe" to local councils, the SNP, like Labour, passed on these cuts and what followed were severe reductions in public services and further privatisation through the contracting out of vital services for groups such as the elderly.

Most recently the SNP were put to the test in 2013 when bosses at the Ineos petrochemical plant in Grangemouth provoked a major confrontation with workers and the Unite union. Ineos boss Jim Ratcliffe victimised the union convenor, and then threatened to close the plant unless workers accepted a pay freeze, an end to their final salary pension scheme and worse conditions. Alex Salmond's response was not to pile in behind the workers or to threaten to renationalise such a vital economic asset. Instead he spoke of protecting the "national interest" and abandoned workers at Ineos. The final rotten deal was accepted by workers at the plant. According to the SNP's Joan McAlpine, Salmond "negotiated a deal to reduce the cost of Ineos's gas by £40 million".

There are other examples that illustrate how far the SNP are willing to go to side with the employers against workers. During the 2011 pensions strike the SNP finance secretary was happy to gloat that "I don't support the strike action and I've already crossed a picket line."

These examples are important to highlight as they point to the dangers for the left in Scotland of adopting an uncritical approach to the SNP in the coming period. Over 30,000 people joined the SNP in the ten days after the referendum, taking its membership to over 60,000. It is now bigger than the Lib Dems across the UK and looks likely to continue growing. The thousands of new members flocking to the SNP see it as a viable and more radical "social democratic" alternative to Labour and the Tories in Scotland.

Yet, unlike the Labour Party, which Lenin described as a "bourgeois workers' party", that was historically "the political expression of the trade union bureaucracy", the SNP is not, nor does it pretend to be, a party rooted inside the working class or with any serious links with the trade union movement. The SNP is a bourgeois nationalist party. It did not arise out of a struggle against colonial oppression. Its emergence coincided with the decline of British imperialism on the world stage. As Iain Ferguson notes: "The SNP was founded in 1934 to unite the different strands of the nationalist movement. It brought together left wing activists who supported independence and former Tories who favoured some form of home rule".[7]

A key issue for the left is how to relate to the SNP and the thousands of activists engaged by the independence movement—many who have joined the SNP believing it can either be pushed further to the left, or to punish the Labour Party at the next election, or in the belief that it can be the vehicle for bringing independence back onto the agenda again.

A wee whiff of Tahrir

Anybody who was fortunate enough to witness the gatherings of thousands of people in Glasgow's George Square in the days running up to the referendum will confirm how electrifying and joyful the atmosphere was. Ordinary people would speak on an open microphone about their hopes for a better society. Large crowds of young people, many of them first time voters, spoke of a world without nuclear weapons, of the urgent need to save the planet and stop fracking. Working class women got up and spoke about how they were politically active and engaged for the first time and how things would never be the same again. There was a festival atmosphere in towns and cities across Scotland at the prospect of building a different kind of society that put

---

7:    Ferguson, 2014.

people before profit. Social media also played an important role in countering the BBC and other mass media lies. There was a demonstration of over 5,000 people at the BBC protesting at its biased coverage.

Across the country mass canvasses of big working class housing schemes organised by the Radical Independence Campaign not only mobilised the Yes vote but drew thousands of new people into a wide range of activism. Socialist Workers Party members played a key role in these canvasses and worked closely with groups like Scottish Asians for Independence in the Pollokshields area of Glasgow. We also leafleted workplaces like Govan shipyards, the big hospitals and key council work-places in Edinburgh and Glasgow. The SWP shared platforms in Aberdeen, Dundee, Motherwell, Paisley and Edinburgh with Tommy Sheridan in the inspiring Hope Over Fear tour. These meetings were massive with several hundred attending each one. English and Welsh comrades played their part by coming to Scotland and campaigning for a Yes vote as one that they welcomed and that would give confidence to English and Welsh workers to fight austerity and the Tories. This message was very well received on the doorsteps in working class areas and among the activists.

There was an explosion of interest in socialist ideas. Sales of *Socialist Worker* were the highest they have been since the great West of Scotland strike-wave of 1974-5 with around 1,000 copies sold each week in the last fortnight of the campaign. The *Socialist Worker* pamphlet *Yes to Independence—No to Nationalism* sold 2,500 copies. The SWP also engaged in the debates with those who supported a No position. These debates involved Labour councillors and key trade union officials and activists. We did not treat No voters as scabs or class enemies. We argued that they were wrong and engaged seriously with them.

The SWP also played a significant role alongside others in linking up the independence movement with wider internationalist struggles. In the solidarity movement for Gaza, for example, we argued that an independent Scotland should boycott Israel and open a Palestinian embassy. We success-fully put pressure on the SNP government to send direct aid to Palestine. The Scottish government announced that it supported a boycott in pro-curing any contracts from companies based in illegal Palestinian settlements. The Palestinian flag was hoisted over Glasgow City Council for a day.

Along with other activists in the anti bedroom tax federation we exerted a huge and successful amount of pressure on the SNP and Labour Party in Holyrood to find an extra £50 million fully to mitigate the effects of the bedroom tax—effectively killing the bedroom tax in Scotland.

Promoting the united front approach to campaigning against the

Scottish Defence League and UKIP was a key area of activity for socialists during the referendum campaign. We appealed to Yes and No voters to oppose UKIP leader Nigel Farage's toxic brand of racism and trips to Scotland. We did not shy away from the need to challenge racism and racist scapegoating.

Where next after the referendum?

"The genie is out of the bottle" and "Things will never be the same again" are common expressions among the Yes movement activists. The desire to keep the movement alive is evidenced by the continuing demonstrations, public meetings and conferences that are planned for the autumn. Tens of thousands of people have been energised and are refusing to return to "normal life". There is a determination not to let the anger against the Tories, the Labour Party, big business, the BBC and the Westminster establishment dissipate or fragment.

Already tens of thousands are joining political parties. The main beneficiary to date has been the SNP. The Green Party report that their membership has doubled and the Scottish Socialist Party (SSP), Tommy Sheridan's Solidarity and the SWP have seen thousands inquiring about membership. This should be welcomed as a sign that thousands of activists want to remain organised and continue to fight.

The significant challenge and immediate task for the left in Scotland is to create a new political vehicle that can organise a radical anti-capitalist alternative to both Labour and the SNP. Although the social movement for resistance to austerity in Scotland has not been on the same scale as in countries like Greece or Spain there is, however, a unique opportunity to build a new left formation that can pull together and organise thousands of the best activists and trade unionists. It is unsurprising that the SNP, the party that put the referendum centre stage, should initially act as the biggest pole of attraction for many people.

Of course, the left should welcome and support those SNP MPs who voted at Westminster against bombing Iraq. We must continue to force it to the left whenever possible. But the left in Scotland should also be under no illusion that the SNP will deliver on the hopes of millions. As a nationalist party that promotes the "national interest" it will continue to promote alliances with the likes of union-busting billionaire chair of Stagecoach Brian Souter and the billionaire owner of Clyde Blowers engineering, Jim McColl. Confronted with the logic of capital and an acceptance of the impeccable laws of the market the SNP will adapt by saying that it has no choice but to implement Westminster cuts. When the next round of austerity kicks in the

SNP will impose its own package of cuts and "efficiency" savings on workers' living standards while promoting tax breaks for big corporate interests.

That is why the SWP does not support calls from Tommy Sheridan and others to vote SNP at the next general election, avoid standing radical left candidates against it and instead wait until the Scottish general election in 2016. To reduce this new social movement or the existing radical left to being the unofficial political wing of the SNP is a flawed strategy. It will only provide a left wing cover for the SNP and cost valuable time by postponing the urgent task of building a new left party. Let's strike while the iron is hot!

There is an urgent need and a mood among a wide layer of activists to build a new party. This process could begin bringing together all those inspired by the Hope Over Fear tour, those mobilised by the Radical Independence Campaign and Labour Supporters for Independence into the same room to discuss a way forward. A blockage to this kind of realignment needs to be addressed. Any new party cannot be defined by the splits in the SSP a decade ago. Many younger activists are demanding a united left alternative and see no sense in separating into competing left groups when there is a crying need for the left forces in Scotland to unite. A broad anti-capitalist and anti-austerity politics can mobilise the working class for the class battles that are on the horizon and offer a serious electoral alternative in the upcoming elections.

The SWP will be taking part in these debates at the Solidarity and RIC conference in the autumn. We will continue to build support for strikes and resistance to the next wave of austerity. The challenges ahead for the left are considerable and the stakes are high but the prize is well worth fighting for.

References

Ashcroft, Michael Lord, 2014, "How Scotland voted and why" (19 September), http://lordashcroftpolls.com/2014/09/scotland-voted/

Burn-Murdoch, John, and Aleksandra Wisniewska, 2014, "Scottish Referendum: Who Voted Which Way?" (19 September), http://tinyurl.com/kr4rfys

Ferguson, Iain, 2014, "The Limits of Scottish Nationalism", *Socialist Worker* (9 September), http://socialistworker.co.uk/art/38927/The+limits+of+Scottish+nationalism

Grice, Andrew, and Oliver Wright, 2014, "Scottish referendum results: Cross-party consensus collapses amid Tory-Labour spat on the 'English question'", *Independent* (19 September), http://tinyurl.com/lnstkkd

Philip, Andy, 2014, "Henry McLeish Warns Labour are in Danger of Dying Out in Scotland unless Radical Action is Taken Now", *Daily Record* (24 September), http://tinyurl.com/ksu673s

Herald, 2014, "Salmond: I Quit as First Minister and SNP Leader", *Herald* (19 September), http://www.heraldscotland.com/news/home-news/salmond-i-quit.1411139324

Wintour, Patrick, 2014, "David Cameron raises West Lothian Question after Scotland Vote: 'English Votes for English Laws'", *Guardian* (19 September), http://tinyurl.com/m3hn2xn

Out now from Bookmarks

DECIPHERING CAPITAL
Marx's Capital and its destiny
Alex Callinicos

£12 from Bookmarks (rrp £14.99)

Marx's Capital is back where it belongs, at the centre of debate about Marxism and its purchase on the contemporary world. Here Alex Callinicos offers his own substantial contribution to these debates. He examines Marx's method in Capital, its relation to Hegel and Ricardo, value theory, labour and crisis. He engages with Marxist thinkers past and present, from Gramsci and Althusser to Harvey and Jameson.

"Callinicos's excellent book is a significant contribution to the revival of Marxian political economy for 21st century struggles against capitalism, with important insights into Capital and the nature of revolutionary subjects in late capitalism" – Fred Moseley, Professor of Economics, Mount Holyoke College

Bookmarks—the socialist bookshop
1 Bloomsbury Street, London WC1B 3QE
020 7637 1848
www.bookmarksbookshop.co.uk
info@bookmarksbookshop.co.uk

The multiple crises of imperialism

Alex Callinicos

If the United States remains the command centre of global capitalism, a multiplicity of crises has been flashing up on its screens in the past few months. Let's consider them in ascending order of importance from the perspective of US decision makers. First, there was Israel's latest war on Gaza—not a crisis for Washington, more the kind of violent outburst through which a kind of equilibrium is re-established, but for growing numbers of people around the world an outrage and a crime. Secondly, there was the war—now halted by an uneasy ceasefire—between the pro-Western government in Kiev and Russian-backed forces in south eastern Ukraine. Thirdly, there is the US bombing campaign to halt the advance of the jihadi group that calls itself the Islamic State, but which we will continue to call ISIS, in Iraq and Syria. And, finally—not yet a crisis, but potentially the most serious conflict—there's the increasingly intense interstate competition in East Asia in response to China's growing power.[1]

One interesting thing about this list is that two of the items—the war in Ukraine and the rise of ISIS—wouldn't have figured in anyone's predictions at the beginning of 2014. This is a sign of the volatility of the international situation, which is a consequence of power shifts among the leading capitalist states. But it's also quite frightening. Christopher Clark in his influential recent book on the outbreak of the First World War argues

1:   Thanks to Anne Alexander, Joseph Choonara, Phil Marfleet, Judith Orr, John Rose and Camilla Royle for their comments on this article in draft.

that, despite the polarisation of Europe into two rival power blocs, in the summer of 1914 "the danger of a conflict between the great alliance blocs seemed to be receding, just as the chain of events that would ultimately drag Europe into war got underway".[2] War can take even the greatest powers by surprise, as we can see now in Barack Obama's reluctant redeployment of US military power in Iraq.

But for many on the left internationally this reluctance is feigned. For them, the unifying theme in these different crises is the assertion of American power to maintain and even expand Washington's global domination, in the process pulverising states such as Iraq, Syria and Ukraine. This diagnosis often dovetails into a revival of what was called "campism" during the Cold War—that is, political support for states that, because they resist the US geopolitically, are seen as in some sense progressive.

The Ukraine war has, as Rob Ferguson discusses elsewhere in this issue, been accompanied by an outburst of campism, with the highly respected Russian Marxist Boris Kagarlitsky going so far as to claim about the Russian-backed forces in south eastern Ukraine: "What is happening in Novorossiya is a revolutionary movement, though it's not yet a revolution in terms of social change".[3] In the Middle East campism takes the form of support for the alliance orchestrated by the Islamic Republican regime in Iran, including notably the regime of Bashar al-Assad in Syria and Hizbollah, the Shiite Islamist movement that dominates Lebanon. More generally, many on the left look to Russia and China as counterweights to the US.

The problem with this complex of ideas is simultaneously factual, theoretical and political. We'll return to the politics. Factually: the US has often harboured expansionist designs. This was true in broad terms after the Cold War, when successive administrations sought, by exporting neoliberalism and expanding NATO, to create a global order economically and politically dominated by the US.[4] And, more specifically, the administration of George W Bush in the neocons' heyday after 9/11 sought to seize Iraq in order to entrench US domination of the Middle East, topple hostile regimes in Syria

---

2:   Clark, 2012, p364.

3:   Kagarlitsky, 2014. *"Novorossiya"*—the name adopted by the pro-Russian rebels for the territories under their control—is a symptom of how much their movement is permeated by imperial ideologies. It was the name given to what is now south eastern Ukraine after it was conquered by Russia under Catherine the Great in the late 18th century. The Tsarist regime settled the area with colonists, many of whom were Ukrainians, thereby unintentionally helping to define the boundaries of modern Ukraine.

4:   Gowan, 1999.

and Iran, and spread bourgeois democracy neoliberal style to the Arab world.[5]

But the Middle East today is shaped above all by the failure of this vainglorious project and by the Arab revolutions and the reactionary attempts to crush them. The Obama administration is profoundly conscious of this. This doesn't mean that it won't inflict more evils on the region, or collude in them (for example through its support for Israel), but, as we will see in more detail below, its current aims are primarily defensive.

Understanding imperialism today

The problem is also theoretical. For much of the left imperialism is equated with US domination. But this is not how it was understood by the classical theorists of imperialism—and not because they were writing a hundred years ago, long before the onset of American hegemony. For them, imperialism had two crucial features. First of all, it involved a system of geopolitical rivalries among the Great Powers. As the Liberal J A Hobson (a major influence on Lenin) put it, "the novelty of recent imperialism regarded as a policy consists chiefly in its adoption by several nations. The notion of a number of competing empires is essentially modern".[6]

Secondly, the emergence of these rivalries was a consequence of a specific phase of capitalist development, as Lenin underlines in his pamphlet *Imperialism*. The concentration and centralisation of capital that Marx identifies in *Capital*, Volume I as one of the main tendencies arising from the capitalist accumulation process led by the beginning of the 20th century to the intersection of economic and geopolitical competition. Capitals, increasingly large in scale and operating internationally, came to depend on the support of their nation state to defend their interests; equally, to maintain themselves against their rivals, states had to promote the industrial capitalist economies that alone could provide complex modern weapons systems and the infrastructure of war. The growing interdependence of states and capitals gave rise to the intensification of geopolitical rivalries that exploded into world war in August 1914 and that produced a second bout of carnage in 1939-45.[7]

So from a Marxist perspective, modern imperialism is a *system* of intercapitalist competition and rivalry. Lenin's key contribution to the theory was the concept of uneven development. Capitalism doesn't grow uniformly: some states and regions leap ahead; others lag behind. This

---

5:   Callinicos, 2003.
6:   Hobson, 1938, p6.
7:   The idea that capitalist imperialism is defined by the intersection of economic and geopolitical competition is a refinement of the classical theory simultaneously formulated by David Harvey and myself: Harvey, 2003, and Callinicos, 2003 and 2009.

unevenness defines the hierarchy of power in the world. But, crucially, the uneven development of capitalism redistributes power among the leading states. This means that the balance of power is constantly shifting, creating the circumstances of new conflicts. The key geopolitical development in the first half of the 20th century was the shift in relative power between Britain, hitherto the dominant capitalist state, and the US and Germany; today another shift in relative power is taking place between the US and China. Changes of this nature, Lenin insisted, make the peaceful transnational integration of capitals that Karl Kautsky called "ultra-imperialism" and Michael Hardt and Toni Negri have more recently named "Empire" impossible: the redistribution of power among states undermines the deals that would be needed to make such integration work.[8]

Why have so many on the left lost sight of the systemic character of imperialism? It may have to do with two optical illusions. The first has to do with the Cold War. This journal was unusual in regarding the Soviet Union as state capitalist and therefore its long struggle with the US as a form of inter-imperialist rivalry. Those on the left who understood the USSR instead as a socialist society or a degenerated workers' state or in some vaguer sense "post-capitalist" couldn't see the Cold War as a conflict between imperialist powers. Isaac Deutscher, for example, developed a highly influential interpretation that portrayed the geopolitical and ideological struggle between Western and Eastern blocs as a "great contest" between "antagonistic social systems", respectively capitalism and communism, in which the Soviet Union, however imperfectly, represented the revolutionary interest on a world scale.[9] This kind of thinking survives in a residual identification of Russia as an "anti-imperialist" power, despite the cynical brutality with which it crushed the Chechen independence movement and the crude fusion of the high command of the state and unrestrained predatory capitalism in Moscow.

The second optical illusion comes from the so-called "unipolar moment" at the end of the Cold War, when the US enjoyed overwhelming military superiority over all other powers combined and, in the late 1990s and mid-2000s, experienced significant economic booms. But even at the time there was a contradiction between the Pentagon's military supremacy and continuing US relative economic decline, masked by a boom that was already being driven by a financial bubble—initially in the stock market and

---

8: See, on Lenin, ultra-imperialism, and uneven (and combined) development, Callinicos, 2009, pp62-66, 88-93.
9: Deutscher, 1961, pp99-100. Compare Binns, 1983, and Callinicos, 2009, pp165-187.

then in the mid-2000s in housing.[10] The bursting of the latter bubble, coinciding with US defeat in Iraq, has made American weakness visible. Not only did the global economic and financial crisis start in the US, but China and other "emerging market" economies recovered much more rapidly. Between 2007 and 2012 the advanced economies grew by 3 percent, the emerging and developing countries by 31 percent, and China by 56 percent.[11] It is precisely during the crisis that China has emerged as the second biggest economy in the world as well as lead manufacturer, exporter and consumer of energy.

The divergence in growth rates is making possible a narrowing of the gap in military capabilities between the US and the rest. In 2013 the US defence budget was a vast $600.4 billion, still dwarfing that of the runners up, China ($112.2 billion), Russia ($68.2 billion), Saudi Arabia ($59.6 billion) and Britain ($57 billion). But since the crash defence spending has risen sharply in some leading "emerging market" economies, while it has stagnated or fallen in the West. In 2008-13 real net defence spending rose 43.5 percent in China, 31.2 percent in Russia, 10 percent in Brazil, 6.6 percent in Japan, 0.3 percent in France, 0.1 percent in the US, -4.3 percent in Germany, -9.1 percent in Britain and -21 percent in Italy. Between 2001 and 2013 the official budget of the People's Liberation Army (which significantly understates Chinese defence spending) rose by 700 percent.[12] The International Institute of Strategic Studies estimates that, on present trends, and depending on the growth rates extrapolated and spending definitions, the US and Chinese defence budgets will converge sometime between 2023 and 2028.[13]

Of course, such extrapolations need to be treated with great care. The annual real rate of growth of Chinese defence spending dropped from 10.4 percent in 2003-7 to 7.6 percent in 2009-13.[14] This trend broadly tracks the slowdown in the overall rate of growth of the Chinese economy. Even the lower growth rate has depended on a debt-driven investment boom engineered by the government in response to the Great Recession of 2008-9. But now analysts are predicting China may be facing a "balance sheet recession", in which heavily indebted companies concentrate on cutting their debts, thereby reducing effective demand and output.[15]

But whatever the future holds for the Chinese economy, the gap

10: Brenner, 2002.
11: Wolf, 2014, p12.
12: All figures from International Institute for Strategic Studies, 2014.
13: International Institute for Strategic Studies, 2013, p255.
14: International Institute for Strategic Studies, 2014, p210.
15: Wildau, 2014.

separating it from the American remains, in reality, large. Earlier this year the World Bank announced that Chinese GDP was now higher than that of the US. This estimate relied on the controversial purchasing power parity (PPP) measure of national income, which adjusts for differences in costs between countries. But China has a population of 1,356 million, while that of the US is only 319 million. Even using the PPP measure, which weights the comparison in China's favour, in 2013 US GDP per capita was $52,000, while China's was $9,800.[16] The American state continues to preside over a far richer economy than China's. It is, moreover, at the centre of the global financial system, issues the main reserve currency and orchestrates a network of international alliances that bind the advanced capitalist states to its political and military leadership.[17]

Nevertheless, the global redistribution of economic power is leading to an intensification of geopolitical competition. The second of the crises listed above, Russia's intervention in Ukraine in defiance of the US, NATO and the European Union, is the most visible example of this development, but from the longer term view what's happening in East Asia—the fourth of those conflicts—is much more significant. Much attention is focused on the build-up of Chinese naval power in the Western Pacific and a host of territorial disputes in the South and East China seas. The most serious of these pits China and Japan, the second and third biggest economies in the world, against each other over ownership of the uninhabited Diaoyu/Senkaku islands.

Beyond nationalist symbolism and the energy reserves scattered across the area lies the strategic significance of the South China Sea. According to the geostrategist David Kaplan:

> The South China Sea functions as the throat of the Western Pacific and Indian oceans—the mass of connective economic tissue where global sea routes coalesce. Here is the heart of Eurasia's navigable rimland, punctuated by the Malacca, Sunda, Lombok and Makassar straits. More than half of the world's annual merchant street tonnage passes through these choke points, and a third of all maritime traffic worldwide.[18]

16: www.cia.gov/library/publications/the-world-factbook/rankorder/2004rank.html. For the pitfalls of PPP measurements of income, see Wade, 2014, pp315-319.

17: Callinicos, 2009, chapter 5.

18: Kaplan, 2014, Kindle location 222. Kim, 2013, offers a Marxist analysis of inter-imperialist rivalries in East Asia. See also Friedberg, 2012, Luttwak, 2012, and Dyer, 2014. Although these and Kaplan's books are written from the perspective of US imperialism, this does not prevent them offering valuable information and insights.

Economic globalisation, by increasing states' dependence on transnational flows of goods, has made maintaining access to key sea routes vital. The saying went in the 15th century, when South East Asia was valued by European states as a source of rare and expensive spices: "Whoever is the Lord of Malacca has his hand on the throat of Venice".[19] More recently Hu Jintao, Chinese president 2002-12, has spoken of a "Malacca dilemma", since so much of China's exports of manufactured goods and imports of energy and raw materials has to pass through these straits connecting the Indian Ocean and the Pacific. This has encouraged China to invest in alternative land routes to the Indian Ocean through Burma and Pakistan that bypass the straits.[20]

In the meantime, the sea routes on which China's position as the world's biggest industrial and exporting economy depends are protected by the US Navy, which has dominated the Pacific since the defeat of Japan in 1945. This situation is not acceptable to China's rulers, as is indicated by the expansion of the People's Liberation Army Navy and heavy investments in weapons systems (for example, a submarine fleet that by 2020 will match that of the US and the DF-21 missile that can hit moving targets at sea such as aircraft carriers) that can deny American warships access to the seas along the Chinese coast. Kaplan quotes Paul Bracken of Yale University to the effect that "China isn't so much building a conventional navy as an 'anti-navy navy' designed to push US sea and air forces away from the East Asian coastline".[21]

But what is happening in Asia is a lot more than a binary confrontation between the US and China. States are generally expanding their military spending as they assert their interests against each other. Particularly since the right wing nationalist Shinzo Abe took over as prime minister in 2012, Japan has been positioning itself as the leader of an anti-Chinese coalition. China, Taiwan, Vietnam, Malaysia and the Philippines, which all have disputed territorial claims over the energy-rich Spratly islands, have built structures in the islands for use by their navies. Kaplan points out that

it isn't just China that is improving its military, so are Southeast Asian countries in general. Their defence budgets have increased by about a third in the past decade, even as European defence budgets have declined. Arms imports to Indonesia, Singapore and Malaysia have gone up by 84 percent, 146 percent and 722 percent respectively since 2000. The spending is on

---

19: Dyer, 2014a, p26.
20: Kaplan, 2010.
21: Kaplan, 2014, Kindle location 706.

naval and air platforms, surface warships, submarines with advanced missile systems and long-range fighter jets. Vietnam recently spent $2 billion on six state of the art Kilo-class Russian submarines and $1 billion on Russian fighter jets. Malaysia recently opened a submarine base on the island of Borneo, even as China is developing an underground base for 20 nuclear submarines on Hainan Island on the other side of the South China Sea. While the United States has been distracted by land wars in Greater East Asia, military power has been quietly shifting from Europe to Asia, where authentic civilian-military, post-industrial complexes are being built, with an emphasis on naval forces.[22]

The old Cold War divisions no longer fit a region where, for example, Vietnam looks to the US to balance against China, and South Korea is attracted towards China as a counterweight to its old colonial power, Japan. Japan itself has been extending feelers towards North Korea, whose rulers sometimes lob test missiles in its direction. As Kaplan puts it, "world-wide multi-polarity is already a feature of diplomacy and economics, but the South China Sea is poised to show us what multi-polarity in a military sense actually looks like".[23]

The burdens of global empire

In itself, the entry of East Asia into a period of more intense interstate competition is not a direct threat to US hegemony. On the contrary, greater Chinese assertiveness may have the effect of pushing more Asian states than Vietnam towards the US.[24] The deeper problem arises from the very feature that distinguishes the US from all other states—namely, that it is the only genuinely global power, maintaining a dominant position in all the key regions of the world economy (North America, Western Europe, East Asia and the Middle East). Putting it crudely, the more widespread the crises, the harder it is for Washington to devote the attention and resources required to resolve any of them.

This problem was a crucial determinant of the decline of America's predecessor as the hegemonic capitalist power—Britain—between the late 18th and early 20th centuries. Britain's ability to manage the European balance of power depended crucially on the combination of its economic strength (as the first industrial capitalist economy and as centre of the

---

22: Kaplan, 2014, Kindle location 383.
23: Kaplan, 2014, Kindle location 319.
24: This is the burden of Luttwak, 2012.

international financial and trading system) and of the resources provided by the empire, above all the money and manpower the Raj extracted from India. At the beginning of the 20th century British hegemony came under pressure thanks to the emergence of the US and Germany as industrial and naval competitors. But what, more than anything else, broke the empire's back was the threat of geopolitical challenges emerging simultaneously in three key regions—continental Europe, the Mediterranean and East Asia. In the late 1930s this threat became reality in the shape of the Axis between Nazi Germany, fascist Italy and Japan. The strategies employed by successive prime ministers—appeasement under Neville Chamberlain and fighting the Axis in alliance with the US under Winston Churchill—both failed to save the British Empire.[25]

American economic and military power is still far greater than Britain's ever was. But the US begins to face the same kind of problem, as it has to deal with China's rise, a reassertive Russia and continuing turmoil in the Middle East. The contours of the problem were already clear when Obama took office.[26] His solution was twofold: first, to liquidate Bush's failed wars in western Asia (pulling US troops out of Iraq in 2011 and, after a futile initial "surge", from Afghanistan next year), and secondly, to effect the famous "pivot" to Asia, giving priority to the Asia-Pacific region in Washington's diplomatic efforts and military capabilities (eg 60 percent of the US Navy).[27] But beyond this reorientation in geographical priorities, Obama has drawn the lesson from the neocons' failure that the US should be much more cautious in using military power. This was already evident in his refusal (despite the pressure from then secretary of state, Hillary Clinton) to intervene too much in the Syrian civil war and in the eagerness with which a year ago he seized on Congressional opposition to abandon his threat to mount air strikes to punish the Assad regime for using chemical weapons.

In a speech at West Point Military Academy in May Obama sought to generalise from this experience, developing what was touted as a new strategic doctrine:

> Here's my bottom line: America must always lead on the world stage. If we don't, no one else will. The military…is and always will be the backbone of that leadership. But US military action cannot be the only—or even

25: See Darwin, 2009, especially chapters 8 and 11.
26: Callinicos, 2010, chapter 2.
27: For a critique of the latter policy for provoking an aggressive defensive response from Beijing see Ross, 2012.

primary—component of our leadership in every instance. Just because we have the best hammer does not mean that every problem is a nail.[28]

Obama reaffirmed George W Bush's own "doctrine": "The United States will use military force, unilaterally if necessary, when our core interests demand it." But he went on to insist that, "for the foreseeable future, the most direct threat to America at home and abroad remains terrorism. But a strategy that involves invading every country that harbours terrorist networks is naïve and unsustainable," particularly because "today's principal threat no longer comes from a centralised Al Qaeda leadership. Instead it comes from decentralised Al Qaeda affiliates and extremists, many with agendas focused in countries where they operate".[29]

Within a fortnight Obama's words came back to haunt him: on 10 June Mosul, Iraq's second city, fell to ISIS. Far from being a fragmented rabble, in Patrick Cockburn's words:

> Al Qaeda-type movements...today rule a vast area in northern and western Iraq and eastern and northern Syria. The area under their sway is several hundred times larger than any territory controlled by Osama bin Laden, the killing of whom in 2011 was supposed to be a major blow to world terrorism. In fact, it is since bin Laden's death that Al Qaeda affiliates have had their greatest successes.[30]

But ISIS is far from being the only challenge to Obama's attempt to avoid new confrontations. Francis Fukuyama criticised him for saying that "the only direct threat we face is terrorism. He said virtually nothing about long-term responses to the two other big challenges to world order: Russia and China...allies the US is sworn to defend are now threatened by industrialised nations with sophisticated militaries".[31] Fukuyama is quite a good barometer of shifts in American ruling class opinion—announcing the End of History and the triumph of liberal capitalism in 1989, calling for war on Iraq in the late 1990s and jumping quickly off the neocon bandwagon when it became clear that the Bush-Blair adventure had failed.[32] Now he

---

28: www.whitehouse.gov/the-press-office/2014/05/28/remarks-president-west-point-academy-commencement-ceremony

29: www.whitehouse.gov/the-press-office/2014/05/28/remarks-president-west-point-academy-commencement-ceremony

30: Cockburn, 2014, Kindle location 112.

31: Fukuyama, 2014.

32: Anderson, 2006.

recognises that the drive to spread neoliberalism globally has not prevented a revival of geopolitical challenges to the US and its allies.

Of these challenges, the Russian is much the less serious. This is partly because, even under Putin, Russia is a shadow of the USSR, despite his determination to maintain economic and political control over the ex-Soviet republics along its eastern and western borders. But it is also because Ukraine matters much less to the US than it does to Russia. The initiative in precipitating the crisis there came from the European Commission, the pro-Western wing of the Ukrainian oligarchy, and some of the EU's member states in central and eastern Europe, who have scores to settle with Moscow. Susan Watkins nicely captures the reactive opportunism the US has shown:

> For Washington, meanwhile, there is simply the imperial automatism of the global hegemon: if there is a power vacuum in a medium-sized country, the State Department's reflex response is to move in and take charge. In Ukraine, the US has much less to lose than the EU, though also much less to gain than Russia. But once the crisis broke in Kiev, Washington could not resist the opportunity to construct a regime to its liking.[33]

Like all US administrations, Obama's has its hawks—most notably Victoria Nuland, Assistant Secretary of State for European and Eurasian Affairs and a neocon holdover from the Bush administration. She was taped in February discussing how to get the western Ukrainian nationalist Arseniy Yatsenyuk into government (he was duly appointed prime minister after the overthrow of President Viktor Yanukovych) and dismissing Brussels with the immortal line: "You know, Fuck the EU".[34] But the administration's dominant strategy has been to strong-arm a reluctant and divided EU to adopt increasingly tough sanctions packages to punish Russia for annexing Crimea and destabilising Ukraine, but also to avoid a wider confrontation. This is a low-cost approach: the US has far more limited economic ties to Russia than the EU, so the more robust sanctions that Washington has imposed don't hurt much. But a military response (beyond limited steps to bolster up NATO's eastern periphery) has never been on the agenda. Large-scale conventional operations so close to Russia are probably beyond the Pentagon's capabilities and might in any case risk a resort to nuclear weapons by Moscow.

Western policy towards Russia's intervention in Ukraine—enough to wound, but not enough to kill—has played into Putin's hands. Ukraine's

---

33: Watkins, 2014, p11.
34: www.bbc.co.uk/news/world-europe-26079957, see also Dyer, 2014b.

integration in the Western bloc threatens to bring NATO to Russia's borders—a bonus to Washington, but a mortal threat to Moscow. Riding a wave of Russian nationalism, Putin quickly seized Crimea, but elsewhere in Ukraine he used more subtle tactics. A fascinating (if somewhat over-heated) piece in the *Financial Times* at the end of August expressed NATO's frustrations at how Russia was outmanoeuvring it in Ukraine:

In public, NATO chiefs talk of Vladimir Putin's 20th century mentality... But, in private, they are more candid—and worried—about the 21st century tactics Mr Putin is using. Russia's actions in Ukraine have exploded the notion that expansive communications technologies and economic interdependence were fostering a kind of grand bargain.

Instead nationalism, genocide, irredentism and military aggression, which were thought to be in decline, are alive and well, finding new and powerful means of being deployed in Ukraine and beyond... NATO refers to this form of conflict as "hybrid war". The phrase refers to a broad range of hostile actions, of which military force is only a small part, that are invariably executed in concert as part of a flexible strategy with long-term objectives.

Predictably, the most lucid exposition of the concept is Russian. In February 2013, Valery Gerasimov, the newly appointed chief of Russia's general staff, penned an article in the Russian defence journal *VPK*.

War and peace, Mr Gerasimov wrote, in remarks that now seem prophetic, are becoming more blurred.

"Methods of conflict," he wrote, have changed, and now involve "the broad use of political, economic, informational, humanitarian and other non-military measures". All of this, he said, could be supplemented by firing up the local populace as a fifth column and by "concealed" armed forces.[35]

So precisely what Putin did not do, despite endless cliché-ridden denunciations by Western leaders and their media echoes, was send the tanks into Ukraine like the Soviet Union in Hungary in 1956 and Czechoslovakia in 1968. Instead Moscow provided command and control, intelligence, special forces and heavy weapons to the pro-Russian militias in south eastern Ukraine. Only when the Kiev government offensive during

---

35: Jones, 2014b.

the summer threatened to overwhelm its opponents did Russia deploy heavily armed regular troops in mid-August. They sent the government forces fleeing in disarray and gave Ukrainian president Petro Poroshenko little alternative except to negotiate the ceasefire Putin quickly offered. Dmitri Trenin, director of the Carnegie Moscow Centre, explained the Russian president's strategy to the *Financial Times*:

> By stepping up Russia's involvement in eastern Ukraine in recent weeks and deploying regular Russian troops, Mr Putin had sent a message to Kiev that he would not allow Ukrainian forces to defeat the pro-Russian rebels.

> "He put his finger on the scales of the battle, not his entire fist. And that was enough to deny victory to Ukrainian forces," said Mr Trenin. The Russian president's main aim, he added, was to position Moscow to have "enough leverage to weigh in very seriously on what happens in Kiev", and prevent it from joining Western alliances such as NATO.[36]

So even a weakened Russia has been able to outmanoeuvre NATO in its "near abroad". China is a much more difficult proposition. This is partly because of the size and dynamism of its economy and the speed with which, as we have seen, it is expanding its military capabilities. But it is also because, like Russia, its focus is primarily regional, and not global. As Geoff Dyer puts it:

> China has no intention of challenging the US around the globe over the coming decades. It has no interest in establishing a serious naval presence in the Caribbean, for instance, or posting soldiers in continental Europe. Instead, it is focused on Asia... China does not need to match the US dollar for dollar to achieve its goals: it only needs to spend enough to change the strategic balance in the western Pacific. Chinese strategists talk about "asymmetric" warfare, tactics and tools that can allow a weaker and smaller country to inflict huge damage on a bigger rival. China is not preparing for a war with the US. Indeed, the goal is to achieve Beijing's political aims without ever firing in anger. Instead, its military build-up is designed to gradually change the calculations of American commanders, to dissuade them from considering military operations anywhere near China's coast, and to push them slowly farther out into the Pacific.[37]

36: Olearchyk, Farchy and Buckley, 2014. See also Olearchyk and Buckley, 2014.
37: Dyer, 2014b, pp44-45.

Back to the quagmire

As we have already noted, it's not beyond Washington's power to respond effectively to this challenge, through a combination of redeploying military capabilities and exploiting fears of Chinese expansionism among Beijing's neighbours. But this requires a concentration of both attention and resources on East Asia. The advance of ISIS—the third of the crises we listed at the start—is effectively threatening to block this pivot. As we argued in our last issue, the rise of ISIS is essentially a product of two factors. In the first place, the failure of the Anglo-American occupation of Iraq forced the US to transfer control to an increasingly sectarian and authoritarian Shiite regime under Nouri al-Maliki, who so thoroughly alienated the Sunni Arab minority that ISIS was able to seize first Fallujah and then Mosul with comparative ease. Secondly, the sectarian civil war launched by the Assad regime in response to the Syrian Revolution of 2011 gave ISIS the space in which it was able to seize large areas of eastern Syria, from which it was able to launch its attacks into Iraq.[38]

ISIS is a sectarian Sunni jihadi organisation whose original inspiration springs from Al Qaeda. Indeed it developed from Al Qaeda in Mesopotamia. Amid the chaos wrought by the 2003 invasion this group, led by Abu Musab al Zarqawi until he was killed by the Americans in 2006, specialised in vicious sectarian attacks on the Shia majority in Iraq. This strategy helped to prevent the consolidation of a united resistance movement to the US occupation.[39] But ISIS has evolved in ways that are significantly different from Al Qaeda. Jason Burke argues that, at the height of its power, the original Al Qaeda functioned, not as "a coherent hierarchical terrorist group, with a single leader, a broadly uniform ideology and an ability to conceive and execute projects globally", but more like a venture capitalist company that would commission and finance projects proposed to it by different jihadi groups around the world. Following its expulsion from Afghanistan in 2001, "all that remains is the idea of 'Al Qaeda'".[40] Al Qaeda's amorphous nature fitted into fashionable talk about the future of warfare being "asymmetric" conflicts between states and "not-state" actors organised in networks.

But, as its name suggests, ISIS's ambition is to become a state—indeed it has already proclaimed itself the Caliphate. This reflects its desire to restore the polity of the classical Islamic era as an alternative to the ills of modernity

---

38: Callinicos, 2014.

39: Napoleoni, 2005.

40: Burke, 2004, pp231, 232, 290.

and the domination of the West. This is a literally reactionary ideology, but its utopian vision of a transnational Islamic political community has allowed ISIS to attract followers from many countries. It has also legitimised constructing a new state in the areas ISIS controls in eastern Syria and western Iraq, where it is developing very modern systems of accounting and bureaucratic control. From kidnapping ransoms and protection money ISIS is evolving towards more conventional sources of revenue, demanding $2 a month tax from shop owners and introducing utility charges. The seizure last year of Raqqa gave ISIS control of the eastern Syrian oilfield, and it is tapping the extensive smuggling network stretching across the borderlands of Syria, Iraq, Turkey and Iran to sell an estimated 80,000 barrels a day.[41] Many bourgeois thinkers have seen the state itself as a protection racket, in which property owners pay up in exchange for the security of their persons and possessions. ISIS seems to understand this quid pro quo. Early reports that it had robbed the vaults of Mosul's banks proved false: the banks have stayed open under jihadi rule.

Now Obama has pledged to "degrade and ultimately destroy" this proto-state. His strategy faces two fundamental contradictions. The first is to preserve the shreds of his commitment to end America's foreign wars. Obama has pledged that the US contribution to defeating ISIS will be confined purely to air power. But ISIS has a highly mobile and effective fighting force that would need to be defeated by ground troops. In fact, Obama has already sent nearly 1,200 US troops to Iraq and announced the dispatch of another 475 on 10 September. Their mission is to "advise" the Iraqi army, but everyone knows that America's involvement in the ground war in Vietnam started with John F Kennedy sending increasing numbers of "advisers" in the early 1960s.

General Martin Dempsey, chairman of the US Joint Chiefs of Staff, has on more than one occasion refused to rule out the return of American ground troops to Iraq. On 25 September he told a journalist: "If you're suggesting that I might, at some point, recommend that we need a large ground force to counter [the Islamic State], the answer to that is also absolutely." He hastily went on to add: "But it doesn't have to be Americans." The "ideal force" would be one "comprised of Iraqis and Kurds and moderate Syrian opposition".[42]

This solution to the first contradiction—Obama's new "coalition of the willing"—leads to a second one. Evidently the ground troops

41: Jones, 2014a, Daragahi and Solomon, 2014.
42: Rosen, 2014.

aren't going to come from Britain or other NATO states busily cutting their defence budgets. So they will have to come from the region itself. But here there is a morass of political difficulties. Gulf-based capital now dominates the Arab East economically, providing crucial backing for the counter-revolutions in Egypt and Syria.[43] Saudi Arabia and the other Gulf states have played their part in transforming the Syrian Revolution into a sectarian civil war by seizing on the conflict as an opportunity to strengthen Sunni Arab power in the region against their Shia opponents (Assad's Alawite sectarian base is a Shiite offshoot and his regime is closely allied to Iran). Much of the money and weapons they have poured into the Syrian war has ended up in the hands of jihadi groups such as ISIS or the official Al Qaeda affiliate Jabhat al-Nusra. Moreover, the legitimacy of the Saudi monarchy derives from Wahhabism, the ultra-purist interpretation of Islam from which Al Qaeda and its offshoots also draw inspiration.

So—despite the Gulf states' involvement in the air campaign against ISIS—they are too deeply implicated with the jihadis to be relied on. Turkey, supposedly the rising regional power, is in a complicated position that makes it also ambivalent about ISIS. The idea that the Iraqi army could fill the gap is laughable. The Iraqi regime became under the occupation what one Iraqi ex-minister called "an institutionalised kleptocracy".[44] Corruption permeates the army: hence it's no surprise that it abandoned first Fallujah and then Mosul to numerically inferior but highly motivated ISIS fighters, leaving behind for the victors new weapons and vehicles supplied by the US. As for the "moderate" Free Syrian Army, a defector to ISIS claims that "meetings of the FSA military council were invariably attended by representatives of the Saudi, UAE, Jordanian and Qatari intelligence services, as well as intelligence officers from the US, Britain and France".[45] The local committees that emerged from the original rising represent more authentic popular forces, but on the ground the FSA has been sidelined militarily by the jihadis.

That leaves the Assad regime. Its relations with ISIS have been ambiguous. Its forces have tended to avoid fighting the jihadis, concentrating their attacks on the more secular wing of the revolution. Moreover, according to the *Financial Times*, ISIS "sells oil to the Assad regime, according to several independent sources with close knowledge of the matter. The regime 'keeps the lights on' in some ISIS-controlled cities in exchange for barrels, one

---

43: Hanieh, 2011.
44: Cockburn, 2014, Kindle location 417.
45: Cockburn, 2014, Kindle location 585.

Western intelligence official says".[46] But the crisis created by the fall of Mosul fitted perfectly Assad's claims to be in the frontline of the "war on terrorism". Some prominent US policy intellectuals—for example, Richard Haass, director of policy planning at the State Department under the younger Bush, and Philip Bobbitt, who has Democratic Party connections—now advocate a tactical alliance with Assad against ISIS.[47] This has a realist logic, as does the further step of cooperation with Assad's backers in Tehran. But it would infuriate the Saudis and the other Gulf sheikhdoms, and confirm ISIS's claim to defend Sunnis against a hostile and oppressive world.

So the US is being dragged back into military involvement in the Middle East, where it faces a set of deeply unpalatable alternatives. In doing so it is trying to prop up a regional status quo that is cracking up under the accumulated internal tensions. That status quo has many victims, most obviously the Palestinians. Israel's latest assault in Gaza (the first of the conflicts listed at the start of this article) was really simply an episode in the permanent war that the Zionist state must wage in order to perpetuate the dispossession and subjugation of the Palestinians. Although the US maintained its default backing for Israel—resupplying it with the weapons that the Israel Defence Forces (IDF) were using indiscriminately to slaughter civilians, the price of these offensives is rising. The IDF were taken by surprise by Hamas's military innovations since their last attacks on Gaza—in particular the complex of tunnels under the territory and the combat training and equipment of Hamas fighters—and Israeli casualties were much higher than previously. But, as Israel's vast military advantage slowly erodes, there is no way out of the structural impasse arising from the dependence of Israeli security on the oppression of the Palestinians.

On a regional scale, the picture is less of deadlock than of fluidity. The same causes behind the rise of ISIS—the catastrophic invasion of Iraq and the Arab revolutions—have destabilised all the Arab regimes. Obama, like his predecessor, is now using American military power to freeze this flux. He is, as we have seen, unlikely to succeed. Along the way, however, this new intervention will no doubt cause much human suffering and political damage, in all probability strengthening rather than weakening ISIS. The successes of the counter-revolutionary forces across the region—and above all in Egypt, the heart of the Arab world—have given the initiative to reaction, whatever shape it takes—the US, Israel, Saudi Arabia, ISIS. In the IDF's bombardment of Gaza, the sectarian massacres in Iraq and Syria,

---

46: Jones, 2014a.
47: Haass, 2014, and Bobbitt, 2014.

the counter-revolutionary repression in Egypt and the US-orchestrated air campaign we see concrete images of the barbarism that Rosa Luxemburg predicted would engulf humankind in the absence of socialist revolution. Much hangs on a new revolutionary wave.

For revolutionaries, opposing Obama's bombing campaign—and whatever other military actions follow—should be straightforward. (We should also, of course, oppose NATO expansion in Central and Eastern Europe.) But this opposition needs to be informed by an understanding that the latest US intervention in the Middle East takes place against the background of a renewal of inter-imperialist rivalries on a scale not seen since the end of the Cold War. Anti-imperialism during that era required, not simply opposing our "own" imperialism, but also refusing to prettify the actions of its rival and acknowledging that it too operates according to an imperialist logic. The same stance is required today, with the complication that today we are seeing multi-polar interstate competition. This is clearest in East Asia. On a global scale, the US remains the only world power, but it faces serious regional challenges from Russia and China, and within the Western bloc Germany and Japan are newly assertive.

Grasping this complexity is not an academic exercise. If we assign a "progressive" role to America's rivals, we lose hold of the thread of class struggle. The main antagonism in the world becomes that between states rather than classes. But, beyond their real conflicts of interest, all the leading capitalist states are united by their common dependence on the exploitation of wage labour. As Lenin and Luxemburg understood so well in 1914, the critique of the imperialist system is an essential political tool in uniting workers against capital.

References

Anderson, Perry, 2006, "Inside Man", *The Nation* (24 April), www.thenation.com/article/inside-man

Binns, Peter, 1983, "Understanding the New Cold War", *International Socialism* 19 (spring).

Bobbitt, Philip, 2014, "Choose Enemies Carefully But Be Less Picky about Allies", *Financial Times* (29 August), www.ft.com/cms/s/0/ad07797a-2ed9-11e4-afe4-00144feabdc0.html#axzz3ERM4pdQy

Brenner, Robert, 2002, *The Boom and the Bubble: The US in the World Economy* (Verso).

Burke, Jason, 2004, *Al-Qaeda: The True Story of Radical Islam* (Penguin).

Callinicos, Alex, 2003, *The New Mandarins of American Power: The Bush Administration's Plans for the World* (Polity).

Callinicos, Alex, 2009, *Imperialism and Global Political Economy* (Polity).

Callinicos, Alex, 2010, *Bonfire of Illusions: The Twin Crises of the Liberal World* (Polity).

Callinicos, Alex, 2014, "Nemesis in Iraq", *International Socialism* 143 (summer), www.isj.org.uk/?id=981

Clark, Christopher, 2012, *The Sleepwalkers: How Europe Went to War in 1914* (Penguin).

Cockburn, Patrick, 2014, *The Jihadis Return: ISIS and the New Sunni Uprising* (OR Books).

Daragahi, Borzou, and Erika Solomon, 2014, "Fuelling ISIS Inc", *Financial Times* (21 September), www.ft.com/cms/s/2/34e874ac-3dad-11e4-b782-00144feabdc0.html#axzz3ERM4pdQy

Darwin, John, 2009, *The Empire Project: The Rise and Fall of the British World System, 1830-1970* (Cambridge University Press).

Deutscher, Isaac, 1961, *The Great Contest: Russia and the West* (Ballantine Books).

Dyer, Geoff, 2014a, *The Contest of the Century: The New Era of Competition with China—and How America Can Win* (Allen Lane).

Dyer, Geoff, 2014b, "US Diplomat Victoria Nuland Faces Questions over Strategy", *Financial Times* (31 July), www.ft.com/cms/s/0/a4f13052-18ca-11e4-80da-00144feabdc0.html#axzz3ERM4pdQy

Friedberg, Aaron, 2012, *A Contest for Supremacy: China, America, and the Struggle for Mastery in Asia* (W W Norton & Co).

Fukuyama, Francis, 2014, "ISIS Risks Distracting US from More Menacing Foes", *Financial Times* (25 June), www.ft.com/cms/s/0/68428a5a-f7c0-11e3-90fa-00144feabdc0.html?siteedition=uk#axzz35qWVRlxl

Gowan, Peter, 1999, *The Global Gamble: Washington's Faustian Bid for World Dominance* (Verso).

Haass, Richard, 2014, "Look to Syria to Halt the Deadly March of ISIS", *Financial Times* (26 August), www.ft.com/cms/s/0/8f5ff39a-2c39-11e4-8eda-00144feabdc0.html?siteedition=uk#axzz3ERM4pdQy

Hanieh, Adam, 2011, *Capitalism and Class in the Gulf Arab States* (Palgrave Macmillan).

Harvey, David, 2003, *The New Imperialism* (Oxford University Press).

Hobson, John A, 1938 [1902], *Imperialism: A Study* (Allen & Unwin).

International Institute for Strategic Studies, 2013, *The Military Balance 2013* (Taylor & Francis).

International Institute for Strategic Studies, 2014, *The Military Balance 2014* (Taylor & Francis).

Jones, Sam, 2014a, "Diverse Funding and Strong Accounting Give ISIS Unparalleled Wealth", *Financial Times* (22 June), www.ft.com/cms/s/0/21e8c922-f95d-11e3-bb9d-00144feab7de.html#axzz3ERM4pdQy

Jones, Sam, 2014b, "Ukraine: Russia's New Art of War", *Financial Times* (28 August), www.ft.com/cms/s/2/ea5e82fa-2e0c-11e4-b760-00144feabdc0.html#axzz3ERM4pdQy

Kagarlitsky, Boris, 2014, "Ukraine's Uprising against Nato, Neoliberals and Oligarchs—an Interview with Boris Kagarlitsky", *Counterfire* (8 September), http://tinyurl.com/pgnpn64

Kaplan, David, 2010, *Monsoon: The Indian Ocean and the Future of American Power* (Random House).

Kaplan, David, 2014, *Asia's Cauldron: The South China Sea and the End of a Stable Pacific* (Random House).

Kim, Ha-young, 2013, "Imperialism and Instability in East Asia Today", *International Socialism* 138 (spring), www.isj.org.uk/?id=882

Luttwak, Edward, 2012, *The Rise of China vs. the Logic of Strategy* (Harvard University Press).

Napoleoni, Loretta, 2005, *Insurgent Iraq: Al Zarqawi and the New Generation* (Constable).

Olearchyk, Roman, and Neil Buckley, 2014, "How Russia Forced Ukraine into a Ceasefire with Rebels", *Financial Times* (12 September), www.ft.com/cms/s/0/3a243bb4-3a5f-11e4-bd08-00144feabdc0.html?siteedition=uk#axzz3ERM4pdQy

Olearchyk, Roman, Jack Farchy, and Neil Buckley, 2014, "Putin and Poroshenko Weigh Ceasefire and Prospect of 'Frozen Conflict'", *Financial Times* (3 September), www.ft.com/cms/s/0/828004a6-3389-11e4-ba62-00144feabdc0.html#axzz3ERM4pdQy

Rosen, James, 2014, "US Combat Role in Iraq Not Off Table, Gen. Dempsey Says" (26 September), www.newsobserver.com/2014/09/26/4184661_us-combat-role-in-iraq-not-off.html?rh=1

Ross, Robert, 2012, "The Problem with the Pivot: Obama's New Asia Policy is Unnecessary and Unproductive", *Foreign Affairs* (November-December), www.foreignaffairs.com/articles/138211/robert-s-ross/the-problem-with-the-pivot

Wade, Robert H, 2014, "Growth, Inequality, and Poverty: Evidence, Arguments, and Economists", in John Ravenhill (ed), *Global Political Economy* (Oxford University Press).

Watkins, Susan, 2014, "Annexations", *New Left Review*, II/86, newleftreview.org/II/86/susan-watkins-annexations

Wildau, Gabriel, 2014, "China Risks 'Balance-Sheet Recession' as Stimulus Impact Wanes" (21 September), www.ft.com/cms/s/0/14404880-3fdb-11e4-a381-00144feabdc0.html?siteedition=uk#axzz3ElXCsvNj

Wolf, Martin, 2014, *The Shifts and the Shocks: What We've Learned—and Have Still to Learn—from the Financial Crisis* (Penguin).

The case of the disappearing Lenin

Kevin Corr and Gareth Jenkins

What, if anything, do modern day socialists have to learn from Lenin? Capitalism is mired in its deepest and longest crisis since the 1930s, producing bitter discontent that in places overflows into mass resistance and even revolutions. With Stalinism all but dead and traditional reformist parties offering little beyond doing austerity in a fairer manner, revolution from below would seem to be an idea whose time has at long last returned. Yet the working class seems "slow" to fulfil the role allotted it by classical Marxism. It has, perhaps, even "accepted" neoliberalism. Many activists do not believe that class or political parties define anti-systemic movements. The idea of working class revolution led by a revolutionary party to smash the state seems the quaint property of irrelevant groups unable to break out of the far-left ghetto.

This mood has affected the revolutionary left. For some the problem is the kind of party they used to believe in. Perhaps it is wrong to insist on a rigid distinction between "revolutionary" and "reformist". Perhaps "mixing" the two can reconstruct a radical left able to fill the gap between a declining parliamentary reformism and a "Leninist" left that cannot grow. This seems to be what lies behind moves to create broad left parties that have the kind of appeal that, for example, Syriza (the Coalition of the Radical Left) in Greece and the Front de Gauche in France enjoy. A *rapprochement* with and re-evaluation of what the revolutionary left termed "left reformism" is therefore required.

This, then, is the context for taking seriously the intellectual debate initiated by the outstanding Canadian Marxist scholar, Lars Lih. Lih has shown that there is nothing in the real Lenin that can be made to justify the ideology of "Leninism" that was fabricated after Lenin's death to justify the growing power of the Soviet bureaucracy. But his defence of Lenin has led him to interpret Lenin as making no fundamental contribution to Marxism—at least nothing that goes beyond the Marxism of the Second International (the International that united all Social Democratic[1] parties before the First World War), as embodied in its most important representative thinker, Karl Kautsky.

What started as a debate primarily about the real meaning of Lenin's 1902 pamphlet *What Is To Be Done?* (hereafter *WITBD*) has become a much broader debate about whether it is possible to deduce from his ideas and practice a distinct theory of revolutionary organisation—whether, in other words, it is possible to rescue a genuine Leninism from its Stalinist caricature. Lih has come to assert that, contrary to appearances, Lenin never broke fundamentally from Kautskyan Marxism. This claim, if true, poses a fundamental challenge to the revolutionary left's view of Lenin as renewing a Marxist tradition that the Second International's greatest theorist had emptied of revolutionary content.

This article argues against the "Kautskyanisation" of Lenin. Lenin may well have thought he was implementing the Marxism he took from Kautsky. The Bolsheviks may, initially, have seen themselves as part of the Social Democratic family (even if Tsarism made them slightly peculiar cousins). Yet they were the only significant social democratic Party not to collapse into chauvinism in the First World War and the only Social Democratic Party to lead a successful revolution. The explanation for this has to be, we shall argue, that though they may have shared (formally) the same Marxism as Kautsky, in practice they did not. This difference in practice resulted in a theoretical renewing of the Marxism that Kautsky had reduced to a dead letter. This renewing is the distinctive Leninism we want to defend. Assessing its validity in terms of what Lenin did, over and above what his language sometimes seems to indicate he thought he was doing, seems to us perfectly correct—even though we recognise that Lih would not agree.

Lenin rediscovered

In his *Lenin Rediscovered: What is to be Done? in Context*, Lih argues convincingly that mistranslations and misunderstandings[2] of *WITBD* have produced a distorted picture of the revolutionary party Lenin wished to create.

1:    The parties of the Second International (1889-1914) were committed, in principle, to the revolutionary overthrow of capitalism. Only later did Social Democracy take on its modern, reformist meaning.

2:    See Lih, 2008a, pp613-658 in particular for a discussion of "spontaneity" and other key terms in *WITBD*.

According to this Cold War "textbook interpretation"[3] Lenin "feared the 'spontaneous' development of the workers' movement", demanded that the movement "be 'diverted' from its natural course" and that it "be directed 'from without' by...bourgeois revolutionary intellectuals"[4] organised in a "hyper-centralised" party and "dedicated to conspiracy".[5] Thus *WITBD* was "a profound theoretical and organisational innovation, the charter document of Bolshevism, and the ultimate source of Stalinism".[6] On the contrary, Lih says, *WITBD* reflected mainstream European socialist thought in the period. Lenin, "a passionate advocate of political freedom",[7] believed that workers would "respond...with acceptance and enthusiasm"[8] to the socialist "good news" message and that the Russian workers' movement, like its Western counterparts, would play the same role in emancipating society.

Lih demystifies the formulations that most seem to favour in the textbook interpretation—Lenin's contention that "class political consciousness can be brought to the workers *only from without*".[9] Lih proves decisively that when Lenin spoke of "spontaneity" and the need to "divert" it[10] (to use the standard translations), we should not take this to mean that workers had to be forced by socialist intellectuals into taking the road to revolution against their natural bent. Rather we should understand this as meaning that the workers' movement was capable of more than fighting for its own immediate interests, that it could become conscious of its power to transform society. Lenin was rephrasing Kautsky's Erfurt Programme (the 1891 programme of the German Social Democratic Party) about the task of Social Democracy being "to lend this workers' class struggle a conscious and united character and to point it towards its necessary goal".[11]

Lenin himself wrote in 1899 in his *Draft Programme of Our Party*: "We are not in the least afraid to say that we want to imitate the Erfurt Programme";[12] and "when we so often hear opportunist and equivocal criticism of that programme, we consider it our duty to speak openly in its

---

3: Lih, 2008a, p13, for first mention.
4: Lih, 2008a, p15.
5: Lih, 2008a, p17.
6: Lih, 2008a, p18.
7: Lih, 2008a, p8.
8: Lih, 2008a, p6.
9: Lenin, 1901, p422. Lenin makes a similar point several times over in the course of *WITBD*, including quoting Kautsky.
10: Lenin, 1901, p384. Lih argues convincingly that "divert" is another, distorting mistranslation (See Lih, 2008a, pp628-631).
11: Erfurt Programme, quoted in Salvadori, 1990, p30.
12: Lenin, 1899, p235.

favour".[13] In other words, Lenin appealed to Kautsky to give authority to his own battle against the Russian "economist" version of revisionism: the ideology that "systematically restricts the worker movement to defending its sectional interests".[14]

Lih's detailed rebuttal of the textbook interpretation was widely, and rightly, welcomed on the revolutionary left.[15] However, Lih's target was not only the textbook interpretation. In his sights was also what he called the "activist interpretation"[16] over what he saw as its negative attitude towards Kautsky. For the activist interpretation, there is an *intrinsic* difficulty in the phrase Lenin took from Kautsky (about the relationship between "spontaneity" and "consciousness"), *irrespective* of whether it has been misused in the textbook interpretation. The danger is of a one-sidedness that comes from understanding socialist theory as something formed separately from workers' practice (and then introduced into the workers' movement). As John Molyneux argues, the truth of socialist theory "must be intimately related to, and influenced by and based upon the activity of the working class".[17] What is problematic about Kautsky's formulation (one that *separates* consciousness from spontaneity) is that it risks incorporating an elitist view of the party's relationship to the class.

For the activist interpretation, this one-sidedness may not have mattered while the emphasis had been on steering against kowtowing to spontaneity (the theme of *WITBD*). But it did matter when revolution approached in 1905. The context was now very different. Hard on the heels of Russian military defeat by Japan, the social and political crisis was itself having a profoundly revolutionising effect on workers. Now the spontaneity of the rising movement had to be brought *to* the party: the

---

13: Lenin, 1899, p235.

14: Lih, 2008a, p594. This ideology is, as Lih points out, the real meaning of *tred-iunionizm* for Lenin (the standard, misleading translation is "trade unionism").

15: See, for example, the generally favourable reception accorded to *Lenin Rediscovered* in the symposium edited by Paul Blackledge in *Historical Materialism*, volume 18, issue 3, 2010. See also Blackledge's review, "What Was Done", of *Lenin Rediscovered* in this journal (Blackledge, 2006a). It should be noted that Chris Harman's contribution to the symposium argued that by portraying Lenin as an "Erfurtian" Lih himself bends the stick too far in the direction of proving Lenin's orthodoxy (Harman, 2010).

16: Lih, 2008a, p18. Lih refers mostly, here and elsewhere, to the Trotskyist tradition, to Tony Cliff, John Molyneux and Chris Harman, from the International Socialist tradition, and to Paul Le Blanc and Ernest Mandel, from the Fourth International tradition. He also refers to Marcel Liebman's libertarian reading of Lenin. Puzzlingly, he does not refer to Hal Draper's analysis of *WITBD* (see Draper, 1990).

17: Molyneux, 1986, p49.

party stalwarts needed to be "taught" by the workers rather than, as the Kautskyan formulation suggested, the other way round. The structures of the party previously needed to resist accommodation to economism were now a hindrance. This was at the heart of the debate at the 1905 April Congress between Lenin and the "committee men", which Lenin lost. Returning to the theme in November that year, Lenin made it very clear that "a sudden influx of large numbers of non-Social-Democrats" would not mean that "the party would be dissolved among the masses" (which had been his argument in *WITBD* against the economists). The renewal of a militant worker intelligentsia in the party would be the much more likely outcome of this more ideologically driven wave of spontaneous class struggle. Now, he emphasised, "the heroic proletariat has proved by deeds its readiness to fight, and its ability to fight...in a purely Social-Democratic [ie revolutionary] spirit... The working class is instinctively, spontaneously Social-Democratic".[18]

This activist interpretation has been roundly condemned by Lih. The "activist writers", Lih says, "talk as if they knew Lenin's beliefs better than he did himself"; he dismisses the idea of Lenin "bending the stick" as "the activist tradition's favourite device for explaining away anomalies". He criticises Molyneux for presupposing that Lenin "remained completely unaware that he diverged in fundamental ways from Kautsky", despite deep familiarity with his writings. "I am not sure", he adds ironically, "whether we are supposed to explain this by Kautsky's deceitfulness, Lenin's inability to understand what he read, or Lenin's unawareness of his own beliefs".[19] This "ends up making Lenin look like a rather incompetent and incoherent leader", and Cliff is similarly criticised for giving an unattractive picture of Lenin as an exaggerated stick-bender.[20]

Yet "stick-bending"—or to use Draper's formulation, "exaggerating in every way that side of the problem which points in the direction it is necessary to move now"[21]—enables a serious socialist party to intervene as circumstances change. Unless it does so, revolutionary principle remains sterile—as Kautsky's "consistency" came to demonstrate.

In particular, Lih dismisses Tony Cliff's claim that Lenin had to

---

18: Lenin, 1905c, p32. Lenin made it clear that the clarity of revolutionary principle and organisational discipline that the party had created over many years was why fear of an influx of workers was misplaced (see Lenin, 1905c, p31).

19: Lih, 2008a, p25.

20: Lih, 2008a, pp25-27.

21: Draper, 1953.

persuade his supporters to abandon positions held in 1903 as "totally false".[22] What the record shows, according to Lih, is not an opposition *in principle* to Lenin's proposal to recruit workers to the party committees, only a disagreement over its *practicability* (the committee men criticised it "because it merely affirmed an axiomatic goal (worker recruitment) without showing ways and means", to use Lih's language).[23]

But for all Cliff's reliance on a particular source,[24] did he get it as wrong as Lih claims? At the Congress Lenin complained, according to the *Collected Works*, that "the inertness of the committee-men has to be overcome"—a statement that was met with applause and booing. Lenin went on to argue that "to place workers on the committees is a *political*, not only a pedagogical, task".[25] Lenin's emphasis on the political importance of getting workers onto the committees suggests that the opposition of the committee-men ran deeper than practicalities.

In addition there are the memoirs of Nadezhda Krupskaya, Lenin's wife and an important Bolshevik in her own right, who was present at the Congress. She reported Lenin as saying, after the debate was concluded: "I could not sit still and listen to them saying that there were no workers suitable to be members of committees. The question drags on, and it shows there is a malady in the party. Workers must be brought onto the committees".[26]

"Bending the stick", then, as a metaphor that shouldn't be taken too literally,[27] makes sense of the shifts in Lenin's practice—particularly here. Lenin himself warned, in his own comments on the re-publication of *WITBD* in 1907, against treating the pamphlet outside the "concrete historical situation" of a past stage in the party's development. Its "incorrect or exaggerated ideas on the subject of an organisation of professional revolutionaries" could be criticised but this was to miss the fact that they no longer applied to the present.[28]

Noting such shifts, as here between the period of *WITBD* and that of 1905, is not to depict Lenin negatively—as an incompetent or incoherent

22: Lih, 2008a, p540. Cliff's account is in Cliff, 1975, pp168-183. See also Lih 2010c, pp147-157 where Lih criticises those who share Cliff's account, eg Harman and Molyneux.
23: Lih, 2010c, p152.
24: Lih disputes the reliability of Solomon Schwartz, a Bolshevik at the time of the 1905 conference who soon after became a Menshevik, and also accuses Cliff of plagiarising.
25: Lenin, 1905a, p408 (our emphasis).
26: Krupskaya, 1970, p116.
27: Lih has a rather long-winded discussion of the metaphor aiming to prove textually its inapplicability to Lenin (Lih, 2008a, p26).
28: Lenin, 1907b, p101.

leader who did not know his own mind as Lih claims. It is, rather, to show that Lenin bent the stick, when required, to ensure particular organisational forms did not hinder the party from growing when conditions changed. This flexibility should not be confused with manoeuvring. Where Lenin *was* inflexible was in his single-minded determination to build a party capable of overthrowing capitalism. The relationship between tactics and principle was a dialectical process of preserving past gains while overcoming one-sidedness.

Was Lenin a Kautskyan?

Since *Lenin Rediscovered* Lih has pushed the idea of Kautsky's influence on Lenin to the point of challenging what seems an obvious problem: Lenin's open rupture with the "renegade" Kautsky after 1914. However, says Lih, "Lenin felt that Kautsky had changed, not himself. He saw no reason to abandon the outlook he shared with Kautsky just at the time when, in his eyes, events had justified it completely".[29] Contrary to appearances, Lenin's writings even after 1914 owe an "enormous debt" to Kautsky's "scenario of global revolutionary interaction" (over the national question, imperialism, and political and social revolution).[30] Lih says this is proved by the praise Lenin gave in 1915 to Kautsky's 1909 *The Road to Power*.

It wasn't Lenin, then, who broke with Kautskyanism; it was Kautsky. As Lih puts it: "Lenin's political outlook and strategy from 1914 on stemmed from a definition of the situation that he took lock, stock and barrel from the writings of 'Kautsky when he was a Marxist'".[31] Indeed, "aggressive unoriginality"[32] is how Lih describes Lenin's general relationship to Kautsky, one that presents a picture of a Lenin who remains strangely unchanging in his Kautskyism.

This view of Lenin, echoed in Lih's biography of Lenin,[33] seems to have become received wisdom by some on the left, if the review by a leading North American socialist activist, Charlie Post, is anything to go by. Post says Lih is right to argue, among other things, that "Lenin remained a relatively consistent 'Kautskyan' Marxist through 1921", that he "never developed an original 'theory of the party'—he merely adapted the SPD model to 'Russian conditions'", that his strategy for the Russian Revolution was not "unique" but one already outlined by Kautsky in 1906 and that with the failure of the post-war European revolutions, the failure

---

29: Lih, 2008b.
30: Lih, 2012c.
31: Lih, 2012c.
32: See Lih, 2009a, and Lih, 2009b.
33: Lih, 2011c.

of the peasantry to split between kulak and poor peasant, and the failure of the Soviet state to conform to Lenin's expectations in *The State and Revolution*, Lenin was forced to "reconsider 'the textbook à la Kautsky'".[34]

Graciously, Post concedes: "While there is little of Lenin's theory with the exception of *State and Revolution* and *Left-Wing Communism* that is either original or of enduring value, the *practice* of the Bolsheviks through 1917 remains relevant".[35] How so big an exception does not invalidate both the main proposition and its relevance to 1917 is a mystery.

The notion of "aggressive unoriginality" underlies Lih's revisionist understanding of the significance of Lenin's 1917 *April Theses*. In the activist interpretation, the *Theses* mark a sharp break from "old Bolshevism" and a rearming of the party that would make the October Revolution possible. It was a "bending of the stick" that faced even greater resistance than that put up by the committee-men in 1905.

Lih rejects this, arguing that the "most famous of historical narratives", in which Lenin "arrives" in April, the Bolsheviks "are baffled with his new vision", he "faces them down" and then, after a month's debate, "everyone gets on board the new line" is simply wrong. Mutual misunderstandings and questions of timing apart, there was general agreement on the basic message, which was to "protect the revolution, respond to the national crisis, carry out the basic programme of the revolution".[36] The *April Theses* are not even as original as some claim. Lenin was influenced by his reading of a recent article of Kautsky's, which Lih calls "a concise précis of old Bolshevik strategy". The verbal echoes "add weight to the strong circumstantial case for seeing Kautsky's article as the catalyst for Lenin's greatest innovations in his ideological outlook".[37] (In other words, Kautskyanism underpinned whatever was really new.) More damningly, it is wrong to assume that Lenin won the debate over the *April Theses* against the old Bolsheviks. On the contrary, Lih concludes, "old Bolshevism triumphed in 1917", something that Lenin "came close to explicitly acknowledging" after the event.[38] The only conclusion to be drawn from this is that, just as the conflict between Lenin and the committee-men in 1905 had been over the practicalities of worker representation, so the conflict between Lenin and the "old Bolsheviks" in 1917 was a pragmatic one over the best way to bring about the Kautskyan revolution.

34: Post, 2011.
35: Post, 2011.
36: Lih, 2012b.
37: Lih, 2010a.
38: Lih, 2011b, p201.

This has very profound implications for our understanding of the October Revolution itself. Lih argues that the message referred to in the previous paragraph (about protecting the revolution) "could be summed up as *Vsya vlast' sovyetam* ('All power to the soviets')" but that he found the phrase *Vsya vlast' naridu* ("All power to the people") more often in the Bolshevik party's pamphlets.[39] Furthermore, Lih claims that "in the months leading up to the revolution, socialism was downplayed" (even if after October steps towards it were "prominent"). The Bolsheviks had to "downplay socialism" before the revolution because "if they thought socialist revolution would appeal to [the people], then they would have called for it. They must have known that it would not appeal." The Bolsheviks may have wanted the revolution to lead to socialism, but they necessarily remained cautious and pro-peasant. What this "urban radical party" achieved was the creation of "a great peasant army" that "would win the civil war". This was the realisation of the "original Bolshevik scenario".[40]

Lih argues that the left, for all its familiarity with the idea that 1917 was a worker-peasant revolution, is wrong to "choose to emphasise *discontinuity* in 1917"; "they are hung up...on the juxtaposition between democratic revolution and socialist revolution. In my view there is certainly a shift, but the discontinuity has been overstated".[41] If Lih is correct, then the soviet seizure of power cannot truly be called a socialist revolution in the sense of workers taking power in order to *break* with capitalism and begin constructing a socialist order. The only conclusion we can draw from this is that October was a popular-democratic revolution—a better, if not qualitatively different, version of February—but one that did not and indeed could not challenge capitalism except partially.

So if Lenin was always deep down a Kautskyan, then the October Revolution itself was a realisation of the (Kautskyan) old Bolshevik 1905 scenario. But if this is true, why should Lenin's Kautskyanism have created a party capable of overthrowing the state? Was this simply a subjective factor, a matter of Lenin sticking to his Kautskyanism, while Kautsky turned his back on it?

To answer this, we need to turn to the question of whether "democracy" meant the same thing to Lenin as it did to Kautsky. At issue here is the nature of the state under capitalism, the role of electoral politics, and the significance of the soviet form of power. As we hope to show, whatever their common commitment to political freedom as the goal of

---

39: Lih, 2012b.
40: Lih, 2012b.
41: Lih, 2012b.

revolution, a much deeper divergence explains why Lenin was capable of building a party that could bring revolutionary change, whereas Kautsky not only could not but finished up on the wrong side.

Kautsky's road to power

Lenin certainly admired the Kautsky of *The Road to Power* and before. But does this prove that Kautsky must be considered a revolutionary Marxist before 1914 even if he ceased to be one afterwards? Some have argued he was never, even at an early stage, a revolutionary in the sense that Lenin was one. Massimo Salvadori, for example, argues that "by the end of the 19th century" Kautsky held a view of the state and democracy "that would inevitably clash with Soviet theory and the practice of the government of the Bolsheviks". Kautsky "had always regarded the dictatorship of the proletariat as a regime which, although it would represent the power of the proletariat alone, would be established by free elections [and] would be based on the use of parliament for socialist purposes".[42]

In his writings, however, Kautsky stressed that only through proletarian revolution could capitalism be defeated and socialism introduced.[43] How was this commitment to revolutionary Marxism reconciled with an equally repeated commitment to the "so-called peaceful method of class struggle, which confines itself to the non-military method of parliamentarism, strikes, demonstrations, the press, and similar means of exerting pressure"?[44] The justification for this new method of struggle ("at least in countries with reasonably democratic institutions"[45]) was that, though *revolution* was still the goal, its insurrectionary form, characteristic of the period of *bourgeois* revolutions, no longer fitted.

There is an obvious tension here between ends and means: peaceful methods of struggle seem the antithesis of revolutionary methods. Kautsky tended to finesse the tension. The "democratic-proletarian method of struggle"[46] was not a substitute for the class struggle required for socialism, as "democracy cannot eliminate the class antagonism of capitalist society".[47] On the other hand, parliamentarism represented the only way to marshall one's forces—under existing circumstances—until the day of capitalism's

---

42: Salvadori, 1990, p12.
43: We are paraphrasing a key section of *The Road to Power*, which itself is an extract from an article published some 16 years earlier (see Kautsky, 2007, pp41-42).
44: Kautsky, 2007, p44.
45: Kautsky, 2007, p43.
46: Kautsky, 2007, p44.
47: Kautsky, 2007, p43.

revolutionary overthrow arrived (this could be said to be a crude, mechanical version of Engels's position[48]).

But Kautsky also offered a justification for the peaceful method of struggle that opened the door to the idea that the revolution could be achieved peacefully. In chapter 5, section 9 of his 1892 commentary on the Erfurt Programme, he wrote that "whenever the proletariat engages in parliamentary activity as a self-conscious class, parliamentarism begins to change its character. It ceases to be a mere tool in the hands of the bourgeoisie".[49] This was an ambiguous formula, admitting both a revolutionary and a reformist interpretation. On the one hand, it implied that once the working class began to compete for votes parliamentarism was no longer a terrain reserved for the bourgeoisie—a position consistent with a stress on the *limits* of parliamentarism (the inability of bourgeois democracy to eliminate class antagonism). On the other hand, it might also imply that parliamentarism, under pressure from the working class, might lose its bourgeois class character altogether. If so, the prospect of the proletariat establishing its power through parliament (by filling it with a different class character) was still a possibility. Kautsky's formulation, in other words, allowed an accommodation with reformism.

This tells us something about the nature of Kautsky's Marxism. Though his reputation as a Marxist rested on a decade-long theoretical struggle against revisionism in the German party, his Marxism offered virtually nothing to the working class except faith in the peaceful method of struggle. One day the decisive battle between bourgeoisie and proletariat might come, but as for what workers in the meantime should do for themselves, Kautsky had little concrete to say. This meant (in the absence of revolutionary theory as a guide to action) that the parliamentarist terrain he operated on was that of his revisionist opponents. Their parliamentarism had no need for revolution as the goal justifying their practice. But nor, in effect, did Kautsky's, as the goal of revolution was forever postponed till the time was right (which it never was). Kautsky was bold in calling for irreconcilable opposition to the existing order in a new era of revolutions,[50] but timid when reality demanded it. As Gary Steenson argues, his opposition to the right wing of the party gave "his work a radical flavour that at times belied the moderation of his true position".[51] Dick Geary argues something similar when he claims that

48: see Engels, 1990.
49: Kautsky, 1892.
50: See the last chapter, "A New Age of Revolutions", in *The Road to Power* (Kautsky, 2007, pp91-106).
51: Steenson, 1991, p102.

"though certainly not intentionally, Kautsky too was a 'revisionist'"[52]—as long as by "revisionist" we understand this to mean that Kautsky's defence of Marxism failed to preserve its revolutionary content.

There was, then, a deep ambiguity about what parliamentarism expected from "democracy". Was it no more than the best terrain on which socialists should fight—without expecting socialism to come through parliament? Or did electoral success mean it could? The painful business of revolution might be avoided altogether by a peaceful "revolution" through parliament. The almost constant rise of German Social Democracy to become the biggest party in the Reichstag by 1912 seemed good enough—proof that "democracy" was making socialism (in general terms) irresistible. As long as capitalism remained relatively "peaceful" and parliament the focus for challenging the hegemony of bourgeois politics (in terms of votes cast and MPs elected), the test of whether or not parliamentarism brought real power for the working class could be avoided.

But the intensified crisis of imperialism changed that. In theory, Kautsky understood that revolution was more necessary than ever if society was not to descend into war and barbarism. But he was incapable of breaking with the parliamentarism that he had so long championed ("failing to bend the stick", one might say) and that had been the bedrock of German Social Democracy. The deep ambiguities in his Marxism became clearer—at least to the German Social Democratic left, who had the advantage of observing Kautsky at closer quarters than Lenin.

Russian exceptionalism

One reason why Lenin admired Kautsky (before 1914) was because of Kautsky's response to the 1905 Russian Revolution.

That has to do with the fact that, as far as "peaceful methods" of struggle were concerned, the exception for Kautsky was Russia. There "older" methods of revolutionary struggle would have to be used precisely because, in the absence of meaningful democratic institutions, peaceful methods of struggle were self-evidently not possible. Democracy (even bourgeois democracy) could only come as a result of revolution—it could not be a way to, or a substitute for, revolution. This "exceptionalism" allowed Kautsky to think, for a time, beyond his habitual attachment to parliamentarism. It led him to support Lenin and the Bolsheviks in 1905 and oppose the Mensheviks. In 1917 the reverse was true: "democracy"

52: Geary, 1987, p14. It should be noted that neither Geary nor Salvadori draws "Leninist" conclusions from Kautsky's "revisionism".

excluded the possibility of socialism through the soviets.[53]

The disagreement between socialists (at least between Bolsheviks and Mensheviks in the 1905 period) was not over the *nature* of the forthcoming revolution: given Russian backwardness, the common socialist belief was that it could not be other than a *bourgeois* one, bringing about the free development of capitalism and therefore the development of a working class able to bring about a future socialist revolution.[54] Where Bolsheviks and Mensheviks disagreed was over *how*, in practice, Tsarism was to be overthrown. Earlier, Plekhanov, the founder of Russian Marxism, had argued that the Russian bourgeoisie was too cowardly to lead its own revolution and so the cultural and political tasks of leadership would "fall to the lot of the proletariat"[55] as the most revolutionary class in society, tiny though it was. The logic of this position was that socialists should strive to preserve the political independence of the working class.

Yet the Mensheviks (and Plekhanov himself) now reneged on that logic. Instead they looked for an alliance with the liberal bourgeoisie, in which the working class was to play a politically subordinate role. It should stiffen the backbone of the liberals but not frighten them with excessive anti-capitalist demands. The Bolsheviks rejected that strategy as both dangerous (the liberals would always prefer compromise) and liquidationist (the class interests of the proletariat would be sacrificed). The Bolsheviks looked, instead, for allies among the oppressed peasantry.

Looking for allies among a "backward" class, more likely to be pro-monarchist than pro-liberal, made the Bolshevik position appear unorthodox from a Marxist point of view. However, Kautsky, when appealed to as a Marxist authority by Plekhanov, dashed Menshevik expectations and sided unequivocally with the Bolsheviks.[56] Lenin was delighted. In his "Preface to the Russian Translation of K Kautsky's Pamphlet: *The Driving Forces and Prospects of the Russian Revolution*", he wrote: "A bourgeois revolution, brought about by the proletariat and the peasantry in spite of the instability of the bourgeoisie—this fundamental principle of Bolshevik

53: See, for example, *The Dictatorship of the Proletariat* (Kautsky, 1918).

54: The exception among socialists was Leon Trotsky. Almost alone, Trotsky saw that if the working class led the revolution, it could not but overstep the limits of a bourgeois revolution. But detailed discussion of his theory of permanent revolution, which came into its own in 1917, lies beyond the scope of this article.

55: Quoted in Cliff, 1957.

56: See Blackledge, 2006b, pp354-356, for a discussion of Kautsky's intervention in the debate around 1905.

tactics is wholly confirmed by Kautsky".[57]

It wasn't only the question of social forces that led Kautsky to distance himself from parliamentarism. The huge strike wave that swept over Russia (and Poland, then one of the most industrialised parts of the Russian Empire) led Kautsky to a positive revision of his view of the armed insurrection. Given that the mass strike had undermined the discipline of the army and the state could no longer rely on its armed forces to control the working class, he could no longer affirm that "armed insurrection...will no longer play a decisive role in the future revolution"[58]—a tortuous way of saying it might.

Kautsky's preparedness to endorse (albeit cautiously) the mass strike as a *political* weapon set him on a potential collision course with the reformist trade union and parliamentary leaders of the German party, for whom such a strategy risked provoking the class enemy and undermining the gains made by parliamentarism. This was the high-water mark of his revolutionary Marxism.

But his boldness was conditional upon Russian "exceptionalism"—upon the difference from "democratic" countries where parliamentarism was the norm. Thus, though Kautsky was prepared to concede that the political mass strike was, in theory, generalisable beyond the borders of Russia, in practice he fairly rapidly retreated from the idea. When the German left, and Rosa Luxemburg in particular, began to agitate in 1910 for the party to adopt the political mass strike as a demand that would take the movement forward, she was opposed by Kautsky, who argued that conditions were not right in Germany. But the way he framed his argument was to suggest that this was more than a tactical question:

> The more democratic the constitution of a country, the less there exist conditions for a mass strike, the less necessary for the masses does such a strike become, and therefore the less often it happens. Where the proletariat possesses sufficient electoral rights, a mass strike is only to be expected as a defensive measure—as a means to protect voting rights or a parliament with strong social-democratic representation, against a government that refuses to obey the will of the people's representatives.[59]

In other words, the growth of "democracy" was making the mass strike obsolete as a political strategy—at best it could only supplement

---

57: Lenin, 1907a, p411.
58: Quoted in Salvadori, 1990, p107.
59: Quoted in Anderson, 1976. From "Zwischen Baden und Luxemburg", 1910, (www.marxists.org/deutsch/archiv/kautsky/1910/xx/luxemburg.htm). Kautsky was thinking of its use in Belgium to extend the franchise.

parliamentary work. Luxemburg may have been wrong tactically about the political use of the mass strike in Germany in 1910 (on this point Lenin agreed with Kautsky) but she spotted, as Lenin did not at the time, the fundamental flaw in Kautsky's "nothing but parliamentarism".[60]

Democracy and the state

Russian "exceptionalism" allowed Kautsky no more than a temporary deviation from his habitual parliamentarism. It also meant he did not have to confront the question of the state. For if the Russian Revolution was a "democratic" one then so was the state that issued from it: the most the working class and its peasant allies were fighting for was parliamentary democracy.

Yet the pre-war German left, in the debate about the mass strike, began to question this. Anton Pannekoek, for example, argued that "the struggle of the proletariat is not simply a struggle against the bourgeoisie *for* state power, but a struggle *against* the power of the state".[61] This distinction made clear something that parliamentarism ducked: namely, that the bourgeois state, however democratic, cannot be captured (through control of parliament) and imbued with a different class content. What Russia in 1905 threw up, and what 1917 repeated on an incomparably bigger scale, was the soviet.

Kautsky failed to grasp its political significance. This was understandable in 1905—virtually no socialist who accepted the bourgeois nature of the revolution did. Lenin, however, saw its potential as an embryonic "democratic dictatorship" by the workers and peasants. He argued that "the soviet should proclaim itself the provisional revolutionary government of the whole of Russia as early as possible, or should *set up* a provisional revolutionary government (which would amount to the same thing, only in a different form)".[62] In other words, it could be a *new* form of state power, embodying the democratic rule of the exploited and the oppressed over society.

What, however, was its relationship to the *goal* of the revolution in Russia? For the Mensheviks, the soviet was at most an instrument to help put power in the hands of the bourgeoisie—certainly not a new form of *political* power, given the goal of the revolution was the establishment of parliamentary democracy. Lenin's position was, therefore, superior to that

---

60: Quoted in Anderson, 1976.
61: Quoted in Geary, 1987, p77.
62: Lenin, 1905b. This was no passing comment—he amplifies and repeats the point over several pages. It follows on his defence of the soviet as a broad, non-party organisation (as opposed to some Bolsheviks who were hostile to it precisely because it was not subordinated to the party).

of the Mensheviks. But it had a weakness. The "democratic dictatorship" of soviet rule might be the only way in which power could be wrested from Tsarism but it could not be other than an *episodic* state form, given the assumption that the revolution was constrained by its bourgeois limits. The "democratic dictatorship" would have to give way to a constituent assembly and the introduction of parliamentary democracy.

It was this ambiguity (about the primacy or otherwise of the soviet form of power) that was at the heart of the conflict between the "old Bolsheviks" and Lenin in 1917. The "old Bolsheviks", true to the 1905 scenario of the "democratic dictatorship", gave critical support to the provisional government insofar as it maintained the gains of the revolution, and was backed by the soviet. Lenin's argument was that the scenario had been made obsolete by the actual course of events. The danger lay in the soviets "voluntarily ceding power to the bourgeoisie, voluntarily making itself an appendage of the bourgeoisie".[63] The new task facing the Bolsheviks, then, was to *reverse* that process of ceding power—by getting the masses to see "that the Soviets of Workers' Deputies are the *only possible* form of revolutionary government" and through "patient, systematic and persistent explanation" prepare the way, not for a parliamentary republic ("a retrograde step") but for a soviet one.[64]

Lenin was surely right. Lih claims, however, that "old Bolshevism" was the real victor in 1917 and that "old Bolshevism" was Kautskyan. Yet what would have happened to the revolution if Lenin had not broken with "old Bolshevism"? The key issue was soviet power. Lih implies that the old Bolsheviks were as ready as Lenin for the soviets to take power. Yet that is open to question. The logic of the old Bolshevik position (of semi-support for the provisional government on the grounds that the revolution had yet to complete its bourgeois–democratic phase) was to *defer* seizure of power by the soviets and put the revolution in jeopardy. It was an adaptation to the Menshevik argument about "stages": first the bourgeois, then the socialist revolution (an idea to prove fatal in the Chinese Revolution of 1925-27).

This also tells us something about Kautsky's understanding of state power in 1917. He fell back on his "exceptionalist" logic: non-parliamentary force was required to bring about a revolution but only insofar as it guaranteed the emergence of parliamentarism. Bourgeois parliamentary democracy, in effect, was as good as it was ever going to get for Kautsky. It was not just the form of democracy best suited for socialists to organise

---

63: Lenin, 1917c, p46.
64: Lenin, 1917b, p23.

under capitalism. It became, for Kautsky, the *highest* form of democracy, the *only* form through which socialism could be realised. There was no other route to socialism except the "democratic" one (of parliamentary majorities). The soviet, therefore, when it came to realise its potential in 1917, was something Kautsky had to reject as *less* than being fully democratic—which is why he criticised the Bolsheviks in 1918 for dispersing the Constituent Assembly and not letting an elected government replace Soviet power, a criticism he sought to justify as Marxist orthodoxy.[65] This is also why in the course of the German Revolution in 1918 to 1919 Kautsky "was willing to accept the [workers'] councils as revolutionary, and therefore temporary bodies, but in politics he thought their utility strictly limited to the period of transition from the old Reich to the new republic".[66]

Rosa Luxemburg's riposte to Kautsky's accusation that the Bolsheviks were against "democracy" because the soviets did not operate on universal suffrage is the right one:

> The party of Lenin was the only one which grasped the mandate and duty of a truly revolutionary party and which, by the slogan—"All power in the hands of the proletariat and the peasantry"—insured the continued development of the revolution.
>
> Thereby the Bolsheviks solved the famous problem of "winning a majority of the people", which problem has ever weighed on the German Social Democracy like a nightmare. As bred in the bone disciples of parliamentary cretinism, these German Social Democrats have sought to apply to revolutions the homemade wisdom of the parliamentary nursery: in order to carry anything, you must first have a majority. The same, they say, applies to revolution: first let's become a "majority". The true dialectic of revolutions, however, stands this wisdom of parliamentary moles on its head: not through a majority to revolutionary tactics, but through revolutionary tactics to a majority—that is the way the road runs.[67]

Lenin's insistence that soviets rather than the parliamentary republic were the democratic way forward was, then, not just an aspect of his earlier break with Kautsky. It was also, whatever Lih claims, a root and branch break with *Kautskyanism*.

65: See, for example, his 1920 preface to *The Road to Power* (Kautsky, 2007, ppli-lxvix).
66: Steenson, 1991, p216.
67: Waters, 1970, p374.

Early on in *The State and Revolution* Lenin demonstrated how far Kautsky's Marxism excused a reformist view of the state:

> "Theoretically", it is not denied that the state is an organ of class rule, or that class antagonisms are irreconcilable. But what is overlooked or glossed over is this: if the state is the product of the irreconcilability of class antagonisms... it is clear that the liberation of the oppressed class is impossible not only without a violent revolution, *but also without the destruction* of the apparatus of class power which was created by the ruling class.[68]

Lenin calls this Kautsky's "*systematic* deviation towards opportunism precisely on the question of the state".[69] As a result, "the most essential distinction between Marxism and opportunism on the subject of the tasks of the proletarian revolution was slurred over by Kautsky!"[70] Lenin locates this "deviation" (a systematic one, it should be noted), not as something of recent appearance, but as something that emerged *as far back as 1899*, in other words, at a time when, according to Lih, Kautsky for Lenin "was still a Marxist".

Kautsky's Marxism could look impressive—while untested in practice. Lenin's *Fifth Letter from Afar* (in early 1917) refers to the Kautsky article that Lih claims influenced him. Lenin quotes Kautsky: "Two things are urgently needed by the proletariat: democracy and socialism." "Unfortunately," Lenin adds, "Kautsky advances this absolutely incontestable thesis in an exceedingly general form, so that in essence he says nothing and explains nothing".[71]

The Leninist party

The shortcomings in Kautsky's politics are reflected in his model of the party. The German SPD, as he famously put it, was "a revolutionary party, but not a revolution-making party".[72] The general truth of this statement (that revolutions cannot be produced at will but are determined by historical conditions) was in practice, as Pannekoek put it, a "theory of action-less waiting... of passive radicalism".[73] The working class was to do very little on its own account other than trust in parliamentarism to build a revolutionary party that

---

68: Lenin, 1917d, p393.
69: Lenin, 1917d, p482 (our emphasis). Lih claims that, despite the impression left by *The State and Revolution*, there was no essential difference between Kautsky and Lenin on what was really meant by smashing the state—see Lih, 2011a.
70: Lenin, 1917d, p483.
71: Lenin, 1917a, pp341-342.
72: Kautsky, 2007, p41.
73: Quoted in Geary, 1987, p71.

would achieve power on its behalf (Chris Harman noted that Kautsky seemed to have "an almost pathological fear of what the workers would do without the party and of the associated dangers of a 'premature' revolution").[74]

A theoretical commitment to revolution in general, and resistance to revisionism in particular, did not entail a corresponding organisational form. If all that really mattered was how successful the party's parliamentarist strategy was, then the priority was unity in the sense of breadth rather than unity in the sense of ideological cohesiveness. A party representing the class as a whole would unavoidably *reflect* its unevenness of consciousness. And this would not ultimately matter, given that history guaranteed socialism.

Compare this with Lenin's very different practice of party building. At the 1903 Russian Social Democratic Party conference, he criticised an opponent, who "*lumps together* in the party organised and unorganised elements...the advanced and the incorrigibly backward",[75] as producing dangerous confusion. On the contrary, Lenin argued:

> the stronger our party organisations, consisting of *real* Social-Democrats, the less wavering and instability there is *within* the party, the broader, more varied, richer, and more fruitful will be the party's influence on the elements of the working class *masses* surrounding it and guided by it. The party, as the vanguard of the working class, must not be confused, after all, with the entire class.[76]

This distinction was at the root of the difference between him and Martov over membership rules. The point was the party should not reflect the inevitable unevenness of the consciousness of the class *inside* the party but organise its most revolutionary section only—the better to intervene in the broader working class movement. Lenin, in Paul Frölich's much later words, "wanted a firmly and tightly organised party which, as the vanguard of the class, would be closely connected with it, *but at the same time clearly distinct from it*".[77]

Organisation for Lenin, then, was an expression of politics—not something of secondary importance. But taking organisation seriously (the permanent need to ensure ideological clarity the better to intervene) also meant that any particular form of party organisation was only good insofar as it made intervention by the vanguard more effective. Hence the shifts

---

74: Harman, 1968/9, p25.
75: Lenin, 1904, p256.
76: Lenin, 1904, p258.
77: Quoted in Molyneux, 1986, p53 (our emphasis).

(the stick-bending) we have already argued as essential to understanding Lenin. What needs stressing here is that it is wrong to suppose that stick-bending was simply a pragmatic response to circumstances (a kind of make it up as you go along version of the party). If that were so, the case against a stick-bending Lenin as making him look unprincipled would be correct—whereas the principle behind each bending was whether the party improved its capacity to lead the working class to revolution. For the same reason, it is mistaken to cherry-pick Lenin.

Take, for example, "democratic centralism". By decontextualising this, one can create almost any Leninism one wishes to. Where bits of *WITBD* were once used to construct an ultra-centralist, proto-Stalinist Lenin, now other passages are used to construct an ultra-democratic Lenin. Those who insist on centralism as the dialectical condition of effective party democracy tend to be confronted with this from Lenin: that the Central Committee "has absolutely no right to call upon the party organisations to accept its resolution" and that "discipline does not demand that a party member should blindly subscribe to all the resolutions drafted by the Central Committee".[78]

If we put this statement in context, Lenin's preoccupation was not some general democratic right to disobey the Central Committee but the specific need to preserve revolutionary politics in conditions where the Mensheviks had become the majority following the 1906 Stockholm (Unity) conference and were using their control of the Central Committee to push support for the right wing constitutional democratic ministry appointed by the Tsar. Anatoly Lunacharsky reported Lenin as saying to him before the conference: "If we have a majority in the Central Committee we will demand the strictest discipline. We will insist that the Mensheviks submit to party unity." In the event of the Mensheviks winning a majority Lenin replied: "We won't permit the idea of unity to tie a noose around our necks and we shall in no circumstances permit the Mensheviks to lead us by the rope".[79] Lenin was determined to preserve the revolutionary tradition through preserving Bolshevik organisational "autonomy" within a party dominated by a liquidationist leadership in this period.

These were the "muddy years", as Paul Le Blanc puts it, and only by comprehending what Lenin did during this period "will we be able to grasp the revolutionary organisational principles that are vitally relevant for our own time".[80] The defeat of the 1905 Revolution involved Lenin

78: Lenin, 1906, pp500-504.
79: Quoted in Cliff, 1975, pp277-278.
80: Le Blanc, 1993, p133.

in a battle on two fronts as Russian Social Democracy splintered under the pressure of Tsarist reaction and the retreat of the working class. The Mensheviks wanted a purely legal party with no commitment to revolution. The ultra-lefts wanted a purely underground party that turned its back on the few legal opportunities open to revolutionaries (electoral work, for example). The outcome of Lenin's struggle against both tendencies—and against those who wanted to conciliate the different wings in the name of party unity (Trotsky was the chief culprit in this respect)—was that Lenin was able to reconstitute Russian Social Democracy as the kind of party he had talked of in 1903, one whose ideological cohesiveness would allow it to intervene effectively. At the Prague Conference of 1912 the party was reborn as effectively a purely Bolshevik one.

Lih dismisses the idea that this represents the emergence of a "party of a new type", describing this as a "dumbed down version of a Stalin-era slogan" which "became a staple of western textbooks".[81] The formal position of Lenin and his comrades may well have been that this was not a different type of party and that its nearly all-Bolshevik character was a reflection of the Mensheviks' self-exclusion. Yet something had fundamentally changed. Lenin's report in 1914 to the Second International was clear about what unity in this "Bolshevik Party" now meant. Previously tolerated positions were "deemed deserving of condemnation" or "incompatible with membership in the party"[82]—which was not the same as saying that minorities did not have rights to voice disagreements before the whole party.

Paul Le Blanc argues that this reflected Lenin's earlier view (around 1904 and 1905), when he had favoured "an uncompromising organisational split from the Mensheviks".[83] He had revised this view in the hope that the wave of revolution would push them towards the Bolsheviks. The fact that the contrary had happened, and that a bitter factional war against liquidationists and conciliators had had to be fought, convinced Lenin, who "reverted to the split perspective, which he believed was necessary for the future effectiveness of a genuinely revolutionary vanguard".[84] So surely Le Blanc is correct to conclude that this split perspective constituted a "veering away from the classic example of German Social Democracy", in which revolutionaries and reformists coexisted.[85] A party of a new type, then, in reality if not in name, had been created.

81:   Lih, 2010b. See also a more extended discussion in Lih, 2012a.
82:   Lenin, 1914a, p519.
83:   Le Blanc, 1993, p167.
84:   Le Blanc, 1993, p168.
85:   Le Blanc, 1993, p168.

Paul Le Blanc's summary of the positions of the Mensheviks, of Kautsky and of Lenin's Bolsheviks seems to us essentially correct:

> With the Mensheviks, based on a dogmatic adherence to the notion that Russia could only go through a democratic-capitalist transformation (that a working class socialist revolution would not be on the agenda until many years later), they became committed to a worker-capitalist alliance, which naturally created pressures that forced them to compromise the class struggle elements of Marxism.
>
> For Kautsky, by 1910, it became clear that he would become marginalised within the increasingly bureaucratic-conservative German Social Democratic movement unless he subtly but increasingly diluted his seemingly unequivocal and eloquent commitment to revolutionary Marxism. By 1914, when the German Social Democratic Party supported the imperialist war policies of the Kaiser's government, and in 1917 in the face of the Bolshevik revolution, Kautsky became utterly compromised.
>
> What is distinctive about Lenin's Bolsheviks is that they did not compromise, they doggedly followed through to the end the implications of the revolutionary Marxist orientation—expressed in *What Is To Be Done? The State and Revolution* and so much else in Lenin's writings.[86]

The activist Lenin

The activist interpretation has always sought to defend Lenin against the image of him as either the demiurge of Stalinist imagination or the demon of Western Cold War warriors. In so doing it has also sought to show that Lenin's practice, understood critically and creatively, can be theorised beyond its immediate context. Indeed, without Leninism and without a Leninist party, no revolution can hope to overthrow capitalism and bring about socialism.

Lih's Kautskyanisation of Lenin essentially denies this—and along with that denies the October Revolution as the product of Leninism. Lih may not go so far as Kautsky's negative verdict on the Bolsheviks[87]—that the soviet regime was a denial of "democracy", and therefore necessarily a dictatorship *over* the proletariat (and the rest of society), rather than *of* it. But nevertheless,

---

86: Le Blanc, 2011.

87: Salvadori gives a useful account of Kautsky's own evolving views from relative to absolute hostility (see Salvadori, 1990, pp251-277).

implicit in this Kautskyanisation is the idea that "Leninism" is at best a figment of the activist imagination or at worst a deviation from Marxism.

If, then, we are to discard the Leninist approach and see the October Revolution through a Kautskyan prism, what is accentuated is its "exceptionalist" nature, its *difference* from the kind of revolution required in advanced, bourgeois-democratic Europe. Bolshevism seems limited, confined to explaining the specific reasons as to why Lenin and his comrades succeeded in 1917. More broadly, though, the point of this Kautskyanisation is to deny the possibility of forming out of the experience of Lenin and the Bolsheviks a theory that can serve as a guide to action for the overthrow of capitalism more generally. Any attempt to do so, we are warned, means endorsing "Leninism" as the product of a degenerating Communist International. What, then, we are left with is a Catch-22 choice; either the "real" Lenin, the Kautskyan Lenin or a constructed Lenin, the proto-Stalinist Lenin.

Yet there is plenty of evidence in Lenin's own thinking and practice that, when he broke from Kautsky in 1914, he was determined to renew Marxism as a living practice. The clue lies in how Lenin began to rethink the kind of International needed after the collapse of the Second International in 1914. This rethinking also involved a very different view of the kind of parties that should constitute a new International.

In late 1914 Lenin made it clear that he was opposed to patching up the old International. Getting the leaders who had lined up with their respective ruling classes round the same table would not do. It would not address the deep-seated failings of an International that had so adapted to "peaceful" conditions that it had fallen apart when capitalism's descent into war made Kautsky's call for revolution in an imperialist epoch an urgent, practical necessity. A qualitatively different type of International was needed—one that would demand "a complete break with the chauvinists and with the defenders of social-chauvinism"[88] (among the defenders he clearly had Kautsky in mind), not one which tolerated unity with them. And therefore the kind of party it needed was qualitatively different from the one that had tolerated opportunists in its ranks. Writing in early 1915, he inveighed against the kind of "unity" that had typified the Kautskyan parties making up the Second International:

Typical of the socialist parties of the epoch of the Second International was one that tolerated in its midst an opportunism...that kept itself secret, adapting

88: Lenin, 1914b, p99.

itself to the revolutionary workers, *borrowing* their Marxist terminology, and evading any clear cleavage of principles. This type has outlived itself.[89]

He reinforced the point about the relevance of Bolshevism when he wrote in 1918 in *Proletarian Revolution and the Renegade Kautsky* that "Bolshevism *has created* the ideological and tactical foundations of a Third International, of a really proletarian and Communist International, which will take into consideration both the gains of the tranquil epoch [that of the Second International] and the *epoch of revolutions, which has begun*".[90]

The Bolshevik model, then, was not just about creating a party committed to soviet power. It was also about using "the gains of the tranquil epoch" in a revolutionary not opportunist way—the point of "*Left Wing*" *Communism—an Infantile Disorder.* The famous 21 conditions of membership of the International (also of 1920) were not just an attempt to make sure that Social Democratic parties, for which the Comintern had become "popular", could only join as long as they broke with their reformist wing. They also implied a radically different way of operating under bourgeois-democratic conditions—one that required applying Bolshevism creatively and critically.

The question of how to create communist parties reflecting a combination of inflexible principle and tactical suppleness was also at the heart of Lenin's comments on the 1921 Comintern resolution (which he had played a role in composing) on how Bolshevik parties should organise and operate. It was, said Lenin in his very last speech to the Communist International in 1922, "an excellent one". But "it is almost entirely Russian" and so "quite unintelligible to foreigners, and they cannot be content with hanging it in a corner like an icon and praying to it".

This is sometimes offered as proof that Lenin rejected the resolution as a mistaken attempt to generalise Bolshevism to countries where it did not (and so perhaps could not) apply. Lenin certainly emphasised what was mistaken about it: its incomprehensibility kept it a dead letter, blocking the way to further success. For all that he was insistent that the "resolution must be carried out" and that foreign communists "must assimilate part of the Russian experience" he also argued: "Just how that will be done, I do not know... We Russians must also find ways and means of explaining the principles of this resolution to the foreigners. Unless we do that, it will be absolutely impossible for them to carry it out".[91] Lenin, then, was still

---

89: Lenin, 1915, p110.
90: Lenin, 1918, p292-293.
91: Lenin, 1922, p431.

emphasising the vital importance of making the foreigners learn despite the difficulties with the resolution's present "unintelligibility".

The need for the parties of the Comintern to absorb the experience of Bolshevism and apply it organisationally should not in any way be confused with the kind of internal regime Grigori Zinoviev (and later Joseph Stalin) insisted these parties should adopt. "Bolshevisation" was a product not of "Bolshevism" but of the degeneration of the Comintern following the defeat of the German Revolution in October 1923. The Comintern stopped being an instrument of revolutionary internationalism and turned into a tool of Russian foreign policy. Alas, Lenin's worst fears were realised. "Bolshevism" became a ritual of bureaucratically arrived at decisions from on high to be blindly obeyed.

Conclusion

Why, finally, does this argument matter today? The Kautskyanisation of Lenin has been offered as proof that there is no such thing as the "Leninist" revolutionary party. The chief target is Cliff, particularly his account, in volumes 1 and 2 of his political biography of Lenin, of how Lenin built the party and prepared it for October 1917.

The critique goes beyond saying Cliff got this or that aspect wrong, or that he exaggerated or neglected parts of Lenin's political life. It argues, in effect, that the *practice* of organisations that look to the "Leninist" model is bound to be at fault because the model advanced by Cliff owes more to the Zinoviev–Stalin interpretation of "Bolshevism" than to anything else.

In one way, this returns us to the old lie that Lenin led to Stalin, and that Leninists are all Stalinists (if only closet Stalinists). But for a left that has lost whatever confidence it had that a revolutionary party rooted in the working class is possible, a Kautskyan Lenin makes sense. On the one hand, as against a *discredited* reformism that no longer talks of an alternative to capitalism, it preserves a commitment to socialist aims and demands; on the other, it sees this commitment being fulfilled in the creation of a party that, while supporting and seeking a basis in mass action, sees the parliamentary framework as the route through which change comes. That, then, is a way to paint left reformism red.

Is there a historical precedent for this? Actually, there is in the Eurocommunist project of the 1970s. This involved more than de-Stalinisation. It involved a theoretical shift: a repudiation of the Soviet model of power as no longer appropriate or operable in "democratic" countries. Socialism was not a matter of "overthrowing the state" but of using parliamentarism to create a mass force that would stop the state being used to block social advance. John H Kautsky has argued persuasively that his grandfather's view of the relationship between "democracy" and "socialism" played a key role at the time in the intellectual underpinning of Eurocommunism.[92]

One descendent of Eurocommunism is Syriza, currently riding high in the Greek polls. Those who espouse the model embracing reform and revolution hold this party up as the party to follow. But the Eurocommunist road to socialism proved unable to deliver even modest reforms—and in a situation where the crisis of capitalism is now much deeper a new improved left reformism will fare no better. It may be hard but the task of patiently building Leninist parties rooted in workers' struggles remains the only way to overthrow capitalism. Lih's Kautskyanisation of Lenin ultimately detracts from this undertaking. In his otherwise laudable attempt to unpick the real Lenin from the ideology of "Leninism" Lih has lost sight of the theoretically sophisticated interventionist conception of political practice that was Lenin's fundamental contribution to Marxism.

References

Anderson, Perry, 1976, "The Antinomies of Antonio Gramsci", *New Left Review*, I/100 (November-December), www.newleftreview.org/I/100/perry-anderson-the-antinomies-of-antonio-gramsci

Blackledge, Paul, 2006a, "What Was Done", *International Socialism* 111 (July), www.isj.org.uk/?id=218

Blackledge, Paul, 2006b, "Karl Kautsky and Marxist Historiography", *Science and Society*, volume 70, number 3 (July).

Cliff, Tony, 1957, "Plekhanov: The Father of Russian Marxism", *Socialist Review* (January), www.marxists.org/archive/cliff/works/1957/01/plekhanov.htm

Cliff, Tony, 1975, *Lenin*, Volume 1, *Building the Party, 1893-1914* (Bookmarks), www.marxists.org/archive/cliff/works/1975/lenin1/

Draper, Hal, 1953, "The Myth of Lenin's 'Revolutionary Defeatism'", *New International*, www.marxists.org/archive/draper/1953/defeat/index.htm

Draper, Hal, 1990, "The Myth of Lenin's 'Concept of the Party'," www.marxists.org/archive/draper/1990/myth/index.htm

Engels, Frederick, 1990 [1895], "Introduction to K Marx's *The Class Struggles in France, 1848-1850*", in Marx, Karl, and Frederick Engels, *Collected Works, volume 27* (Progress).

Geary, Dick, 1987, *Karl Kautsky* (Manchester University Press).

Harman, Chris, 1968/9, "Party and Class", *International Socialism* 35 (first series, winter), www.marxists.org/archive/harman/1968/xx/partyclass.htm

92: Kautsky, 1994, pp161-204.

Harman, Chris, 2010, "Lenin Rediscovered?", *Historical Materialism*, Volume 18, Issue 3.

Kautsky, John H, 1994, *Karl Kautsky: Marxism, Revolution and Democracy* (New Brunswick).

Kautsky, Karl, 1892, *The Class Struggle (Erfurt Program)*, www.marxists.org/archive/kautsky/1892/erfurt/index.htm

Kautsky, Karl, 1918, *The Dictatorship of the Proletariat*, www.marxists.org/archive/kautsky/1918/dictprole/index.htm

Kautsky, Karl, 2007 [1909], *The Road to Power* (Center for Socialist History), www.marxists.org/archive/kautsky/1909/power

Krupskaya, Nadezhda, 1970, *Memories of Lenin* (Panther History).

Le Blanc, Paul, 1993, *Lenin and the Revolutionary Party* (Humanities Press).

Le Blanc, Paul, 2011, "Lenin and Us: Into the Past, Back to the Future", *Links: International Journal of Socialist Renewal* (14 June), links.org.au/node/2364

Lenin, V I, 1899, "A Draft of Our Party Programme", in *Collected Works*, volume 4 (Progress), www.marxists.org/archive/lenin/works/1899/dec/draft.htm

Lenin, V I, 1901, "What is to be Done?" in *Collected Works*, volume 5 (Progress), www.marxists.org/archive/lenin/works/1901/witbd/

Lenin, V I, 1904, "One Step Forward, Two Steps Back", in *Collected Works*, volume 7 (Progress), www.marxists.org/archive/lenin/works/1904/onestep/i.htm

Lenin, V I, 1905a, The Third Congress of the RSDLP", in *Collected Works*, volume 8 (Progress), www.marxists.org/archive/lenin/works/1905/3rdcong/18.htm

Lenin, V I, 1905b, "Our Tasks and the Soviet of Workers' Deputies", in *Collected Works*, volume 10 (Progress), www.marxists.org/archive/lenin/works/1905/nov/04b.htm

Lenin, V I, 1905c, "The Reorganisation of the Party", in *Collected Works*, volume 10 (Progress), www.marxists.org/archive/lenin/works/1905/reorg/i.htm

Lenin, V I, 1906, "Let the Workers Decide", in *Collected Works*, volume 10 (Progress), www.marxists.org/archive/lenin/works/1906/jun/01.htm

Lenin, V I, 1907a, "Preface to the Russian Translation of K Kautsky's Pamphlet: *The Driving Forces and Prospects of the Russian Revolution*", in *Collected Works*, volume 11 (Progress), www.marxists.org/archive/lenin/works/1906/dec/00b.htm

Lenin, V I, 1907b, "Preface to the Collection *Twelve Years*", in *Collected Works*, volume 13 (Progress), www.marxists.org/archive/lenin/works/1907/sep/pref1907.htm

Lenin, V I, 1914a, "Report of the CC of the RSDLP to the Brussels Conference and Instructions to the CC Delegation", in *Collected Works*, volume 20 (Progress), www.marxists.org/archive/lenin/works/1914/jun/30.htm

Lenin, V I, 1914b, "Dead Chauvinism and Living Socialism", in *Collected Works*, volume 21 (Progress), www.marxists.org/archive/lenin/works/1914/dec/12.htm

Lenin, V I, 1915, "What Next?", in *Collected Works*, volume 21 (Progress), www.marxists.org/archive/lenin/works/1915/jan/09.htm

Lenin, V I, 1917a, "Letters from Afar: Fifth Letter", in *Collected Works*, volume 23 (Progress), www.marxists.org/archive/lenin/works/1917/lfafar/fifth.htm

Lenin, V I, 1917b, "The Tasks of the Proletariat in the Present Revolution (April Theses)", in *Collected Works*, volume 24 (Progress), www.marxists.org/archive/lenin/works/1917/apr/04.htm

Lenin, V I, 1917c, "Letters on Tactics", in *Collected Works*, volume 24 (Progress), www.marxists.org/archive/lenin/works/1917/apr/x01.htm

Lenin, V I, 1917d, "The State and Revolution", in *Collected Works*, volume 25 (Progress), www.marxists.org/archive/lenin/works/1917/staterev/

Lenin, V I, 1918, "The Proletarian Revolution and the Renegade Kautsky", in *Collected Works*, volume 28 (Progress), www.marxists.org/archive/lenin/works/1918/prrk/

Lenin, V I, 1922, "Fourth Congress of the Communist International", in *Collected Works*, volume 33 (Progress), www.marxists.org/archive/lenin/works/1922/nov/04b.htm

Lih, Lars, 2008a [2006], *Lenin Rediscovered: What Is to Be Done? in Context* (Haymarket).

Lih, Lars, 2008b, "Lenin and Kautsky: the Final Chapter" *International Socialist Review* (May-June, online), www.isreview.org/issues/59/feat-lenin.shtml

Lih, Lars, 2009a, "Lenin, Kautsky and 1914", *Weekly Worker* (10 September), www.cpgb.org.uk/assets/files/resources/Lenin_Kautsky.pdf

Lih, Lars, 2009b, "Lenin's Aggressive Unoriginality", *Socialist Studies*, volume 5, number 2 (autumn), www.socialiststudies.com/index.php/sss/article/view/86/83

Lih, Lars, 2010a, "Prospects of the Russian Revolution (1917) by Lars Lih and Karl Kautsky", *Weekly Worker (supplement)* (15 January), www.cpgb.org.uk/assets/files/resources/April%20Theses.pdf

Lih, Lars, 2010b, "How a Founding Document Was Found, or 100 years of *Lenin's What Is To Be Done?* Part III: 'Party of a New Type,' 1931-77", Kasama Project (26 June), http://tinyurl.com/noc73en

Lih, Lars, 2010c, "Lenin Disputed", *Historical Materialism*, Volume 18, Issue 3.

Lih, Lars, 2011a, "The Book that Didn't Bark", *Weekly Worker* (27 April), http://weeklyworker.co.uk/worker/863/the-book-that-didnt-bark/

Lih, Lars, 2011b, "The Ironic Triumph of Old Bolshevism: The Debates of April 1917 in Context", *Russian History*, volume 38.

Lih, Lars, 2011c, *Lenin* (Reaktion).

Lih, Lars, 2012a, "The Non-Geometric Elwood", *Canadian Slavonic Papers (Revue Canadienne des Slavistes)*, volume 54, numbers 1-2 (March-June).

Lih, Lars, 2012b, "April Theses: Before and After April 1917", *Weekly Worker* (22 November), http://weeklyworker.co.uk/worker/939/april-theses-before-and-after-april-1917/

Lih, Lars, 2012c, "Lenin, Kautsky and 'the New Era of Revolutions'", *Weekly Worker* (22 December), http://weeklyworker.co.uk/worker/895/lenin-kautsky-and-the-new-era-of-revolutions/

Molyneux, John, 1986, *Marxism and the Party* (Bookmarks), www.marxists.org/history//etol/writers/molyneux/1978/party/index.htm

Post, Charlie, 2011, "Lenin Reconsidered", *International Viewpoint* (3 November), www.internationalviewpoint.org/spip.php?article2361

Salvadori, Massimo, 1990, *Karl Kautsky and the Socialist Revolution 1880-1938* (Verso).

Steenson, Gary, 1991, *Karl Kautsky, 1854-1938: Marxism in the Classical Years* (University of Pittsburgh Press).

Waters, Mary-Alice (ed), 1970, *Rosa Luxemburg Speaks* (Pathfinder).

Ukraine: imperialism, war and the left

Rob Ferguson

And when war is waged between two groups of predators and oppressors merely for division of the spoils of plunder, merely to see who will strangle more peoples, who will grab more, the question as to who began this war, who was the first to declare it and so forth, is of no economic or political significance.

Lenin: "In the Footsteps of *Russkaya Volya*", 13 April 1917.[1]

In every country preference should be given to the struggle against the chauvinism of the *particular* country, to awakening of hatred of one's *own* government, to appeals...to the solidarity of the workers of the warring countries, to their *joint* civil war against the bourgeoisie. No one will venture to *guarantee* when and to what extent this preaching will be "justified" in practice: *that is not the point*... The point is to work on those *lines*. *Only* that work is socialist, not chauvinist. And it *alone* will bear socialist fruit, revolutionary fruit.

Lenin: "Letter to A G Shlyapnikov", 31 October 1914.[2]

1:   Lenin, 1917.
2:   Lenin, 1914.

The most powerful military alliance in the world met in Newport, Wales, at the beginning of September. It was, arguably, the most significant meeting of the NATO alliance since the fall of the Berlin Wall. Two issues dominated the NATO agenda: the rise of Islamic State and, beyond all expectations, the apparent success of Vladimir Putin's strategy in Ukraine.

Armed conflict has raged over eastern Ukraine for five months. Over 3,000 have been killed and more than 6,000 injured. The United Nations Refugee Agency estimates over a million people have been displaced, 94 percent of them residents of Ukraine's two eastern regions. Some 15 percent of the local population have fled their homes, either to Russia or elsewhere in Ukraine. Intensive shelling of residential areas has inflicted major damage, and many who remain have little access to food, water or electricity.[3]

A few weeks before the NATO summit the separatists of eastern Ukraine had appeared on the verge of defeat and Putin faced humiliation in Russia's "near abroad". Yet in mid-August the separatists successfully mounted a counter-offensive, equipped with Russian weaponry and supplies and supported by significant numbers of Russian troops (or "volunteers"). The Ukrainian government claimed that Russians spearheaded the attack and that it was they who turned the tables, not the separatists. Whatever the precise combination of forces, the Ukrainian army and its militias were thrown into retreat. Newly elected Ukrainian president Petro Poroshenko agreed a ceasefire on 5 September. Vladimir Putin has reminded the West that, though weakened, Russia is still an imperialist power to be reckoned with, especially in its own backyard.

It is not over. Whether or not the fighting resumes in the country itself, a "frozen conflict" in Ukraine has huge implications for Russia's entire southern flank from the Baltic states to Central Asia. Renewed tensions are mounting between Armenia and Azerbaijan and between the central Asian states. Russia and the West have their own stake in each and Georgia and Moldova also remain potential flashpoints.

In the wake of the Ukraine crisis NATO is establishing a "rapid reaction force" in the Baltic states and Eastern Europe; United States president Barack Obama has insisted NATO is open to new members on Russia's borders, however unlikely that may now seem. The Baltic states and Poland have demanded permanent NATO bases as opposed to the current temporary ones. Russia for its part has announced large-scale strategic nuclear missile exercises this September and Putin has reminded the West that "Russia is one of the most powerful nuclear nations. This is a reality, not

---

3:   Cumming-Bruce, 2014, and UN High Commissioner for Refugees, 2014.

just words".[4] As winter approaches, both Europe and Russia face continuing economic crisis and the prospect of a sanctions and energy supply war.

This does not mean Armageddon is round the corner. The West and Russia both face real limits on their ability to manoeuvre, and their current strategy is premised on avoiding direct military conflict. The establishment of permanent bases in the Baltic republics and Poland is still not certain. NATO leaders made it clear to Poroshenko that they would not supply Ukraine with the military hardware needed to roll back the counter-offensive, precisely for fear this could lead to a full-scale invasion by Russia and threaten a wider conflict. It was this that forced an ashen-faced, humiliated Poroshenko to agree to a ceasefire.

Russia for its part has no wish to get bogged down in eastern Ukraine as a permanent occupying military force. So Putin has exerted authority over his own proxies, finally moving against the mainly Russian leadership of the separatists, who had provided cover for arms-length Russian intervention in Crimea and eastern Ukraine, but whose fantasies of restoring the Russian empire made them strategically unreliable at the endgame. Paradoxically, it was only once they were replaced with a leadership more compliant to Moscow that Putin committed the logistical support and the detachments of Russian troops needed to turn the tide, confident that he could control the outcome and impose a ceasefire broadly on his terms.

A quarter century after the end of the Cold War, Russia and the West are facing each other down across Ukraine. Despite their wish to avoid direct military conflict or wider regional instability, we should remember, a century after the First World War, that military and economic rivalry have a habit of escaping beyond the intentions and best laid plans of the contenders. After all, the current crisis took Ukraine, Russia, the European Union (EU) and the United States *all* by surprise and unprepared.

While it would be a mistake to conclude that we are on the brink of a European war, this is not a conflict that will simply blow over. We are at a turning point; the rivalry over Ukraine poses real dangers and presents a serious challenge to the left and to the anti-war movement.

In his 1999 book, *Ukraine and Russia: A Fraternal Rivalry*, Anatol Lieven wrote that he was generally optimistic about Ukraine as long as three conditions were met:

1. That the Ukrainian state was not perceived by Russian speakers and ethnic Russians as having caused a breakdown with Russia.
2. That Russia did not attempt to spread an ethnic chauvinist

---

4:    *Stratfor*, 2014a.

version of Russian nationalism beyond its borders.

3. That the West did not pursue a "balance of power" strategy leading to confrontation.[5]

All these three conditions lie in shreds. Lieven, it has to be said, believed then if not now, in the possibility of a benign Western foreign policy and, for that matter, a benign Russian one too. However, a Marxist analysis cannot start from wishful thinking. We have first to situate national conflicts in the context of dynamics of global and regional power. We live in an imperialist world system, a system of competing capitals and competing capitalist states. This was the starting point for Lenin and his fellow revolutionaries when addressing the position socialists should take towards imperialist war in 1914. It remains an indispensable starting point for socialists today.[6]

Second, when looking at a conflict of the kind we have witnessed in Ukraine, we must ask how the unity of workers across national and ethnic divides is to be achieved. This cannot be reduced to an abstract formula but is a question we must look at concretely.

Ukraine: A history of imperialist rivalry and slaughter

Ukraine means, in a literal sense, borderland. Throughout its history imperialist armies have marched across its territory; in the modern era the Tsars, the Poles and the Austro-Hungarian Empire. During the Russian Revolution some of the most critical battles of the civil war were played out in Ukraine between the Red and White armies, and Polish and German forces. The Bolsheviks' attitude to the national question was put to perhaps its severest test, in circumstances where counter-revolution was organised under the banner of "an independent Ukraine".

After a political struggle by Lenin and others, the Bolsheviks granted Ukraine's right to self-determination. The immediate post-revolutionary period saw a flourishing of Ukrainian art and culture. But at the end of the 1920s Joseph Stalin launched his counter-revolution. In 1928 the campaign to forcibly collectivise agriculture began. Vast resources of food and land

---

5: Lieven, 1999, pp7-9. Lieven is not of the left but has written interesting and informed work on Chechnya and Ukraine.

6: For a discussion of how the classic theories of imperialism should be applied, see Harman, 2003. Elsewhere Harman specifically addresses the argument that Russia cannot be seen as an imperialist power (Harman, 1980) and takes a critical look at Nikolai Bukharin's approach (Harman, 1983). Also see the debate between Alex Callinicos and Leo Panitch and Sam Gindin (Callinicos, 2005; Panitch and Gindin, 2006; Callinicos, 2006). On the latter debate also see Rees, 2006, pp212-17 (this is of particular interest in the light of recent differences between myself and John Rees over Ukraine).

were expropriated from the peasantry, and Ukraine, the most fertile area of the Soviet Union, was plunged into a famine that left 3 million dead.

The counter-revolution swept away the entire gains of the revolution including all forms of national and language rights. The old Bolshevik leadership of Ukraine, associated with the post-revolutionary period of "Ukrainisation", were purged. Almost the entire central committee and politburo of Ukraine and an estimated 37 percent of Communist Party members, about 170,000 people, perished.

Imperialist rivalry was also a driver of Stalin's purges.[7] The purges of the Ukrainian and Polish Communist Parties were particularly intense, even by the grotesque standards of the Great Purge. They came as Stalin contemplated his strategy for the oncoming carve-up of Europe that culminated in the Stalin-Hitler pact.[8] In Vinnytsia a mass grave was unearthed by the Nazis containing the bodies of 10,000 people shot between 1937 and 1938. The massacre could not be referred to officially in the Soviet Union and was not acknowledged until 1988.

During the Second World War an estimated 7 million Ukrainians lost their lives, including 900,000 Jews at the hands of the Nazis. Again imperialism ripped Ukrainian society apart, setting ethnic Ukrainian against ethnic Russian, against Pole and, of course, against the Jews. The experience of Soviet occupation under the Stalin-Hitler pact and the sufferings of the Stalin period led a minority of Ukrainians to see the Nazis as "liberators". A reactionary Ukrainian nationalist movement emerged, including many fascists, which collaborated with the Nazis and massacred Jews and Poles as well as Ukrainians.

Trotsky raged at the disastrous consequences of the carve-up and Stalin's decimation of Ukraine:

Since the latest murderous "purge" in the Ukraine no one in the West wants to become part of the Kremlin satrapy which continues to bear the name of

---

7:    Communist Party of the Soviet Union, 1939, pp331-52. This final chapter of "The Short Course", *The History of the Communist Party of the Soviet Union (Bolsheviks)* begins with the international situation and concludes with the "Liquidation of the Remnants of the Bukharin-Trotsky Gang of Spies, Wreckers and Traitors".

8:    Trotsky predicted an alliance between Stalin and Hitler in 1937, documenting attempts by Stalin to reach an understanding with the Nazi regime—Dewey Commission, 1937. Also Broué, 1997, p716. Pierre Broué argues that the purges of the Polish Communist Party were motivated in part by Stalin's need to clear the path for a deal with the Nazis to carve up Poland; under the terms of the pact Stalin seized the Ukrainian regions of Galicia and Volhynia, including Lviv. If Broué is right, similar calculations would have applied to the Ukrainian Communists. I am grateful to Gareth Jenkins for this reference.

Soviet Ukraine. The worker and peasant masses in the Western Ukraine, in Bukovina, in the Carpatho-Ukraine are in a state of confusion: Where to turn? What to demand? This situation naturally shifts the leadership to the most reactionary Ukrainian cliques who express their "nationalism" by seeking to sell the Ukrainian people to one imperialism or another in return for a promise of fictitious independence. Upon this tragic confusion Hitler bases his policy in the Ukrainian question.[9]

Ukraine's borders and its populations have been repeatedly torn asunder. Now Ukraine finds itself at the fulcrum of an arc of tension that stretches across Russia's southern flank from the Baltics through the Caucasus to Central Asia. Sherman Garnett has termed Ukraine "The Keystone in the Arch", referring to its critical geopolitical location between Western Europe and Russia. The orientation of Ukraine between East and West, Garnett argued, would determine the dynamic of rivalry and conflict from the Baltic Sea to Central Asia. Perceptively he warned that NATO's expansion would lead to internal conflict if Ukraine were torn between Russia and the West. Both Garnett and Lieven argued that any attempt on the part of the West to engage in a tug of war over Ukraine could destabilise not only Ukraine but the entire region.[10]

Ukraine is the largest country entirely in Europe, with the second largest population. It shares borders with Hungary, Slovakia and Poland to the west; Belarus to the north; Russia to the north and east; and Romania, Moldova and its pro-Russian breakaway Transnistria to the south. As the annexation of Crimea highlighted all too clearly, Ukraine has a key strategic coastline on the Black Sea and the Sea of Azov, across which lie Turkey and the Caucasian states of Georgia, Armenia and Azerbaijan (all subject to their own rivalries and conflicts); beyond that lie the Caspian Sea, Central Asia and that other rising, rival imperialism, China.

Class conflict and national divisions

The Maidan protests (which took their name after the central square in Kiev) began in autumn 2013. They were triggered by President Viktor Yanukovych's refusal to sign an Association Agreement with the European Union (EU). The students who made up these initial protests looked to the market, Europe and the West for an alternative to the corruption of the

---

9:   Trotsky, 1939.
10:   Garnett, 1997; Lieven, 1999. See also Goodby, 1998. For a strong post-Maidan analysis from the same "realist" school see Trenin, 2014.

Ukraine

Russian sphere: Belarus; Kazakhstan; Armenia
EU sphere: Moldova; Georgia
Between spheres: Azerbaijan; Turkmenistan; Uzbekistan

Ukrainian elite and their smashed hopes of a post-Communist economic future.

It is important to note that this was not the first protest movement to challenge a Ukrainian regime. In 1990 a group of students also occupied the Maidan. They were inspired by two key events: first, the miners' strikes that shook the Soviet Union in 1989, when tens of thousands of miners occupied their town squares, including in Donetsk in eastern Ukraine, banging their helmets, their eyes rimmed with black coal dust, demanding soap and democracy. Second, by the Chinese students in Tiananmen Square. They set up a tent city, began a hunger strike and demanded sovereignty for Ukraine (not independence) and democratisation. The protests became known as the "Revolution on Granite" after the granite paving of the Maidan. The protests reached hundreds of thousands, part of a wave of mass movements demanding national independence across the Soviet empire.[11]

By mid-October 1990, however, there was a stand-off. The government refused to negotiate and the threat of reaction loomed as the regime prepared to use force. The turning point came when a large column of workers from Kiev's largest factory, a core part of the Soviet military-industrial complex, employing tens of thousands of workers, marched on parliament in support of the students. As Bohdan Krawchenko describes:

> On 18 October, unexpectedly, a large column of workers from Kiev's largest factory marched on parliament in support of students. They chanted only one word, their factory's name—"Arsenal". Workers tipped the balance. That evening the government reported that it would meet all student demands. Kiev celebrated the victory into the early hours of the morning. The students had stopped the march of reaction in its tracks.[12]

The struggles for independence, democracy and the strikes over economic demands across Ukraine demonstrated the potential for united resistance. The Donbass miners' strikes were supported in the West, and joined by important mining centres in the heartlands of western Ukrainian nationalism. The referendum on independence in 1991 had a turnout of 84 percent. Even in the industrialised regions in the east such as Donetsk and Luhansk where the majority were Russian speakers and with the highest numbers of

---

11:   Harman and Zebrowski, 1988; Harman, 1990. These two articles, written as the Soviet Union entered its final collapse, contain a classic analysis of the roots of the crisis, and the part played by the national movements in the former Soviet republics.
12:   Krawchenko, 1993.

Figure 1: Gross Domestic Product (GDP) compared to 1993
Source: World Economic Outlook

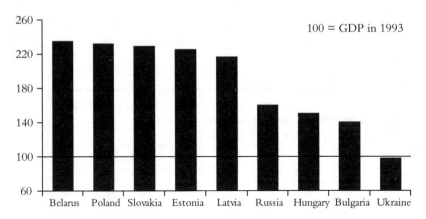

ethnic Russians, support for independence did not dip below 83 percent. The one exception was Crimea, a military bastion of Soviet imperialism, and even here 54 percent of the ballot was cast in favour of independence.

However, the post-Soviet economic collapse began to fuel divisions. The hopes of 1989–1991 were dashed on the rocks of shock therapy and hyperinflation, exceeding even the horrifying descent of the Russian economy. Annual inflation in Ukraine for the period 1993–5 averaged 2,001 percent per year (the figure for Russia for the same period was 460 percent).[13] Living standards plummeted and lifetime savings and pensions evaporated; Ukraine was at the eye of the neoliberal economic storm. Today Ukraine is the only Eastern European state whose level of production stands at pre-1993 levels (see figure 1).

A minimal recovery after 2000 was followed by the 2008 crisis: world steel prices fell; national debt on vast foreign loans mushroomed; reserves evaporated. The economy contracted by 15 percent and the currency lost 40 percent of its value. Per capita income (2013) and average life expectancy in Ukraine compared to its neighbours give an indication of what this means.

However, as workers in both east and west saw their futures evaporating, one group of Ukrainians did very well indeed amid the post-Soviet collapse. The oligarchs, who rose from the ranks of the old Soviet ruling class

---

13:   Gillman, 1998, p398.

Income per capita (US dollar equivalent)
Source: World Bank

Ukraine	3,900
Hungary	12,560★
Poland	13,432
Russia	14,612

★2012 data

Male life expectancy (2014 estimates)
Source: CIA World Factbook and The Lancet

Ukraine	63.78 (61.2 years in east Ukraine)
Hungary	71.73
Poland	72.74
Russia	64.37

(the *nomenklatura*) who were joined by new rising entrepreneurs cum gangsters, acquired vast wealth in the privatisation fire sale of state assets and new business interests.

Rinat Akhmetov, for example, now the wealthiest oligarch, built his fortune in the mining and steel industries in the east. He has interests in both Russian and Western markets and, like most oligarchs, is keen to keep both Russian and Western competitors out of the sectors where he makes his profits. He is worth (advisedly) over $14 billion. He controls more than 50 percent of the country's electricity and energy coal production, with interests in ore mining, steel, media, real estate, oil and natural gas.

There is another side to Akhmetov's wealth. Ukraine has the highest mining death rate in the world. The death rate per million tonnes of coal dug is three times that of China, ten times that of Russia and 100 times that of the United States—all for less than £200 a month. At one of Akhmetov's mines, the Sukhodilska-Skhidna pit, 127 miners died in a methane gas explosion in 2011. A miner, Smetanin Ihor Vladimirovich, described the conditions that caused the accident:

> Yesterday I helped bring up the dead guys to the surface. I cried half a night after this. I overheard someone say there was 5 percent of methane instead of a half-percent. If there is a leak, nobody can leave. They just push in some fresh air and keep you working. Otherwise, you lose your job.

I'm paid Hr 1,300[14] for a hellish job in the shaft; there is a lot of coal dust and no air circulation. In winter time, the shower has no heating… We get treated like animals…

I saw those dead guys. They had no shoes. One was missing half a head. I worked the whole day, but in the evening I collapsed and cried till three in the morning. I never cried at anyone's funeral. I am really sorry for them as a human. Really sorry.

And they died because [they tell us] "Come on! Faster! Give us coal output. Give us a new shaft! Give us millions!"[15]

The obscene wealth of the oligarchs was epitomised by the family of President Yanukovych: when protesters broke into his mansion they wandered stunned at the pure copper roof, private zoo, underground shooting range, 18-hole golf course, tennis courts, bowling alley and a gold plated bidet. Among the invoices were found $30 million for chandeliers with $5 million small change spent on switches and fittings. This is in a country where 35 percent of the population live below the poverty line.

After 1991, as the crisis wrecked the lives of ordinary Ukrainians, oligarchs and politicians encouraged regional and ethnic loyalties and divisions. Even where political leaders attempted to balance rival economic and regional interests they increasingly resorted to playing the ethnic and nationalist card in order to secure a political base against their rivals and to deflect popular anger away from themselves.

The growing splits between these groups of equally corrupt politicians and oligarchs culminated in the so-called "Orange Revolution" of 2004. Although it was triggered by a rigged election, neither side cared about democracy. Western leaning politicians knew of the fraud, which was an open secret, and planned mass protests, although they were by no means confident of winning support or resisting a crackdown. However, the numbers flocking into the square far exceeded expectations and the pro-Western politicians found the lever they needed. As the crisis grew, the ruling elite in the east threatened separation but backed down. At no point did the movement break from the grip of the elite on either side.

After the crisis of 2008 elements of the ruling class employed a divide and rule strategy with a vengeance. The Russian speaker in east Ukraine was

---

14: 1,300 Ukrainian Hryvnia, about £62 at the time of writing.
15: Vladimirovich, 2011.

portrayed by Ukrainian nationalists as a "coloniser", belonging to a foreign fifth column, who had conspired to destroy Ukrainian culture and language, guilty by association with the famine and the purges. The Ukrainian speakers in the west were portrayed as filthy Galician Nazi collaborators, who hated ethnic Russians and Russian speakers, and were out to suppress their language and rights. Ethnic and national divisions were deepened by the impact of crisis and the role of the elites. They are not written into Ukrainians' historical genes but had to be forged and fostered.

Under pro-Western president Viktor Yushchenko the government promoted an ultra-nationalistic reworking of history. The Nazi collaborators of Stepan Bandera were rehabilitated and Bandera himself was posthumously awarded the title "Hero of Ukraine" in 2010. Meanwhile the mainstream media gave increasing coverage to the Nazis of Svoboda.[16] This did not help Yushchenko, however. By the end of his presidency he was totally discredited, scoring 5 percent in the 2010 presidential elections. Up until 2009 ordinary Ukrainians' concern about ethnic conflict was declining. But, as figure 2 shows, there was a sudden upturn in the wake of the crash and the stoking of tensions by the elite.[17]

Nonetheless, as political geographer Evan Centanni observes, the mainstream media have misrepresented the divisions in Ukraine. In response to an article by the *Washington Post*'s Max Fisher,[18] Centanni writes, "There's not, as Fisher preposterously claims, 'an actual, physical line' splitting Ukraine in half. Instead, there's a gradual shading of mixed populations whose ethnic identities and voting history don't always correlate to the country's current political divisions".[19]

The language question has also been subject to much misrepresentation. There was systematic suppression of the Ukrainian language under Soviet rule. By 1988 only 28 percent of all Ukrainian children were taught in Ukrainian language schools compared to 89 percent in the late 1930s.[20] Yet prior to the Maidan crisis many old divisions of language and ethnicity were breaking down, especially among Ukrainian youth. Between 2003 and 2010 the percentage of young people using only Ukrainian or only Russian dropped significantly. The category that increased was the bilingual use of both the Russian and Ukrainian languages, rising from 18.9 percent

---

16: Rudling, 2013, pp228-231.
17: Pew Research Centre, 2014, p10.
18: Fisher, 2013.
19: Centanni, 2014.
20: Lieven, 1999, p16.

Figure 2: Ukrainians' concern about ethnic conflict
Source: Pew Research Centre—Spring 2014 Global Attitudes Survey

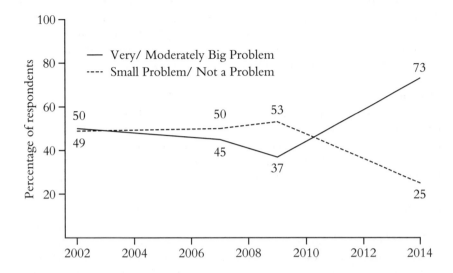

in 2003 to 40.3 percent in 2010.[21] The truth is that over a vast swathe of Ukraine, including the east, ethnic Ukrainians speak Russian, intermarry with ethnic Russians and they all converse in both languages at home, work and with friends and neighbours.

Similarly, the most important issues for young Ukrainians were the right to work; the right to a home; the right to education; freedom from arbitrary arrest; freedom of speech; freedom of movement and freedom of conscience respectively.

This helps explain the inability of the far-right Ukrainian nationalists to attract more than minority support, overwhelmingly confined to the far western regions of Galicia and Volhynia. Likewise the great Russian chauvinists have proved incapable of winning support beyond the two eastern regions of Donetsk and Luhansk and parts of the south. The political appeal of movements based on a narrow chauvinism is limited. Before May 2014, despite rising tensions, the majority of ethnic Russians were opposed to separation. Overall only 14 percent of Ukrainians wanted to allow regions to secede. In the eastern regions this rose to 18 percent and even among Russian speakers

---

21: Diuk, 2012, pp120-121.

in eastern Ukraine only 27 percent wanted to allow secession.[22]

The struggles of 1989-91 and growing social integration had demonstrated the potential for unity among ordinary Ukrainians. Two factors undermined this process: first, in the face of ongoing political and economic crisis, rival sections of the ruling elite fostered regional and ethnic division; second, these rival camps were in turn pulled by both the West and Russia who each wanted to forge Ukraine as a "buffer" state against their rival.

Maidan

By the end of 2013 the Ukrainian ruling class were desperate. The central bank had two months of foreign reserves left and Ukraine was judged twice as likely to default as Greece.[23] The ruling class desperately needed a bailout from either the EU and IMF or Russia. Either would come at a heavy price; both would offer nothing but continuing misery for Ukraine's workers. After some hesitation Yanukovych turned to Russia, refusing to sign the Association Agreement that had been negotiated with the EU.

This triggered a reaction that had its roots in the shared rage at the crisis and hatred for the oligarchs common to both east and west. However, the protests could never develop into a national movement as long as their demands were hitched to the EU and the West. The seeds of division had already been sown. The nature of the demands meant that the student-led protests of early autumn were reaching a limit beyond which they were unlikely to generalise further. Arguably, by the end of November the protests were on the wane. But on 30 November Yanukovych and his supporters made a fateful decision.

In two years Yanukovych had seen his support slump from 42 to 14 percent; he feared the protest movement might just be sufficient to dislodge him. Memories of the "Orange Revolution" of 2004 and the precedent set by the "Revolution on Granite" of 1990 had more than a symbolic resonance for Ukraine's rulers. Yanukovych decided to sweep the protesters from the square in an action that he hoped would bring the protest to a rapid end. He sent in the notorious interior ministry troops: the "Berkut" (Golden Eagles) to disband the students violently. The Berkut had their roots in the Soviet OMON formed at the end of the 1980s to take on the miners and the independence movements. They were paid double the wages of the ordinary police and had a deeply anti-Semitic culture. They went on a violent rampage not only clearing protesters from the square but pursuing them through the streets with clubs and laying siege to St Michael's

---

22: Pew Research Centre, 2014, p4
23: Rao, 2013.

Monastery where many took sanctuary.

Demonstrations of tens of thousands were transformed into demonstrations of hundreds of thousands and more. By early December up to half a million demonstrated. The motivation of the demonstrators is instructive. In a poll conducted among 1,037 demonstrators in and around Maidan square on 7-8 December, 70 percent said they came to protest against the police brutality of 30 November; 53.5 percent in favour of the EU Association Agreement; 50 percent "to change life in Ukraine"; 40 percent "to change the power in the country". Only 17 percent protested for fear that Ukraine would enter Russia's Customs Union or against the possibility of a turn back towards Russia. A negligible 5.4 percent said they answered the calls of opposition leaders.[24] As David Cadier observes: "The protests, while initially prompted by the rejection of the Association Agreement, grew considerably bigger and more determined after the police had repressed them; they became less about allegiance to either the EU or Russia than they were about denouncing a corrupt and inefficient political executive".[25] Once at the square the demands of the political opposition came more to the fore. But nonetheless when asked to choose which three political demands they most supported, signing the EU agreement came fourth with less than half the protesters including it as a demand. First, by a significant margin, was the release of those arrested on the Maidan and an end to repression; second, the dismissal of the government; third, the resignation of Yanukovych and early presidential elections.[26]

Confrontations and demonstrations continued through the winter. Then on 16 January the government passed a series of anti-protest laws, soon called "the dictatorship laws", that included ten-year jail terms for blockading government buildings, one-year jail terms for slandering government officials or "group violations of public order", amnesty from prosecution for the Berkut and law enforcement officials who had committed crimes against protesters, and a host of other measures. This triggered a further wave of mass protest against which the Berkut launched its most vicious and murderous onslaught. Over 100 protesters were killed. The fascists and ultra-right were able to present themselves both as victims and as the most determined defence against the Berkut and came to the fore in many of the confrontations that ensued.

The government strategy backfired disastrously. Yanukovych fled and the ruling Party of the Regions all but collapsed as the oligarchs and

---

24: Ilko Kucheriv Democratic Initiatives Foundation, 2014.
25: Cadier, 2014.
26: Ilko Kucheriv Democratic Initiatives Foundation, 2014.

deputies cut loose. The beneficiaries were the pro-Western oligarchs and politicians who brought the fascists of Svoboda and the Right Sector on board, appointing them to key ministerial posts.

This process has been depicted by a section of the left as a putsch from beginning to end. This is dangerous nonsense, and at best confuses outcome with intention. It ignores the role of the Berkut and the slaughter of demonstrators in much the same way as some pro-regime supporters ignore the massacre of anti-Kiev activists in Odessa by a pro-Kiev mob and the Right Sector. But it was not Svoboda, the Right Sector or the pro-Western politicians who turned the early demonstrations into mass protests—it was the turn to deadly force by Yanukovych and his supporters, a decision that led to his downfall, leaving a vacuum that the pro-EU, pro-Western politicians stepped into.

Ukraine: between East and West

Ever since the fall of the Soviet Union, the EU and NATO have sought to expand their sphere of influence into the former Soviet bloc, while Russia has sought to retain influence and, where possible, restore its own dominance over its "near abroad"—the former republics of the Soviet Union that won independence after 1991.[27]

The balance has long been in the West's favour and Russia could do little or nothing as one by one Eastern European countries, including the Baltic states, signed up to the EU and NATO. By 2009, 12 former Communist states had joined NATO, 11 of them joining the EU. In 2014 Georgia, Moldova and Ukraine all signed an EU "Deep and Comprehensive Free Trade Agreement".

It is important to grasp that the gathering tensions over the membership of rival trade blocs in Eastern Europe and the Russian periphery are not incidental, nor simply a matter of an aggressive foreign policy on the part of the EU; neither are they simply a sentimental attachment to former empire or just fear of encirclement on the part of Russia. This is not a matter of joining a "club" in order just to get some attractive offers or deals. The rivalry over these regional economic blocs is an expression of the economic competition between capitals on a world scale.

At stake are vast resources and markets. Each bloc is compelled to seek maximum competitive advantage against its rivals and to strengthen its competitive position in the world market. The European Union was formed precisely so that its member states could compete against other major

---

27: Stewart, 1997, pp18-21.

economies such as the US, Japan, the south-east Asian states and now China. With the end of the Cold War, it was inevitable the EU would turn eastwards.

David Cadier, albeit in the language of an academic economist, has quite astutely traced the dynamic of competition between the EU and the Russian sponsored Eurasian Customs Union (ECU) and the contradictory pressures this competition exerts on the states they wish to "integrate". As in the case of Ukraine, none of these states fall neatly into one economic sphere of influence or the other. They all have conflicting interests in both Russia and its ECU partners and in EU markets[28] most are also heavily dependent on Russian gas and energy supplies. The principal rivals themselves are also highly interdependent on one another.

Despite this, both "partnerships" are mutually exclusive; their rules preclude membership of both regional blocs. As Lenin and Bukharin observed a century ago in arguing against Karl Kautsky, increasing economic integration on a world scale does not *reduce* competition. On the contrary, the pressure to seek advantage at the expense of a rival capital, or seize the resources and markets it controls, means that competition will always reassert itself, however "illogical" this may appear.

Cadier argues that these economic "partnerships" are "two competing region-building endeavours" aimed at the same group of countries in Russia's "near abroad"; both Russia and the EU therefore attempt to shape the economic, administrative and, to some extent, political structures of the states of their common neighbourhood, albeit by different means and with differing records of success".[29] In Marxist terms, we are back to the classic analysis of imperialism—the development of economic competition between blocs of capital—and military rivalry between states.

It is no accident that competition between the EU and Russia came to a head over Ukraine, even though neither side anticipated the outcome and both miscalculated badly. The world economic crisis of 2008-9 has led to greater pressure on the ruling classes of nation states outside the major regional trade blocs to seek "partnership" deals or membership status, whatever the costs. The impact of the crisis on trade and rising deficits increases the need to reduce tariffs (itself a tool of capitalist competition). This combined with rapidly depleting reserves puts immense pressure on these states to sign up to these "partnerships", whatever the terms. The terms, of course, come at a price for the workers of these states themselves.

28: Although in the case of the ECU, the balance of trade is overwhelmingly with Russia. Belarus and Kazakhstan remain bit players.
29: Cadier, 2014.

Ukraine is a classic example. President Yanukovych attempted to balance between the ECU and the EU and keep a foot in both. He sought observer status in the ECU while at the same time negotiating the Association Agreement with the EU. However, Ukraine's looming economic crisis and the "take it or leave it" terms presented by both Russia and the EU would not permit this balancing act to continue. The EU overplayed its hand, and Yanukovych turned to Russia. The balancing act was over and Ukraine toppled.

Russia has always drawn red lines round the bordering states of Belarus, Moldova, Ukraine, Georgia, Armenia, Azerbaijan and Kazakhstan. However, some of these states significantly outweigh others in importance. Ukraine was the jewel in the crown. Ukraine joining the ECU was essential to Putin's regional economic project. Without Ukraine the ECU just leaves Russia, Belarus and Kazakhstan, an altogether reduced project entirely, and one that other states have less incentive to join.

The economic expansion of the EU also carries with it the threat of ever greater military encroachment by NATO. If Ukraine were to slip out of Russia's orbit altogether, Russia's regional and global position would be immeasurably weakened. Putin was never going to let that happen. While he had never calculated on the fall of Yanukovych and his replacement by a pro-Western regime in Kiev, the West for its part grossly underestimated Russia's determination. When Yanukovych fell and Ukraine turned west, Russia's economic levers were no longer sufficient and Putin deployed Russia's geopolitical advantage and military resources to de-stabilise Ukraine and at the very least, prevent it from integrating fully into a Western economic and military alliance.

Russia's strategy over Ukraine followed a pattern of intervention it has adopted since the 1990s. Russia has avoided becoming militarily involved in neighbouring states, with the notable exception of Chechnya, which it invaded after the republic declared independence. The war in Afghanistan and the first war in Chechnya aroused massive opposition in Russia and the legacy continues to hang over Russian foreign policy.[30] Instead Russia fostered national and ethnic conflicts that destabilised neighbouring states and made them dependent on Russian goodwill.

The price of this policy was a series of bloody conflicts across Russia's

---

30: Even in the case of Chechnya, Putin learnt from the experience of the defeat of 1994-6. He took great care at the beginning of the war to foster a strong, local Chechen regime under a former rebel, the brutal Akhmat Kadyrov, succeeded after his assassination in 2004 by his equally brutal and corrupt son, Ramzan. Putin poured billions of dollars into the reconstruction of Grozny in order to cement their rule.

near abroad in which Russia played a key role. These included the separatist conflicts between Georgia and the breakaway regions of Abkhazia and South Ossetia; Moldova and its pro-Russian breakaway Transnistria and the conflict between Armenia and Azerbaijan over the enclave of Nagorno-Karabakh.[31] Rather than committing large numbers of troops and armour, Russia relied on "volunteers", often highly trained, experienced, middle-ranking military and intelligence officers, to lead and direct local forces on the ground and provide a conduit for Russian weaponry and logistical supplies. In the course of these conflicts there emerged a highly ideological layer of deeply reactionary Russian nationalists, motivated by dreams of restoring the Russian/Soviet empire.

Many of these figures gravitated around the far-right "Eurasianist" movement led by the fascist Aleksandr Dugin and the anti-Semitic newspaper *Zavtra* (Tomorrow) and news network *Den* (The Day) led by the far-right reactionary Aleksandr Prokhanov. These were part of a "redbrown" alliance of Stalinists, great Russian chauvinists and outright fascists whose leading figures were cultivated at arms length by the Kremlin.

From 2000 onwards Putin built up a far more professional, paid and better equipped military, on the back of a tide of energy wealth as the price of oil and gas on the world market rose from $30 to $130 a barrel bringing a vast flow of capital. However, these military resources have so far been used to strengthen Russia's strategy in using proxies to destabilise its neighbours rather than supersede it.

Russia's strategy came to a head in 2008 when Russia humiliated the West in a short, sharp five-day war to prevent Georgia from moving to join NATO. Russia used the pro-Russian enclave of South Ossetia as a mechanism for de-stabilising Georgia; Georgia then overplayed its hand thinking that it would have the backing of the West and attacked the South Ossetians. Russia responded with troops and air cover in support of the rebels. Since then Russia has continued to use its economic leverage on Georgia, not least through energy supplies.

Western imperialism and the Russian "bear".

Those who choose to weigh one imperialism against another in favour of whichever they see as "the least bad" often justify their position by overstating the threat from Russia on the one hand or the United States on the other. This is not to say that they are evenly balanced either militarily or economically; the United States and its allies clearly massively outweigh Russia on both counts.

31: For an account of the war in Chechnya and the conflicts of the 1990s, see Ferguson, 2000.

Yet this is not the end of the matter. Imperialist conflicts do not simply disappear because one side is stronger than the other. As we have already insisted, imperialism is a system, not a boxing match. In particular, tensions and conflicts arise as the parameters of competition between capitals shift.

In the current conflict between the West and Russia, each has its own vulnerabilities and its own respective advantages and weaknesses. Some are obvious. The dream of the neoconservatives' "New American Century" lies in ruins on the battlefields of Iraq, Afghanistan and Syria. The US relies heavily on its military advantage to compensate for its relative loss of economic dominance since the Second World War. However, this military advantage has diminishing returns the nearer a conflict zone is to the borders of growing or resurgent rival powers such as China or Russia. The US suffers from overstretch, and NATO has gone to great lengths to avoid getting dragged into putting boots on the ground in Ukraine.

Russia on the other hand has difficulties of its own; its military re-equipment is extremely uneven and beset with problems. Russian growth has gone into reverse and, however popular Putin may appear, past experience shows that getting involved in a war during an economic downturn can soon change that. Some 50,000 people demonstrated in Moscow against war a day before the Crimean referendum. They not only opposed war but many, possibly a majority, opposed the annexation of Crimea itself—an impressive position to take in the circumstances and one that shames many on the Western left.[32]

In this respect both the West and Russia face the same difficulty. The role of the anti-war movement in limiting US, British and allied intervention in Syria and Iran and the huge scale of opposition to the wars in Afghanistan and Iraq are generally acknowledged. Despite the image of a Russian population that adores Putin for restoring Russia's imperial pride, Putin fears he would face serious trouble if Russia were to get bogged down in Ukraine.

On the face of things there appears to be a high level of popular support for Putin's warmongering in eastern Ukraine. However, this is deceptive on a number of counts. It is true that when polled over 50 percent of Russians said Russia should give *support* to the separatist leadership and the fighters in Donetsk and Luhansk, with 20 percent opposed and 20 percent unsure. However, while 40 percent supported sending troops, 45 percent

---

32: The demonstrations were impressive but revealed the weakness of the Russian left which only numbered a few hundred. This has serious consequences for a movement whose political orientation is largely dominated by free market liberals (I am grateful to Ben Neal, who lives in Moscow, and has actively participated in the protests, for this observation).

were opposed.[33] (Another indication of the potential opposition to Putin is the anger among families and relatives at the secrecy and intimidation surrounding the scores of deaths of Russian soldiers in Ukraine while "on holiday").[34]

The first point to make is that such views in current circumstances, with a deluge of government controlled media propaganda and a weakly organised anti-war movement, are incredibly impressive. However, even more significant are the views among youth. Another poll shows the percentage of 18 to 30 year olds opposed to giving *any* support to the separatists exactly matching those in favour, at 41 percent.[35]

Limitations on their ability to achieve quick victories on the battlefield and the risk of mass opposition at home have led both the West and Russia to place great reliance on proxies in their imperialist ventures. The fostering of sectarian, national and ethnic division attains absolute primacy in these conditions, even when unintended consequences such as in Iraq, Syria and Ukraine pose immense difficulty for the ruling class. Such a strategy is highly unpredictable, partly because it involves supporting actors whose own reactionary ideologies often lead them to defy their imperialist patrons. One thing is predictable, however—such a strategy has proved its weight in gold in destroying any prospect of united resistance from below against the ruling class and against imperialism. For this our rulers will pay the price of any "local difficulty".

Whether they get away with it depends in part on the opposition they face, and on the politics of the left and the international anti-war movement. Thus it is critical we understand what is happening in Ukraine and how the left should respond.

Crimea and the east

The ousting of Yanukovych and the collapse of the Party of the Regions had massive consequences. Russia's strategy had been to keep Ukraine, if not firmly within the Russian sphere, at least out of the Western alliance.[36] This was now in jeopardy. The West threw its support behind Kiev, turning a blind eye to the absolutely reactionary character of the regime and the role of Svoboda and the Right Sector.

This continued through the massacre of anti-Kiev Russian nationalists in Odessa on 2 May. Over 3,000 have been killed and a million

---

33: Levada, 2014.
34: Schlossberg, 2014a and 2014b.
35: Goryashko, 2014.
36: See for example, *Stratfor*, 2014b.

displaced in eastern Ukraine as a result of the so-called "Anti-Terrorist Operation". Disaffection within the ranks of the Ukrainian military and their families, and the dilapidated state of the Ukrainian armed forces has forced Kiev to rely on using the Nazis of the Right Sector and other militia formations. Kiev is now detested in the east, particularly in the Donetsk and Luhansk regions, including by many who were previously divided in their loyalties. The divisions between workers in Ukraine now run very deep.

Nonetheless, it is a mistake to see the movement in the east as anti-fascist or any less reactionary than its stronger counterpart in the west. The annexation of Crimea by Russia was key. Crimea houses Russia's vital naval base on the Black Sea, leased from Ukraine. It has been the touchstone for Great Russian chauvinists since the 1980s. Year after year there have been demands, including from within the Kremlin and the Russian parliament, to annex Crimea.[37] This has never had anything to do with the right to self-determination of an oppressed minority, which Russian speakers in Ukraine were not, and everything to do with exerting Russian dominance, not only over Ukraine itself but across Russia's entire periphery.

It was in Crimea that the networks who had earned their military spurs in previous proxy conflicts helped build a political bridgehead for Russia in Crimea and afterwards in eastern Ukraine. These included the deeply reactionary Sergei Aksyonov who took the post of prime minister of Crimea, despite his party only getting 4 percent in the 2010 election; Igor Girkin (also known as Strelkov, "rifleman"), Alexander Borodai, Igor Bezler and Vladimir Antyufeyev were all veterans of previous conflicts, particularly in Transnistria. Antyufeyev, the lesser known but possibly the more significant current figure, served as security chief in Transnistria and was involved in a failed coup attempt in Latvia in 1991.

After the Crimean annexation Girkin and Borodai both moved to eastern Ukraine, where they took the leadership positions of the separatists. Their connections were critical in ensuring a flow of arms, supplies and volunteer fighters from Russia. There is no doubt that the separatists have won an important level of support as a result of political opposition to the government in Kiev and the slaughter initiated by Kiev in the east but this does not alter the fact that they can only exist as a proxy for Russian interests in Ukraine. Active support for the fighters has been limited; Girkin himself complained vehemently of this, accusing Ukrainians in the east of being cowards.

In June 2013 Girkin contributed to a round table held by a pro-Kremlin Russian news agency on Russian military strategy. His central thesis was that

---

37: Stewart, 1997, pp21-6.

Russia needed to wage a new type of war modelled on the "pre-emptive" strikes mounted by Israel against enemies beyond its borders. Incidentally, he went on to talk of the "demographic decomposition of Russian society" among ethnic Russians outside Russia as well as inside; he complained of the threat of immigration and radical Islam, and how the Bolsheviks had succeeded in 1917 supported by "covert and secret international structures" (Jews) because action was not taken early enough to "neutralise" the enemy.[38]

Some on the left seem to be almost willingly fooled by the "anti-fascist" rhetoric of the separatists without understanding that this rhetoric has a long Stalinist and reactionary pedigree. It was used against the East German uprising of 1953 and the Hungarian Revolution in 1956; it was used again by the Warsaw Pact powers to justify support for the invasion of Czechoslovakia in 1968. The charge of "national fascism" has been used to try and whip up Russian antagonism towards the independence movements in the former Soviet republics ever since the end of the 1980s.

This is a much deeper issue than the reactionary predilections of a few individuals. The very character and politics of the separatist movement are based on Great Russian chauvinism and ethnic division, notwithstanding the popular support they have achieved. In fact while the separatists secured substantial passive support against Kiev they never mobilised a mass uprising. The fighting forces and even the largest demonstrations were simply not of that order. They never managed to extend or sustain the occupations beyond some towns and cities in the two regions where the ethnic Russian population is highest.

Both the West and Russia have supported their respective proxies in Ukraine and the result has been a carnival of reaction on both sides of the conflict. Both camps have driven divisions between Ukrainian workers and in doing so strengthened the grip of the rival imperialisms over the whole working class. The pretence of some on the European and Russian left that the movement in the east is based on a progressive articulation of class demands is spurious. It is the *subjective* absence of a class movement in Ukraine that has allowed both these minority chauvinisms to dominate Ukraine's political landscape with such disastrous consequences.

Imperialism and the left

A debate has emerged on the left over how to respond to Russia's role in the conflict. Behind these debates lie differences in approach to the understanding of imperialism in general and, among Marxists, how we should

---

38: Investigate This, 2014.

apply our understanding of the classic theory of imperialism developed by revolutionaries in the early 20th century.

The dominant response, rightly, has been to oppose any interference and intervention on the part of NATO. This has to be the starting point for revolutionaries and anti-war activists in Britain. Disagreements over Russia's role cannot be allowed to impede a united response to our own warmongers, whose hypocrisy is beyond satire. President Obama declared on Russia's annexation of Crimea, "Sending in troops and, because you're bigger and stronger, taking a piece of the country—that is not how international law and international norms are observed in the 21st century." Clearly 21st century norms do not apply to Afghanistan, Iraq or Gaza.

However, this cannot be a reason for socialists to downplay the character of the conflict or Russia's role. To do so can only undermine building an international movement against war in the long run. The difficulty begins with a tendency to view Russia's role through the lens of US military dominance alone. Thus some of the most principled and longstanding opponents of US and British imperialism have argued that Russia is not a culpable party to the conflict or that it is on the "defensive" against the US and NATO. Such positions have been articulated, with different degrees of emphasis, by Noam Chomsky, John Pilger, Jonathan Steele and Seamus Milne of the *Guardian* and Stephen F Cohen, the bane of US Cold War ideologues.[39] This is understandable if mistaken; however, such positions extend to sections of the left who invoke the revolutionary tradition and this has particular consequences for the left in Russia and the former Communist bloc. Within the anti-war movement treating the conflict as an inter-imperialist one has been discouraged, on the grounds that we should concentrate all our fire on our own imperialists and refrain from criticising Russia's role.[40]

However, Russia is not Iraq or Afghanistan and cannot be viewed solely in an isolated relationship to US power and NATO expansion.[41] Russia occupies a vast territory and has its own imperialist interests both in its own region and in other parts of the world including the Middle East. It is a contender, albeit a weak one, in the imperialist world system. Russia is part of a world system of competing capitals and seeks to compete with rival powers in order to dominate and oppress its own workers and people and those of its "near abroad" in particular. Russia is still the world's second nuclear power.

39: Chomsky, 2014; Pilger, 2014; Milne, 2014; Steele, 2014; Vanden Heuvel and Cohen, 2014.

40: German, 2014; Nineham, 2014.

41: See Nineham, 2014 for a comparison of positions on Russia to, for example, Serbia.

It is essential not to confuse *inter-imperialist* conflicts between rival imperialist powers with conflicts between major powers and subordinate or oppressed states. If in the latter case we were to oppose both belligerents equally, we would in effect end up supporting the most powerful. However, it is a mistake to approach an inter-imperialist conflict as if it was a conflict between an imperialist and a subordinate state.

The danger, as in the Cold War, is a descent into "campism", in which one imperialism is seen as a more or less welcome "counterweight" to the other. Here socialists and anti-war activists can be trapped into a position of justifying the ventures of "the least bad" of the rival powers. Such is the position some have taken over both the annexation of Crimea and the separatists in east Ukraine.[42] The danger here is that the anti-imperialist principle so essential to building a mass anti-war movement can become discredited. It also implies that socialists in "the least bad" imperialism are exempt from arguing that "the main enemy is at home". Meanwhile those who hold to opposing their own imperialists, but take a "campist" position, risk falling into ever deeper apologetics on the one hand or, as in the Cold War, suddenly switch position when support for a rival imperialism is no longer tenable.

An insistence on the imperialist character of the rivalry between the great powers is not an abstraction. Nor does it imply a "neutral" position. On the contrary, in the case of Ukraine, it means that even if we suspend reality for a moment and assume Russia were the dominant expansionist power, we would *still* be absolutely opposed to NATO intervention or sanctions. Opposition to our own imperialists does not rest on having to disguise the role of its rivals.

Above all, it is only by insisting that we face an imperialist war that it makes sense to argue, *in every country*, that the main enemy is at home. The aim for socialists is not only to oppose war but to turn the war between nations into a civil war between classes; to unite the workers of every country against the international "gang of robbers".

The position of Russian socialist Boris Kagarlitsky illustrates the problem of excluding Russia from the equation, especially given the pressures on the left in the post-Soviet states. Kagarlitsky was a prominent radical dissident in the 1980s and played an important role in first advocating perestroika and glasnost "from below". He had a high profile internationally and was prominent at anti-capitalist and anti-globalisation forums. However, Kagarlitsky's vulnerabilities were evident before the Ukraine crisis. He took

---

42: Kagarlitsky, 2014a; 2014b; 2014c; 2014d; 2014e.

a dismissive attitude towards the huge "Bolotnaya" protests in 2011 against fraud in the Russian presidential elections, casting them simply as "middle class" protests divorced from the concerns of workers (this is a theme of Kagarlitsky's that he took up again in the case of Ukraine).[43]

Unfortunately, far from arguing that in Russia, as in Britain, "the main enemy is at home", Kagarlitsky has contented himself with attacking NATO while supporting Russia's proxies in eastern Ukraine and praising the ethnic Russians in Crimea.[44] Indeed he has criticised Putin for not intervening forcefully enough and opposed the 26,000 strong anti-war protest in Moscow on 21 September 2014.[45] This is a tragic political position to hold but one in which the Western left also bears some responsibility.

In Ukraine itself the left is disastrously split. One organisation, "Borotba", with a strong Stalinist tradition has collapsed into an alliance of Stalinists and Great Russian chauvinists and called for support for the eastern separatists. Another section, associated with the Fourth International, oriented on the movement that arose out of the Maidan protests. Unfortunately, the latter directed their main arguments against Russia rather than the deep illusions in NATO and the EU in western Ukraine. In the West too the Maidan attracted the hopes of those who elevated the "spontaneous" character of Occupy and other social movements with some casting Russia as the main enemy and Western imperialism as a mere bit player.[46]

Conclusion

While we can speculate as to the outcome of the current ceasefire, what is clear is that economic crisis and imperialist rivalry have deeply divided Ukraine. Nonetheless, the objective *potential* for a united response by workers in the east and west continues to exist. This will depend upon whether a movement and force on the left begins to emerge that challenges not only the oligarchs but the rival imperialisms *and* the rival national chauvinisms they have fuelled.

To side with one chauvinism or another in Ukraine or paint one side or another in fake socialist colouring or to argue that one imperialist camp is defensive is to defy the lessons drawn by revolutionaries in the First World War.

43: Kagarlitsky, 2011. See also Haynes, 2008; Crouch, 2002; Harman, 1994 and Callinicos, 1990 for criticisms of key aspects of Kagarlitsky's approach, not least on the national question and his ambiguous position regarding the Russian "left".

44: Kagarlitsky, 2014a; 2014b; 2014c; 2014d; 2014e.

45: Rabkor, 2014.

46: Žižek, 2014.

It is true that socialists in Ukraine, in Russia and here in the West face different concrete tasks. However, these tasks are informed by two common principles: first, recognition that this is an imperialist conflict; second, that socialists strive to forge the international unity of the working class across every national and ethnic divide. It is from these principles that uncompromising opposition to our own rulers' rivalry in Ukraine flows, while at the same time making no concession to their imperialist rivals or their proxies. This is as true in London as it is in Moscow, Kiev or Donetsk.

In his pamphlet "Socialism and War", Lenin argues:

> From the standpoint of bourgeois justice…Germany would be absolutely right as against England and France, for she has been "done out" of colonies, her enemies are oppressing an immeasurably far larger number of nations than she is, and the Slavs who are oppressed by her ally Austria undoubtedly enjoy far more freedom than those in tsarist Russia, that real "prison of nations". But Germany is fighting not for the liberation, but for the oppression of nations.

Lenin goes on to argue that it is not the business of socialists to help one robber rob another: "Socialists must take advantage of the struggle between the robbers to overthrow them all. To be able to do this, the Socialists must first of all tell the people the truth, namely, that this war is in a treble sense a war between slave-owners to fortify slavery".[47]

The lessons learnt in forging a united international workers' movement in the teeth of war, crisis and national chauvinism on the monumental scale that existed in the First World War needs to be relearnt. The long decades of low levels of class struggle and the rise and fall of the movements have exacted a political price on the left, leading many to turn to other social forces to bring change. Ultimately this leads to the danger of compromise with the existing system itself. Nowhere is this task more urgent than over the question of Ukraine.

The failure to grasp the character of state capitalism in Russia after Stalin's counter-revolution has also returned to haunt us. During the Cold War Tony Cliff first used the slogan: "Neither Washington, Nor Moscow but International Socialism!" to restore the principled positions taken by Lenin and the Bolsheviks during the First World War. Cliff did so in a situation where the left internationally took a "campist" position in favour of supporting one imperialism or another, in particular the state capitalist Soviet empire, and turned their backs on an international working class that

---

47: Lenin, 1915.

had the capacity to bring ruin to their own imperialists, and to the entire "gang of robbers". It is a position the left needs to re-learn in the context of a multi-polar world of rival capitals and states:

> In their mad rush for profit, for wealth, the two gigantic imperialist powers are threatening the existence of world civilisation, are threatening humanity with the terrible suffering of atomic war. The interests of the working class, of humanity, demand that neither of the imperialist world powers be supported, but that both be struggled against. The battle-cry of the real, genuine socialists today must be:

> "Neither Washington nor Moscow, but International Socialism".[48]

48: Cliff, 1950.

References

Broué, Pierre, 1997, *Histoire de L'Internationale Communiste: 1919-1943* (Fayard).

Cadier, David, 2014, "Eurasian Economic Union and Eastern Partnership: the End of the EU-Russia Entredeux", LSE (27 June), www.lse.ac.uk/IDEAS/publications/reports/pdf/SR019/SR019-Cadier.pdf

Callinicos, Alex, 1990, "A Third Road?", *Socialist Review* (February), www.marxists.org/history/etol/writers/callinicos/1990/02/3rdroad.html

Callinicos, Alex, 2005, "Imperialism and Global Political Economy", *International Socialism* 104 (autumn), www.isj.org.uk/?id=140

Callinicos, Alex, 2006, "Making Sense of Imperialism: a Reply to Leo Panitch and Sam Gindin", *International Socialism* 110 (spring), www.isj.org.uk/?id=196

Centanni, Evan, 2014, "How Sharply Divided is Ukraine, Really? Honest Maps of Language and Elections" Political Geography Now (9 March), http://tinyurl.com/orv5vgm

Chomsky, Noam, 2014, "Interview: Noam Chomsky", Chatham House (June), www.chathamhouse.org/publication/interview-noam-chomsky#

Cliff, Tony (as R Tennant), 1950, "The Struggle of the Powers", *Socialist Review* (November), www.marxists.org/archive/cliff/works/1950/11/powers.html

CPSU, 1939, *History of the Communist Party of the Soviet Union (Bolsheviks)* (Foreign Languages Publishing House).

Crouch, Dave, 2002, "The Inevitability of Radicalism", *International Socialism* 97 (winter), www.marxists.org/history/etol/newspape/isj2/2002/isj2-097/crouch.htm

Cumming-Bruce, Nick, 2014, "More than a Million Ukrainians have been Displaced, UN says", *New York Times* (2 September), http://tinyurl.com/jwgx7pn

Dewey Commission, 1937, "The Case of Leon Trotsky, 8th Session" (14 April), http://tinyurl.com/qfjmeec

Diuk, Nadia M, 2012, *The Next Generation in Russia, Ukraine, and Azerbaijan: Youth, Politics, Identity and Change* (Rowman and Littlefield).

Ferguson, Rob, 2000, "Chechnya: The Empire Strikes Back", *International Socialism* 86 (spring), www.marxists.org/history/etol/newspape/isj2/2000/isj2-086/ferguson.htm

Fisher, Max, 2013, "This One Map helps explain Ukraine's Protests", *Washington Post* (9 December), http://tinyurl.com/op4s9ce

Garnett, Sherman W, 1997, *Keystone in the Arch: Ukraine in the Emerging Security Environment of Central and Eastern Europe* (Carnegie).

German, Lindsey, 2014, "Does Opposing our Government's Wars mean we Support 'the Other Side'?" (13 July), http://tinyurl.com/knsfch7

Gillman, Max, 1998, "A Macroeconomic Analysis of Economies in Transition", in Amnon Levy-Livermore (ed), *Handbook on the Globalization of the World Economy* (Edward Elgar).

Goodby, James E, 1998, *Europe Undivided: The New Logic of Peace in US-Russian Relations* (United States Institute of Peace Press).

Goryashko, Sergei, 2014, "Russians do not Understand the Objectives of the Lugansk and Donetsk Republics", *Kommersant* (4 September).

Harman, Chris, 1980, "Imperialism, East and West", *Socialist Review* (February), www.marxists.org/archive/harman/1980/02/imp-eastwest.htm

Harman, Chris, 1983, "Increasing Blindness", *Socialist Review* (June), www.marxists.org/archive/harman/1983/06/bukharin.htm

Harman, Chris, 1990, "The Storm Breaks", *International Socialism* 46 (spring), www.marxists.org/archive/harman/1990/xx/stormbreaks.html

Harman, Chris, 1994, "Unlocking the Prison House", *Socialist Review* (July/August), www.

marxists.org/archive/harman/1994/07/centasia.html

Harman, Chris, 2003, "Analysing Imperialism", *International Socialism* 99 (summer), www.marxists.org/archive/harman/2003/xx/imperialism.htm

Harman, Chris, and Andy Zebrowski, 1988, "Glasnost—Before the Storm", *International Socialism* 39 (summer), www.marxists.org/archive/harman/1988/xx/glasnost.html

Haynes, Mike, 2008, "Valuable but Flawed", *International Socialism* 119 (summer), www.isj.org.uk/?id=471

Ilko Kucheriv Democratic Initiatives Foundation, 2014, "Maidan 2013: Who, Why and for What?" http://dif.org.ua/ua/events/gvkrlgkaeths.htm

Investigate This, 2014, "Ukraine Crisis: Militia Leader Igor Girkin a Hardline Russian Ex-FSB Colonel (Updated)" (15 August), http://tinyurl.com/lbqf4xd

Kagarlitsky, Boris, 2011, "Boris Kagarlitsky: A Very Peaceful Russian Revolt", *Links: International Journal of Socialist Renewal* (11 December), http://links.org.au/node/2663

Kagarlitsky, Boris, 2014a, "Boris Kagarlitsky: Crimea Annexes Russia", *Links: International Journal of Socialist Renewal* (24 March), http://links.org.au/node/3790

Kagarlitsky, Boris, 2014b, "Boris Kagarlitsky on Eastern Ukraine: The Logic of a Revolt", *Links: International Journal of Socialist Renewal* (1 May), http://links.org.au/node/3838

Kagarlitsky, Boris, 2014c, "Solidarity with the Anti-fascist Resistance in Ukraine Launch", (Video Link with Boris Kagarlitsky—2 June), http://tinyurl.com/lg52v87

Kagarlitsky, Boris, 2014d, "Boris Kagarlitsky: Eastern Ukraine People's Republics between Militias and Oligarchs", *Links: International Journal of Socialist Renewal* (16 August), http://links.org.au/node/4008

Kagarlitsky, Boris, 2014e, "Ukraine's Uprising against Nato, Neoliberals and Oligarchs—an Interview with Boris Kagarlitsky", *Counterfire* (8 September), http://tinyurl.com/pgnpn64

Krawchenko, Bohdan, 1993, "Ukraine: the Politics of Independence", in Ian Bremmer and Ray Taras (eds) *Nations and Politics in the Soviet Successor States* (Cambridge University Press).

Lenin, V I, 1914, "Letter to A.G. Shlyapnikov" (17 October), http://tinyurl.com/phfy3gd

Lenin, V I, 1915, "Socialism and War" (July-August), http://tinyurl.com/nmq7nrq

Lenin, V I, 1917, "In the Footsteps of *Russkaya Volya*" (13 April), http://tinyurl.com/psufcxc

Levada, 2014, "Russian Views on Events in Ukraine" (27 June), http://tinyurl.com/on2w23s

Lieven, Anatol, 1999, *Ukraine and Russia: a Fraternal Rivalry* (United States Institute of Peace Press).

Milne, Seamus, 2014, "It's not Russia that's Pushed Ukraine to the Brink of War", (30 April), www.theguardian.com/commentisfree/2014/apr/30/russia-ukraine-war-kiev-conflict

Nineham, Chris, 2014, "Ukraine: Why Being Neutral Won't Stop a War", (23 March), www.counterfire.org/articles/analysis/17119-ukraine-why-being-neutral-wont-stop-a-war

Panitch, Leo, and Sam Gindin, 2006, "Feedback: Imperialism and Global Political Economy—a reply to Alex Callinicos", *International Socialism* 109 (Winter), www.isj.org.uk/?id=175

Pew Research Centre, 2014, "Despite Concerns about Governance, Ukrainians Want to Remain One Country", *Pew Research Global Attitudes Project* (8 May), http://tinyurl.com/pxayt3u

Pilger, John, 2014, "In Ukraine, the US is Dragging us Towards War with Russia", *Guardian* (13 May), http://tinyurl.com/le5v6h4

Rabkor, 2014, "Anti-fascists were Removed by Police from the 'Peace March' in Moscow, Rabkor (21 September), http://rabkor.ru/news/2014/09/21/peace-march

Rao, Sujato, 2013, "Banks Cannot Ease Ukraine's Reserve Pain", *Global Investing* (9 December), http://blogs.reuters.com/globalinvesting/2013/12/09/banks-cannot-ease-ukraines-reserve-pain/

Rees, John, 2006, *Imperialism and Resistance* (Routledge).

Rudling, Per Anders, 2013, "The Return of the Ukrainian Far Right: The Case of VO

Svoboda", in Ruth Wodack and John E Richardson (eds), *Analysing Fascist Discourse: European Fascism in Talk and Text* (Routledge).

Schlossberg, Leo, 2014a, "The Army and the Volunteers", *Novaya Gazeta* (3 September).

Schlossberg, Leo, 2014b, "They weren't just Tricked, They were Humiliated", *Novaya Gazeta* (4 September).

Steele, Jonathan, 2014, "The Ukraine Crisis: John Kerry and Nato must Calm Down and Back Off", *Guardian* (2 March), http://tinyurl.com/mped2pn

Stewart, Dale B, 1997, "The Russian-Ukrainian Friendship Treaty and the Search for Regional Stability in Eastern Europe (Thesis)", Monterey Naval Postgraduate School (December), https://archive.org/details/russianukrainian00stew

Stratfor, 2014a, "Potential New Dangers emerge in the US-Russian Standoff" (3 September), http://tinyurl.com/l8usyt5

Stratfor, 2014b, "Ukraine: Russia Looks Beyond Crimea" (3 March), http://tinyurl.com/ktjaybx

Trenin, Dmitri, 2014, "The Ukraine Crisis and the Resumption of Great Power Rivalry", *Carnegie Moscow Center* (9 July), http://tinyurl.com/kc9uwul

Trotsky, Leon, 1939, "The Problem of the Ukraine", *Socialist Appeal* (9 May), www.marxists.org/archive/trotsky/1939/04/ukraine.html

UNHCR, 2014, "Number of Displaced inside Ukraine more than Doubles Since early August to 260,000" (2 September), www.unhcr.org/540590ae9.html

Vanden Heuvel, Katrina, and Stephen F Cohen, 2014, "Cold War Against Russia—Without Debate", *The Nation* (19 May), http://tinyurl.com/kmnx48d

Vladimirovich, Smetanin Ihor, 2014, "Coal miner: People are Expendable", *Kyiv Post* (5 August), http://tinyurl.com/lg3w963

Žižek, Slavoj, 2014, "What Europe Can Learn from Ukraine", *In These Times* (8 April), http://inthesetimes.com/article/16526/what_europe_can_learn_from_ukraine

South Africa: from Marikana to the "Numsa moment"

Charlie Kimber

O n 16 August 2012 South African police shot and killed 34 striking
workers at the Lonmin mine near Rustenburg.[1] The massacre sent
shockwaves around the world—and the implications of this political
earthquake are far from played out. It is likely to be seen as one of the key
elements that began a process leading to a mass worker-based party to the
left of the African National Congress—a development of global importance.
We are seeing the beginning of a major challenge to the class compromises
of 1994 that saw the end of apartheid and the start of ANC rule.

In 1891 police murdered ten textile workers on a May Day parade
in the small town of Fourmies in France. Parliamentary deputy Georges
Clemenceau warned the ruling class, "Take care, the dead are strong
persuaders. One must pay attention to the dead."

Certainly the Marikana dead deserve attention. The massacre and the
subsequent struggles inspired by the courage of the Marikana strikers are
central factors explaining the political breakthroughs that have taken place
and that are now set to deepen. These struggles, together with the crisis of
capitalism, the turmoil in the ANC and several major trade unions, and the
victorious five-month strike by platinum miners in 2014 have punched a

1:    Thanks to members of Keep Left and the Democratic Left Front in South Africa and to
Anita Khanna, Peter Dwyer, Alan Goatley, Jim Nichol, Sam Ashman and Alex Callinicos for
comments on the draft article.

hole in the tripartite alliance of the ANC, the South African Communist Party (SACP) and the Cosatu trade union federation. There is now a chance for a new beginning—the question is whether it will be seized.

Much of the left across the world has studied the rise of Syriza in Greece and has debated whether this is the essential reference point for how the left should organise today. There has been much less attention on what is happening in South Africa, but it is of at least equal importance.

Of course there was tenacious struggle inside South Africa during the ANC's rule before the Marikana strike and massacre. According to an official South African Police Service report obtained by News24 Investigators, there were more than 3,000 protests over housing, water, electricity, land rights and similar issues between 2009 and 2012.[2] These protests, often met by violence, expressed the deep disillusion with the slow pace of change—or utter lack of change—since the end of apartheid. There were also important strikes, such as the public sector strike of 2010 involving over a million workers for four weeks. None had the same impact as the "Marikana moment"—although in truth it is a process, not a moment.

Why was Marikana so crucial? In a powerful article Peter Alexander points out that:

> Commentators have used different adjectives to underline the event's importance. It has been described as a "watershed moment"...a "turning point"...a "tipping point"...as "seminal"...as a "seismic event"...and as marking a "tectonic shift". Its significance has been likened to the massacres at Sharpeville (1960) and Soweto (1976)...and to the 1973 strikes in Durban... For one US historian, the killings "signalled the quasi-official end of post-apartheid South Africa's revolutionary era".[3]

Anyone who studies the history of South Africa knows that the racist apartheid system sustained its control by the brutal suppression of its opponents. That meant a history of massacres including Sharpeville, Soweto and Bisho and Boipatong, both in 1992. Whatever the shortcomings of life after the end of apartheid in 1994, most people believed that at least the era of massacres had come to an end. Of course, before 2012 the police had attacked protesters and strikers. Banning marches and shooting at service delivery protesters had become a common occurrence. The police had

---

2: Saba and van der Merwe, 2013.
3: Alexander, 2013.

even killed people.[4] But there had not been the mass slayings designed to smash resistance. Now the massacres were back. The trade union federation Cosatu said, "After 18 years of democracy we have witnessed scenes which we had hoped were now only part of our history".[5]

That was a shock for many. But equally shocking in its own way was the reaction from those who during apartheid had been the subject of repression and murder—the ANC and its allies. Instead of blaming the mine bosses and the police, the ANC and its alliance partners directed most of their fire at the strikers themselves and their Association of Mineworkers and Construction Union (AMCU).

Four days after the Marikana massacre, Frans Baleni, general secretary of the Cosatu-affiliated National Union of Mineworkers (NUM), attacked AMCU and spoke of "dark forces who can mislead our members, make them to believe that they've got extra power to make their life to be different overnight".[6] Blade Nzimande, SACP general secretary, wrote that "attempts by the opposition to liken police reaction in Marikana to that of the apartheid regime is outrageous" and that there should be an investigation into "essentially backward beliefs and practices amongst sections of the working class". He condemned "cheap politicking...in trying to lay the blame at the door of government and narrowly the police".[7]

Jeremy Cronin from the SACP wrote:

At least one of the silver linings in this dark cloud has been the widespread public revulsion at the vulture-like behaviour of some of the more demagogic interventions since the tragedy. We trust that those...who had continued to flirt with illusions about "economic freedom fighters" now understand exactly what the SACP said back in 2009 when we characterised this tendency as anti-union, anti-worker and even as "proto-fascist".[8]

Even the Cosatu statement mentioned earlier, which captured the shock of what had occurred, went on to say: "Cosatu is however refusing to use this tragedy to score points. We won't play the blame-game nor will we use the anger workers and their communities are feeling to drive sentiments against government or anyone".[9]

4:   The horrific and well-documented killing of Andries Tatane is one example.
5:   Cosatu, 2012.
6:   NUM, 2012.
7:   Nzimande, 2012.
8:   Cronin, 2012.
9:   Cosatu, 2012.

This is not the place for a full analysis of what happened on the day. Anyone wanting the truth should see the wonderful film *Miners Shot Down* and read some of the excellent analysis that has appeared.[10] The basic facts are that an unofficial strike broke out at the Lonmin platinum mine in Marikana. Some 3,000 rock drillers began the action having seen the success of a similar strike at the start of the year at Impala's platinum mine in Rustenburg. The action was over the poverty pay and appalling conditions suffered by workers whose sweat (and sometimes lives) produced one of the most valuable minerals on earth. But it was also a conscious challenge to the NUM, the once-mighty union that had been at the forefront of the battle against apartheid and whose heroic strike in 1987 was one of the proudest moments of the trade union struggle. The NUM had now been transformed into a pliant partner of management, policing the deals that kept pay low and working with the bosses to prevent alternative workers' organisations emerging.

The strike was therefore a challenge to the neoliberalism that the bosses and the ANC government defend, and to the NUM, a crucial element in the tripartite alliance and Cosatu. These forces were personified in former NUM general secretary Cyril Ramaphosa. During the 1987 strike Ramaphosa led a defiant struggle against mine bosses and the apartheid state. At that time he stated: "I don't know how one shares power with people who have shotguns in their hands, people who have tear gas canisters, and I really don't know how one shares power with people who continue to pay starvation wages." This was in response to the then AngloGold Ashanti chief executive Bobby Godsell's statement about the need for liberal business to share power with black workers. Ramaphosa went on to help draw up South Africa's post-apartheid constitution, becoming, by 2012, a leading figure in the ANC, a top businessman and one of the richest bosses in South Africa with an estimated wealth of $750 million. Crucially for the Marikana strike, he was a non-executive director of Lonmin as well as having a big shareholding through the Shanduka Group. As the strikers targeted the profits and power of the mine bosses, Ramaphosa urged the police to stop treating the Lonmin strike as a labour dispute and to start approaching it as "dastardly criminal" conduct. He was the link between the multinational firms, the police and the ANC.

The miners were murdered in order to break a strike against poverty pay that was also part of a wider wave of resistance to capital. The massacre tore away the myths about post-apartheid South Africa. It revealed it as a

---

10: Alexander, Lekgowa, Mmope, Sinwell, Xezwi, 2013. See also *Socialist Worker*'s coverage at http://socialistworker.co.uk/public/searchByTag/436

bloody neoliberal state that continued to enforce capitalist rule.

This was also the analysis of Marikana by the National Union of Metalworkers of South Africa (Numsa). After its Central Committee met at the end of August 2012 it said:

> The CC was adamant that what happened in Marikana should be correctly understood, and must go down in our history as the first post-apartheid South African state massacre of the organised working class, in defence of the local and international mining bosses and their profits... The actions of the police confirm that we have not, post-1994, transformed the apartheid state and its violent machinery.[11]

The subsequent inquiry into Marikana, the Farlam Commission, was still taking evidence as this article went to press. But it has heard repeated testimony of the deliberate killing of strikers, and it has seen emails detailing Ramaphosa's role in lobbying the state on Lonmin's behalf. The emails showed a toxic collusion between Ramaphosa, Lonmin, ANC mineral resources minister Susan Shabangu's department, the police ministry and the state security agencies leading to the planned murder of black strikers. The exchanges at the commission are captured well by this response from Jim Nichol, a lawyer working with the team representing the murdered miners' families:

Evidence
Cyril Ramaphosa
Deputy President: Republic South Africa
Deputy President: African National Congress
General Secretary: National Union Mineworkers
Director: Lonmin PLC
MacDonalds
Shanduka—shares in every pie
Wealth: US$750 million
2012 bid R19 million for a buffalo
Anti Apartheid Hero

Escorted:
30 or more
Police cars.

11: Numsa, 2012.

A lawyers' posse.
Men in suits
Stand guard

The Auditorium
packed–miners.

and then

T-shirts out
T-shirts on
"McCyril the killer"
Cameras flash

Toy Toying
Singing
"Buffalo Buffalo
blood on your hands"

Families sing
aloft
photographs
loved ones
massacred

Ramaphosa
Picks his teeth.

Commission suspended

Commission resumes

Q. You are a renowned negotiator?
A. Yes.
Q. Lonmin refused to negotiate?
A.Yes
Q. Did you suggest to Lonmin that they negotiate?
A. No.
Q. Why?
A. I was only a non–executive director. I did not want to interfere.

Q. If Lonmin had negotiated killings may not have happened?
A. Agreed.
Q. You in charge Lonmin's housing for miners?
A. Yes.
Q. Lonmin meet its target?
A. 100 percent.
Q. The target was 3?
A. Yes.
Q. 3?
A. 3.

(Evidence continues)

Ramaphosa's journey from militant union leader to militant defender of capitalist violence is not just about one man's failings. The process that ended apartheid in 1992-4 represented a compromise between the ANC and big business. Explosive workers' struggles and mighty unions, combined with sustained uprisings in the black communities, had not only threatened apartheid. They also opened the way to an assault on capitalism itself in South Africa. A section of big business and the political establishment decided that it was better to secure a deal with the black opposition rather than risk losing everything. This was a difficult and protracted process, relying on major concessions by both sides and the ability of leaders to diminish the expectations of their supporters.

At key points Nelson Mandela's leadership came under severe strain. The Boipatong massacre in June 1992 saw 41 people shot or hacked to death by vigilantes from the Inkatha Freedom Party backed by the security forces. It saw all the impatience with the slow pace of change bubble to the surface. Mandela, criticised by the youth for acting "like a lamb while the government butchers our people", called off talks with the white regime. ANC supporters in the trade unions called for strikes. But as soon as the emergency had passed, the negotiations started again.

The murder of ANC and Communist Party leader Chris Hani in 1993 was an even greater trial. The whole country was in ferment. The movement sent a shudder through those who had envisaged a relatively stable movement from apartheid capitalism to capitalism led by the ANC. But Mandela was able brilliantly to express the outrage at the murder and simultaneously continue the negotiations.

The ANC's 1994 election manifesto contained some quite radical promises. But at the same time ANC leaders made it quite clear there was not going to be any assault on capitalism. In a speech to white farmers Mandela insisted they had nothing to fear from ANC rule and that their land would not be nationalised. He told business leaders in London, "We have issued an investment code which provides there will be no expropriation of property or investments. Foreign investors will be able to repatriate dividends and profits." Pallo Jordan, the ANC's mineral and energy policy coordinator, confirmed that nationalisation of mining companies or mineral rights was not under consideration.

The ANC leaders who headed South Africa after 1994 hoped to preside over a "fair" capitalism where black and white would be treated equally. They hoped that "partnership" with the bosses would produce prosperity. But the price for securing the goodwill of the powerful corporations, landowners and bankers, both in South Africa and abroad, was the abandonment of their promises to the masses. The process began even before the elections with the decisions of the ANC-dominated interim government. As the writer Patrick Bond says:

> The very first act of the interim government was to accept an $850 million loan from the International Monetary Fund... The loan's secret conditions—leaked to the main business newspaper in March 1994—included the usual items from the classical structural adjustment menu: lower import tariffs, cuts in state spending, and large cuts in public sector wages.[12]

Two years into its rule the ANC imposed an even more neoliberal economic strategy, based on World Bank advice. Ministers pleaded that this was the only alternative to economic collapse. The ANC knew it could rely on the union leaders and the SACP to do no more than mutter against this turn. They might criticise the ANC, but they would not propose any alternative. Together they sought to squash any systematic opposition. One of the best organised and most militant working classes in the world was held back as the SACP's leadership came to justify the ANC regime's shifts. Trade union militants became caught up in a process of stopping strikes rather than encouraging them.

Neoliberalism has been a disaster. Of course there have been some changes since 1994. There are more homes, more people linked to the electricity grid and more schools and hospitals. But not nearly enough. And real economic power remains with the same corporations as under apartheid. Meanwhile a tiny black elite has made itself fabulously wealthy.

12: Bond, 2004.

Such conditions provoke resistance. And because the state is determined to face down the resistance rather than confront capital, it also means the ANC has turned to repression. The Marikana massacre was a continuation of a wider process, not a break from it. But the fightback will not go away.

Due to the extraordinary courage and defiance of the miners, the Marikana massacre did not end the Lonmin strike. Instead it fuelled a great wave of further resistance. Immediately after the murder a further 23,000 miners in the Marikana complex struck, eventually forcing Lonmin to concede a substantial pay rise. Workers also took strike action at Bafokeng Rasimone Platinum Mine, the Thembelani Anglo Platinum's mine and facility and Eastern Platinum's Crocodile River Mine. A report from the US Geological Survey says:

In early September [2012], unrest spread to Amplats's Rustenburg operations. Rustenburg employed 21,000 workers and accounted for about one third of Amplats's mine production. In early October, the company fired 12,000 striking workers and confirmed labour strikes at its Union and Amandelbult operations... Strikes also spread to other PGM [platinum-group metals], gold, and iron ore producers and to the transportation sector. In September and October, workers went on strike at Atlatsa Resources Corp's Bokoni Mine, Gold Fields Ltd's Beatrix and KDC West Mines, Gold One International Ltd's Ezulwini Mine, Harmony Gold Ltd's Kusasalethu Mine, Kumba Iron Ore Ltd's Sishen Mine, and Village Main Reef Ltd's Blyvoor Mine. AngloGold Ashanti Ltd had strikes at all its gold mining operations.[13]

The strikes spread to lorry drivers, sections of municipal workers and even farm workers in the Western Cape—some of the most exploited and oppressed workers in the country. Trevor Ngwane of the Democratic Left Front (DLF) was right to say:

Marikana is a spark for a new South Africa! It is a spark for a South Africa that works for, affirms and advances the interests of the workers and poor. It is a spark for a worker-led democracy! We say to the ANC ministers, the credit rating agencies, the International Monetary Fund and most importantly the mining bosses—the Marikana moment is here to stay! As long as the rich get richer and workers poorer in South Africa the Marikana moment is here to stay![14]

13:   US Department of the Interior and US Geological Survey, 2013.
14:   Democratic Left Front, 2012.

Wherever miners' strikes took place they involved mainly NUM members. But, just as at Lonmin, the NUM officials ruthlessly opposed the strikes. Workers therefore set up their own independent committees which in some cases began to set up coordinating committees across the mines. This was an extremely important development. The workers rejected not only the NUM but also—in the initial stages—AMCU as well in favour of rank and file committees. The rock drill operators' committees set up from June 2012 were intensely democratic. There were elections, recalls of reps if workers felt they weren't doing their job, and regular re-election of shop stewards. The committees represented thousands of workers concentrated in a handful of strategically crucial workplaces. Workers formulated their own demands for a "living wage" of 12,500 rand. The now-iconic 12,500 rand demand did not come from a union leader or a think-tank or a politician. It came from below based on workers' lives and what they felt they could win. At the Farlam Commission workers have repeatedly been asked: "Who came up with this figure?" Lawyers and others seem to find it inconceivable that it came from the workers. Not surprisingly, employers and the government were terrified that independent workers' committees would take root and spread beyond the mines. In fact they did not become permanent structures, due to intense hostility from the union leaders. But many of these activists became the key organisers in the AMCU union. AMCU was a step forward compared to NUM, a step back compared to the independent committees.[15]

AMCU, formed by miners expelled from the NUM for unofficial militancy, had achieved a foothold in the mines (particularly at Lonmin) before the massacre. Afterwards workers flooded into the new union. In most circumstances revolutionaries oppose splitting activists away from unions that organise the majority of the workforce. But in this case it

---

15: The potential is captured in another of Jim Nichol's responses: *The Marikana Effect*

Who said that?/the employers/their friends/the government/the unions/ the markets/they're frightened/What is it?/22% increase/Is that it?/Nah-read on
Strike committees/independent/elected/democratic/mass meetings/participation of all workers/all unions/they decide
Want more?/Yes please
Contagion/no boundaries
Employers' Demands/Unions must rein in members/Unions: "We agree"
Yes—but what if: Strike committees/become shop stewards' committees/permanent democratic?
Shop stewards committees/meet with other shop stewards committees/as one does
Now there is a problem/for the employers/and their friends
Watch out/the "Marikana Effect"/may be coming to a country near to where you live

became impossible to implement a rank and file strategy inside the NUM. Workers who challenged the existing leadership were met with expulsions and violence. The NUM hierarchy became a byword for corruption and manoeuvre. The union was increasingly integrated into corporate structures with powerful material benefits for those who hung on to their union positions. Greg Marinovich writes:

> Despite the pitfalls of conflicted interests, NUM pushed the mines to pay unionists' salaries. At the lower end, full-time shaft or shop stewards received a few thousand rands extra per month to bring them to a Patterson C level pay grade—roughly R12,000 to R14,000 a month. In addition they received a company petrol card, company cell phone and a company vehicle. Then there were the other perks—*bosberaads* or company get-togethers, international excursions, etc. Obviously, these unionists did not do another underground shift; they were freed from the arduous labour and conditions that had encouraged them to join the union in the first place. The arrangement with the mines that were their original employers was that should shop stewards not be re-elected, they would return to their old jobs. This was not something anyone wished to do.[16]

Accountability went out the window. In its place came a cosy atmosphere of working with the bosses.

The strikes ebbed towards the end of 2012. But the circumstances that had produced them did not. And 2014 has seen two further mass strikes of huge political importance. First came the remarkable all-out strike lasting five months by up to 80,000 workers at Anglo American, Impala and Lonmin, three of the world's major platinum producers. It became the biggest miners' strike in South African history. This was the continuation of the pay battle that started at Marikana—and because its bosses had reneged on the deal won in 2012 and it was utterly opposed by the NUM union, the ANC and the SACP. A great class struggle took place—and they were on the wrong side.

It ended with a deal that, although it did not meet all the miners' demands, was undoubtedly seen by millions of black workers as a victory. The NUM and ANC described it as a defeat. In fact AMCU was not broken by starvation, state repression, the hostility of the media, the lies and slurs from the ANC and the NUM, the armoured cars, the tear gas, the batons and the bullets. It prevailed. It faced down ruthless multinational

---

16: Marinovich, 2013.

capital and won concessions. When bosses sent out threatening text messages to strikers and tried to organise mass scabbing backed up by the might of the state, the workers responded with rallies and meetings, intensive picketing and mobilisations that stopped the scabbing before it began. The "back to work" movement failed utterly. Had other major unions backed AMCU there could have been a total victory that would have completely changed the environment in South Africa. And AMCU, whatever its weaknesses, showed a grassroots style of trade unionism that was far more democratic than the NUM's operations. AMCU leader Joseph Mathunjwa did not dare make any decision about the strike without the broadest consultation with members and stewards. The final acceptance of the offer came after a protracted series of meetings involving tens of thousands of workers.[17]

The success of the AMCU action, despite its abandonment by almost all the other unions, lent weight to the idea that there is a positive alternative to the traditional political forces.

Then came an all-out strike over pay by 220,000 workers in the steel and engineering sectors who are members of Numsa. It began just as the five-month platinum miners' strike ended, and metal workers were undoubtedly inspired by the miners' courage. The strike hit the bosses hard, affected 12,000 firms and, according to the employers, cost companies £25 million a day. Carmakers including Toyota, Nissan, BMW, Ford and General Motors stopped production at some or all of their South African units due to lack of components. The ANC and sections of the top bosses were already shaken by the platinum strike—and the dip in GDP caused by it. The credit ratings agency Moody's commented: "The Numsa strike threatens to bring this year's number of lost workdays close to the 20.7 million record set in 2010. South Africa's reputation among investors is being increasingly damaged by the strike-prone nature of its economy".[18] Metal bosses were therefore in no condition to hold out indefinitely.

The strike ended after four weeks having forced bosses to make major concessions over pay and other matters. Irvin Jim, Numsa general secretary, said: "The settlement offer has been overwhelmingly and unanimously accepted by our members. This is a massive victory given the pittance offer at the point of deadlock."

Faced with this show of workers' defiance and power, top ANC leaders are now demanding new anti-strike laws—ironically similar to those pushed

---

17: Socialist Workers Party members and supporters in Britain sent over R200,000 (£12,000) to the miners and their families as part of the solidarity movement.
18: Williams, 2014.

through by Margaret Thatcher—apartheid's last friend—in Britain. We are likely to see a determined assault on militant workers in order to shore up profits and prevent the "contagion" of inspiration from the platinum miners and metal workers to other groups. Big business are increasingly worried that the "reasonable" unions that they have learned to live with are being replaced by a more militant brand of activists. A few days after the Marikana massacre South Africa's bosses' paper, *Business Day,* ran an editorial saying:

> The new Association of Mineworkers and Construction Union (AMCU) is slowly taking apart the venerable National Union of Mineworkers (NUM) in the platinum industry, mine after mine. That fact, on its own, should be enough to raise alarm bells throughout the South African body politic. The NUM is the thoughtful, considered heart of the union movement here... As a union it is a powerful voice of reason in an often loud and rash movement. It appreciates and values private capital and strong companies. Business everywhere should be hoping the union finds a way to defend itself effectively from AMCU's attacks... There is not going to be any stopping AMCU. That means a solution to the violence has to be found at a high level, and that it has to recognise, for the NUM and for Cosatu and the ANC itself, the extremely uncomfortable truth that there is a power building in the land over which they have little or no influence, and which itself has little or no respect for the powers that be.[19]

Turmoil in Cosatu

At several points in the last 20 years the fury among workers at the ANC's pro-capitalist policies has found a reflection at the top of the unions and come close to seeing serious splits inside Cosatu. But it has never come to a break. Workers quite rightly prize unity, and this is a heavy pressure towards the sinking of secondary differences. But now there is a serious possibility that Cosatu may divide. Much of the media highlights the role of Zwelinzima Vavi, Cosatu's general secretary. Vavi was an important figure in the NUM before becoming Cosatu deputy general secretary in 1993 and then general secretary from 1999. He campaigned for Jacob Zuma to become president but became increasingly critical of him.

Since 2010 Cosatu leaders talked openly of the "predatory elite" and the threat of the emergence of a "predatory state". The federation launched campaigns against neoliberal government policies and targeted not only the

---

19: *Business Day,* 2012.

ANC leaders but also the SACP figures who were loyal members of the cabinet. In January 2012 Cosatu launched Corruption Watch to highlight the misuse of office at the top. Such assaults, from such a respected position, were not ignored. The ANC and SACP leaders turned against Vavi because he represented a much broader sense of anger inside the working class.

Then in 2013 Vavi was accused by a Cosatu employee of rape and sexual assault. He said they had an affair. The woman subsequently withdrew a sexual harassment complaint against him. In August 2013 Vavi was suspended from office, a decision that was recently overturned in court. Numsa and a group of unions that support its position have demanded a special Cosatu conference to discuss and decide the issue, but this has been blocked by ANC-supporting unions that have a tiny majority on the executive.

Last year Zwelinzima Vavi dismissed superficial or personalised explanations of the crisis in Cosatu. The notes for his speech point towards much deeper political issues:

1. The real bases of the crisis in Cosatu are its complex and contradictory class relationships which it finds itself having to deal with, on a daily basis, in the multiclass and unstructured ANC led Alliance, to which it belongs.

2. The second basis is the failure of the liberation movement as a whole, to resolve the national, gender and class questions post-1994, and letting the Black and African capitalists in the liberation movement to win the day. This has led to the strengthening and deepening of the colonial capitalist mode of production in South Africa and its social relations, and thus deepening and worsening unemployment, mass poverty and extreme inequalities.

3. The singular failure to address the property question, in favour of the popular masses post-1994 in point 2 above, threatens to actually overwhelm and destroy the liberation movement as a whole, and Cosatu in particular.

4. The crisis in Cosatu is a reflection of the class contradictions and class struggles that are broadly playing themselves out in South Africa and in the liberation movement and its formations between the South African Black and African proletariat and the forces of South African colonial capitalism and imperialism.[20]

The vituperative divisions inside Cosatu, which may well see Numsa expelled in the near future, are not about Vavi's leadership; they are an echo of the wider arguments inside the working class after Marikana.

20: Vavi, 2013.

The election

At first sight there is no reflection of the "Marikana moment" on the electoral field. But that ignores the long-term fall in the ANC vote, and the emergence of the Economic Freedom Fighters (EFF). Beneath the surface there are major shifts taking place.

At the May 2014 general election the ANC was the clear winner with 62 percent of the vote, only a few percent down from 2009. It retains a huge loyalty from those who see it as the party of Nelson Mandela and the main force that conquered apartheid. The SACP's election poster avoided any class appeal, saying simply: "Do it for Madiba [Mandela]—vote ANC".

But the ANC's vote is ebbing. South Africa's current voting age population—those who could have voted—is approximately 32.6 million. The 11.4 million votes for the ANC in May represent 35 percent of this figure. And by this measure the ANC's support has been falling ever since the end of apartheid. It declined from 54 percent in 1994 to 47 percent in 1999 to 40 percent in 2004 to 39 percent in 2009 and now to 35 percent. The idea of an unchanging ANC hegemony looks far less credible when only one in three of the voting age population vote for them.

The ANC's vote is falling most sharply in the cities. In Gauteng, which includes Johannesburg and is the country's most populous province, the ANC share fell from 64 percent in 2009 to 55 percent in 2014.

The state-funded luxury upgrade of President Jacob Zuma's Nkandla home estate has become a symbol of the corruption of sections of the ANC and the increasing divide between the governing elite, with their opulent lifestyles, and those who had elected them. Archbishop Desmond Tutu famously said that the ANC government had "stopped the gravy train only long enough to get on".

One of the most powerful contributions during the election period came when a group of veterans of the anti-apartheid struggle headed by Ronnie Kasrils said they would not be voting ANC. Kasrils is a former leader of the ANC's armed wing, leading member of the SACP and intelligence minister after the end of apartheid. Now he urged people to vote for progressive alternatives to the ANC, even if they were small parties. If people could not find any organisation they favoured then it was their right not to vote at all.

Such a position flowed from what Kasrils had written in 2013:

From 1991 to 1996 the battle for the ANC's soul got under way, and was eventually lost to corporate power: we were entrapped by the neoliberal economy... What I call our Faustian moment came when we took an IMF loan on the eve of our first democratic election. That loan, with strings attached that precluded a radical economic agenda... To lose our nerve was not necessary or inevitable. The ANC leadership needed to remain determined, united and free of corruption—and, above all, to hold on to its revolutionary will. Instead, we chickened out... To break apartheid rule through negotiation, rather than a bloody civil war, seemed then an option too good to be ignored. However, at that time, the balance of power was with the ANC, and conditions were favourable for more radical change at the negotiating table than we ultimately accepted.[21]

Many South Africans agree with that. The ANC is far from finished. It retains vast reserves of respect and a committed cadre, including some excellent activists. But it is no longer the unchallenged force on the left.

The EFF

The Economic Freedom Fighters (EFF), a party that had existed for only eight months, won well over a million votes (6.5 percent) and secured 25 of the 400 members of the new parliament. This real achievement was based on expressing the deep resentment and frustration with the lack of change since 1994, and hatred of the arrogance and corruption of the ANC's elite. It was undoubtedly a left vote, a radical vote and a sign of what is possible in terms of an alternative to the ANC.

The EFF's approach was uncompromisingly militant, with its activists clad in Che Guevara style berets and red T-shirts proclaiming "Economic Freedom in our Lifetime"—a clear message that the end of apartheid might have meant some political freedom but economic change was still to come. Its posters had slogans such as "Destroy e-tolls physically" (a reference to the automatic charging system that bills drivers for using major roads), "Let's stop Nkandla corruption" and "Nationalise the banks and the mines". The EFF leader (or Commander in Chief as the party calls him) Julius "JuJu" Malema derided the ANC as the "African National Criminals".

To his great credit, Malema gave total support to the Marikana miners in 2012 and called for nationalisation of the mines. The EFF backed the 2014 platinum miners' strike and on 16 August announced that it would build homes for the widows of the Marikana slain.

Malema is in some ways an unlikely character to lead an anti-corruption, anti-ANC elite party. He faces charges of fraud, corruption, racketeering and money laundering. He vehemently denies these but the

---

21: Kasrils, 2013.

evidence is overwhelming. Malema was president of the ANC's Youth League from 2008 until he was expelled from the party in 2012. But Malema's former ties to the ruling party and his wealth have proved no barrier to him effectively expressing the resentments of the poor. He came from a very poor family and when he speaks about poverty and humiliation you can tell he knows what he is talking about.

In truth the EFF's positions are often less far-reaching than its posters suggest. For example, its nationalisation proposals would leave 40 percent of the mines in the hands of private capital. And even then Malema said that although there would be some form of nationalisation "the percentages we are prepared to discuss when we reach the appropriate point". The EFF is also open to populist pressure. When it launched its manifesto it said that it would seek to hold a referendum on the reintroduction of the death penalty. This reactionary policy appealed to more backward elements of its support base but fortunately was quietly sidelined later in the campaign.

More fundamentally the EFF has no real analysis of the state, or of capitalism itself. It simply accepts that a parliamentary majority would be sufficient to implement far-reaching change. Yet any serious assault on the power of capital would be met by a very unparliamentary response—as Marikana precisely demonstrated. And much of the EFF's rhetoric suggests that the problem is that ownership and control are in the hands of white bosses rather than black African ones. It is indeed a scandal that the same bosses who lorded it during apartheid are in many cases still in their positions and still immensely powerful. But putting Cyril Ramaphosa in the director's padded chair has clearly made little difference. Installing Julius Malema or his friends as chief executives would be equally ineffective. The EFF promotes a sort of state capitalism with change from above but little initiative from below.

However, there is no doubt the EFF is having a big impact and is reaching out primarily to the poor. It has caused a huge stir by refusing to obey the stuffy procedures of parliament. Whenever he sees the ANC bowing and scraping to some pompous nonsense inherited from Westminster-style parliaments, Malema's instinct is to ridicule it and tear it up. Good luck to him. The parliament has a strict dress code that the EFF's MPs subverted from day one. They came for the swearing-in ceremony dressed in red overalls as miners or domestic workers to emphasis that they were there to "go to work" for the people and the revolution. This enraged the other parties. When the EFF tried the same tactic in the Gauteng provincial legislature, they were forcibly expelled. Riot police used stun grenades, rubber bullets and tear gas to eject the EFF from the chamber.

Even more unacceptable to the powerful was Malema's claim in parliament that the ANC had murdered 34 miners in Marikana. He was eventually excluded from the chamber but he certainly did not back off, holding a press conference to announce: "No prison, not even death, can stop this idea that the ANC murdered people."

Of course, stunts and speeches are not enough, but they have made an impact. The EFF is set to do well in the municipal elections in 2015 and has strong support among large sections of the unemployed, young people and casual workers although it is much weaker in the unions and among permanent workers. Its members and supporters could play an important role in Numsa's new socialist party project (which I will discuss shortly).

The EFF has shown a willingness to engage with other parts of the left—including the Trotskyist left. It has, for example, met with the DLF to discuss the possibility of joint campaigns and has drawn in some DLF members to bolster its work. This is positive and underlines that the EFF cannot be ignored by anyone—including Numsa—that wants a new left.

Unfortunately the EFF refused an invitation to take part in a symposium on left parties hosted by Numsa in August this year. It gave two reasons for its non-attendance. One was that Numsa had not made sufficient effort to hold talks with the EFF leadership—hardly a reason to ignore an opportunity to put forward the EFF's view. The second was worse:

> a concern that Numsa still forms part of the alliance with the ruling party, the ANC, through Cosatu. There is no clarity, for instance, whether the current differences in Cosatu are deeper ideological differences, or political differences which can be settled through a process presided by, amongst others, Cyril Ramaphosa, who is an enemy of the working class and responsible for the murder of workers in Marikana.[22]

That is an ultra-left refusal to recognise the immense potential of what Numsa is trying to do and, also, that any left alternative to the ANC and SACP will repeatedly have to enter forums where the ANC operates in order to win its supporters. The EFF will also need to show that the slurs of its critics in the ANC are baseless.

In July ANC secretary general Gwede Mantashe said Malema was a "Hitler in the making", and that there were close parallels between the rise of fascism in Germany in the 1930s and that of the EFF. Days later he reiterated that South Africa has witnessed "the entering of a fascist movement into our parliamentary politics". Earlier in a parliamentary debate on

---

22: Economic Freedom Fighters, 2014.

the budget, deputy minister Buti Manamela said that Malema was a dictator in the making and he feared that Hitler had "risen from the dead".

In case such myths do not work, there have also been moves by sections of the ANC to pose left in order to counter criticisms that they have sold out. In August 2014 Gauteng ANC spokesman Nkenke Kekana said there was "frustration about the slow pace of economic transformation, and that there was a need for a much more radical approach towards the economy". A motion to the 2015 ANC national general council calls for the state to intervene in mine ownership—although in the form of support for black "entrepreneurs" rather than through social ownership. Top ANC figures have also discussed the formation of a state bank, although again this would be through the purchase of one of the major banks rather than through any form of expropriation.

The EFF has put forward a real challenge and mobilised people in an exciting way. There remain serious doubts about how far it can become a genuine anti-capitalist force. But it is one of the forces that the left must engage with very seriously. It will be a test for the DLF, which has brought together activists on the far left. It was formed in January 2011 after a conference at Wits University of 250 delegates representing a diverse range of social move-ments, popular organisations and anti-capitalist formations. This followed a lengthy period of discussion and preparation. The conference declared:

> Post-apartheid capitalism is leaving a trail of hunger, poverty, anger and misery. The wealthy elite, the bosses and their hangers on refuse to concede a single inch to the urgent needs of the majority. They label even the most modest reforms as the thin edge of the wedge of communism. And as always the government shakes and concedes... And a new round of suffering begins for our people.[23]

The DLF has done important work in uniting far-left groups and individuals and then organising solidarity with strikes and protests. It took a lead in backing the miners' struggles in 2012 and 2014. It now has to work constructively with the EFF and, in particular, the Numsa project.

Numsa

If the EFF has caused shudders, the discussions about a new workers' party could bring down the house. I say "could"; there is a long way to go. These discussions centre on South Africa's biggest union, the 320,000-

---

23: Democratic Left Front, 2011.

strong metal workers' union Numsa.

The process of moving to new political formations after Marikana was not instantaneous. But the tensions it produced were too great to contain in the existing structures. Partly this was because of developing turmoil in Cosatu, and partly because the ANC and SACP showed no sign of learning from the uproar after the massacre. The Numsa special congress that met in December 2013 said that four factors had led to the need for a fundamental re-think of past positions. First the ANC had adopted the National Development Plan, whose faults were not that it was technically flawed or needed minor revision. Instead, for Numsa, "it is the programme of our class enemy. It is a programme to continue to feed profit at the expense of the working class and the poor." Secondly, the ANC leadership had shown at recent conferences that it would not allow fundamental challenges to its direction—and it would manoeuvre and trample on procedure to crush challenges. Thirdly, Cosatu had been consumed by internal battles and Numsa "has been continuously vilified and smeared by those opposed to its militant approach". Finally the state had "attacked and killed workers on behalf of capital". In summary "the ANC has been captured by representatives of an enemy class. It has adopted the strategic plan of that class. Its leadership has shown that it will not let the small issue of democracy get in the way of defending its control."

Furthermore the congress went on to say that the tripartite alliance of the ANC, SACP and Cosatu "is dysfunctional, in crisis, paralysed and dominated by infighting and factionalism. It has been captured by right wing forces... There is no chance of winning back the Alliance to what it was originally formed for, which was to drive a revolutionary programme for fundamental transformation of the country." After Marikana Numsa had bitterly criticised the ANC and SACP but had dedicated itself to winning back the SACP so that it became a true party of the working class. This project had now been abandoned.

The conclusion was a call on Cosatu to break from the Alliance: "The time for looking for an alternative has arrived." Numsa would also "lead in the establishment of a new United Front that will coordinate struggles in the workplace and in communities, in a way similar to the UDF of the 1980s. The task of this front will be to fight for the implementation of the Freedom Charter and to be an organisational weapon against neoliberal policies such as the NDP." In addition: "Side by side with the establishment of the new United Front, Numsa will explore the establishment of a Movement for Socialism as the working class needs a political organisation committed in its policies and actions to the establishment of a socialist South Africa."

Then the Numsa congress turned to the coming elections. It acknowledged: "We have traditionally supported ANC in elections. Since 1994, Numsa has invested resources and person-power towards ensuring an ANC victory in elections." But now, given the factors discussed above, "Numsa as an organisation will neither endorse nor support the ANC or any other political party in 2014... Numsa will cease to pay into the COSATU/SACP political levy".[24]

This was a hugely significant development offering a powerful alternative to the ANC. The revolutionary left should wholly welcome discussions towards a "united front and movement for socialism". There will be problems ahead, and I shall come to some of these. But the first reaction has to be unstinting support for the process that Numsa has begun. If there is a party to the left of the ANC and the SACP involving tens of thousands of workers and the poor, based on the organised working class, and committed to the revolutionary transformation of society, then it will be massively significant.

It will offer an important space for serious united activity, immensely fruitful learning in the course of working together, and discussion about how a successful revolution can take place and what socialism really means. It will be a place for all the serious revolutionary forces including Keep Left (the SWP's sister organisation in South Africa), the DLF, and the Workers and Socialist Party (WASP)[25] to act together and to seek to break militants from reformism.

The Numsa process is posing again, and set to resolve in a more positive way, the key issues about politics and trade unionism that were raised and debated in an earlier period. The modern black trade union movement was born out of a series of strikes in Durban in 1973. As the unions grew there was a sharp debate about the relationship with political organisations in general, and the ANC in particular. The activists who headed the Federation of South African Trade Unions (Fosatu) in 1979 consciously rejected the subjugation of workers' interests to those of the multi-class ANC. The experience of Zimbabwe and other national liberation struggles underlined for them the need for an independent workers' movement that was not used as an occasional actor to strengthen the hands of black capitalists who wanted to achieve their own place in the sun. This did not mean they wholly ignored the wider political questions—who could do so

---

24: Numsa, 2013.
25: WASP stood in the national election of May 2014 and received just over 8,000 votes (0.05 percent).

in apartheid South Africa? In 1982 Fosatu played a leading role in the first political strike of the modern era—a half hour stoppage involving 100,000 workers in protest at the death in police custody of trade union organiser Neil Aggett. Fosatu news described it as the "first national work stoppage for nearly 20 years and the first in which workers stopped work simultaneously in their factories and did not just stay away from work".

This pointed the way towards a potential political alternative to the ANC: rooted in the working class and fighting for class interests in the workplace and in the struggle to change society. But without the creation of such an alternative the only force putting forward a strategy to defeat apartheid was the ANC; it might be imperfect but it could not be challenged by a void. The Fosatu unions either in effect tailed the ANC or were, for most of the time, politically abstentionist. There was talk about a workers' party, but it did not happen. In 1982 the Fosatu general secretary Joe Foster told the federation's congress: "It is, therefore, essential that workers must strive to build their own powerful and effective organisation even whilst they are part of the wider popular struggle. This organisation is necessary to protect and further worker interests and to ensure that the popular movement is not hijacked by elements who will in the end have no option but to turn against their worker supporters."

As journalist Martin Plaut writes, the speech:

held out the implicit threat that Fosatu would be the launch pad from which a workers party would be formed—possibly on the lines of the Workers Party in Brazil. The reply was provided by the "African Communist", which was then much more than just the theoretical journal of the South African Communist Party (SACP). It was the mouthpiece of the Congress Alliance. Fosatu was labelled as "syndicalist" and the union federation was accused of attempting to substitute itself for the Communist Party as the party of the working class.

The ANC mobilised to ensure that it not only won the unions to its cause, but to its political perspective. Within four years it had managed to exert enough political muscle to persuade the South African union movement to reform itself as the Congress of South African Trade Unions—Cosatu—adopting the Congress label as an indication that its loyalties lay with the Congress Alliance. They had also managed to arrange a meeting with the new Cosatu leadership in

Zambia, at which the Cosatu general secretary endorsed the exiled movement as the leading element in the liberation struggle.[26]

In 1994 the 170,000 strong Southern African Clothing and Textile Workers Union called on the Cosatu trade union federation to break its links with the ANC after the elections. And against the advice of its leadership, Numsa voted to consider a workers' party and to sever ties with an ANC-led government of national unity. But neither of these led to a decisive break or a new party—and workers have suffered because of it.

Now the question is posed again. What are the central issues that a Numsa-led Movement for Socialism (MfS) will face? The first concerns the nature of capitalism and the state in South Africa. In a very interesting document produced in March 2014, Numsa puts forward its views on basic questions facing the left in the country. It says: "In all essential respects, however, the colonial status of the black majority has remained in place. Therefore we characterise our society as 'colonialism of a special type'".[27] This formulation, popularised by the ANC and SACP, was used to say that change in South Africa had to go through a number of stages—first the national democratic revolution to get rid of colonialism of a special type (apartheid), then eventually socialist revolution. Irvin Jim, in his Ruth First memorial lecture this year, spoke repeatedly of how he believes South Africa remains a colonial country.

Notions of colonialism, whether simple or of a "special type", can be used in different ways. Many in Numsa would say they reject stageism and believe in a simultaneous struggle against colonial control and the capitalist system itself. Irvin Jim spoke recently of "the interrelatedness, the dialectical connectedness, of racial and capitalist oppression and exploitation in South Africa".[28] The problem is that such concepts often obscure the nature of an indigenous and independent capitalist class that has its own interest and its own dynamic. The struggle is not against some particular form of capital: it is capitalism itself that brings exploitation and oppression.

The capitalist state, whether under apartheid or colonialism or "free" capitalism, acts in the interests of the capitalist class and enforces its rule. We saw that state in operation in Marikana as capital; the "bodies of armed men" of which Lenin spoke in *The State and Revolution* and the governing apparatus all conspired and combined to assault the proletariat. Socialism

---

26: Plaut, 2013.
27: Numsa, 2014.
28: Jim, 2014.

in South Africa is possible only on the basis of smashing that state. It is this essential truth that explains why "democracy" after apartheid has not delivered for the vast majority. As Lenin wrote:

> Bourgeois democracy, although a great historical advance in comparison with medievalism, always remains, and under capitalism is bound to remain, restricted, truncated, false and hypocritical, a paradise for the rich and a snare and deception for the exploited, for the poor. It is this truth, which forms a most essential part of Marx's teaching".[29]

The MfS needs to be much more than an SACP Mark 2 based on votes and with a conception of society that evades the need to smash the bourgeois state.

More particularly there are four questions for any new Numsa-launched formation. These matter because it will come under immense pressure from its Alliance rivals. Already the ANC and SACP are encouraging the growth of an alternative union to Numsa which would affiliate to Cosatu if Numsa is expelled or leaves. And a Cosatu congress decision which goes some way towards Numsa's position is likely to be ignored by the right in Cosatu. This will pose huge questions for Numsa and any political alternative it supports. So clarity about its ideas is important.

Elections

The MfS would rightly stand in elections in order to test its strength, mobilise people around its ideas and win representatives to speak out in parliament, the provinces and councils. This would be important. But if it becomes the central and dominant concern it will be disastrous. Here the example of the Brazilian Workers Party (Partido dos Trabalhadores, PT) is instructive. The PT was formed in quite similar circumstances to the MfS: it came from a series of very militant workers' struggles and from opposition to a brutal military dictatorship. It united trade unionists and intellectuals, community groups, indigenous people's movements, landless people's organisations, women's groups and others. Politically it was a left reaction to the conservatism and Stalinism of the Brazilian Communist Party. It was an undoubted step forward. But its focus on elections and securing victory for its presidential candidate Lula led to concession after concession. In order to calm the financial markets before the 2002 presidential election, Lula issued a "Letter to the Brazilian people"—in truth a letter to the Brazilian ruling class. It committed

---

29: Lenin, 1918.

the PT to meeting the budget limits imposed by the IMF. When he took office, he not only did this, but went further and increased the budget surplus from 3.5 percent of GDP to 4.6 percent. Bankers applauded his rule, characterising it as "continuity not change". Lula and the PT have achieved some improvements for the poor, but no more than the ANC delivered. It is a lesson of the dangers of making elections the most important focus. The rightward drift of Syriza in Greece as it comes closer to office and seeks to make itself acceptable to bosses and sections of the right is another example. The MfS must be based on struggle, not elections.

A tribune of the oppressed

Lenin argued that a revolutionary's ideal "should not be the trade union secretary, but the tribune of the people, who is able to react to every manifestation of tyranny and oppression, no matter where it appears, no matter what stratum or class of the people it affects; who is able to generalise all these manifestations and produce a single picture of police violence and capitalist exploitation".[30] The MfS has to connect with all of South Africa's poor and oppressed. It must be based on the power of the organised working class, but has to draw in the unemployed, the school, college and university students, the casual workers, the women. Otherwise there is a danger of a "division of labour" where the EFF draws on the communities and MfS on the workplace.

Organised workers must be at the centre of a new formation. The MfS must fight for full nationalisation of key industries and banks under social control, for jobs, decent pay and workers' rights. But it must also campaign on housing, a national free health service, better transport, against xenophobia and homophobia and for women's liberation.

The failure of the trade unions and most of the left to relate to these issues and to address seriously a decade of rebellion inside working class communities is a tragic mistake. Leonard Gentle writes:

> We have had nearly ten years of working class communities being in what has been called everything from "service delivery" protests to a "revolt of the poor." And this too has passed Cosatu by. We have just had an election in which more than a million people voted for a party—the EFF—which embraces a language of militant left wing politics—nationalisation, redistribution of the wealth, and insisting that ministers and public officials must use public services—and

---

30: Lenin, 1901.

this was the language of Cosatu before. But now it lines itself alongside the government against whom all these slogans are directed.[31]

Gentle undoubtedly makes a powerful point when he rages at the gap between organised labour and the millions of unemployed and never-employed people. He is also correct to point to a "seamless continuity, or rather a toxic cocktail of 'workplace' and 'community issues'" including the appalling living conditions for mine workers in informal camps, that together fuelled militancy around the platinum miners' strike. However, elsewhere in his article he goes too far in writing off the unions and organised labour. Like establed trade unions everywhere, South Africa's unions have a bureaucracy that ultimately plays a conservative role. This should not obscure the truth that workers organised at the point of production are more powerful than in the communities. The platinum miners' strikes cut off the source of profits to the mining bosses. This is what made them such a threat to the system. They were a greater threat than the community unrest. The Marikana massacre was the ruling class's response to the threat posed by a monstrous enemy.

The task for the left will be to fuse workplace power and community revolt. It cannot operate effectively by dividing the two and ignoring community issues.

What sort of party?
Many activists drawn towards the MfS have seen the failings of the ANC and SACP and are suspicious of parties. This fear of bureaucratic command will be intensified by the central role of Numsa, such a big and well-organised force. This can be overcome only by thoroughgoing democracy, respect for minorities and differences while uniting around key themes and campaigns, the right to organise platforms and to push for internal change while not degenerating into a debating society, and so on. Numsa has democratic structures and its leaders have suffered from a lack of democracy in Cosatu. So there is a good basis to begin with. Numsa's symposium of the left in August 2014 showed a refreshing openness to debate and mutual learning. The lesson is that any new project requires compromise, listening and patience. It must be a democratic party of struggle and socialism: only this will open it up to the rich input of worker and community activists.

31: Gentle, 2014.

The union leaders

Even the most left wing union leaders face intense pressure arising from their social position. They negotiate compromises rather than seek to abolish the system. At its worst we have seen the bureaucracy in the NUM become an adjunct of management at certain points in the mines. Numsa has far better leaders. But they did not openly organise solidarity with the 2014 platinum miners' strike and accepted the fudged statement on Marikana at the Cosatu congress. The recent Numsa strike, although a step forward, was organised in a top-down way and the leadership was clearly expecting a short strike. It will have to reassess tactics for longer struggles. This does not diminish the importance of the involvement of leading figures in Numsa in the MfS. But it does mean that the MfS must be organised primarily at the grassroots and rank and file level—and recognise the role trade union leaders play at critical points.

Conclusion

The potential is clear. Can it be fulfilled? In the end that depends on both the objective and the subjective factors. The objective ones are present now, even if they may not be in six months time. The subjective ones—leadership, political organisation, argument that wins others over—are in the hands of parties and individuals. The MfS can play a key role in the struggles ahead. But there is great danger in delay. With every day that passes an opportunity is missed to support a community struggle or act in solidarity with a strike. New political projects cannot be rushed, but there is a momentum in South Africa that exists now and can be focused—must be focused. In the absence of a workers' party it may cohere around the EFF—then the workers' party will be a latecomer on the scene. It is time for decisive action.

References

Alexander, Peter, 2013, "Marikana, Turning Point in South African History", *Review of African Political Economy*, volume 40, issue 138, http://dx.doi.org/10.1080/03056244.2013.860893

Alexander, Peter, Thapelo Lekgowa, Botsang Mmope, Luke Sinwell and Bongani Xezwi, 2013, *Marikana: a View from the Mountain and a Case to Answer* (Bookmarks).

Bond, Patrick, 2004, "From Racial to Class Apartheid: South Africa's Frustrating Decade of Freedom", *Monthly Review*, volume 55, number 10 (March), http://monthlyreview.org/2004/03/01/south-africas-frustrating-decade-of-freedom-from-racial-to-class-apartheid/

Business Day, 2012, "Editorial: A failure of our society on many levels" (17 August), www.bdlive.co.za/opinion/editorials/2012/08/17/editorial-a-failure-of-our-society-on-many-levels

Cosatu, 2012, "Cosatu Statement on Marikana Massacre" (24 August), www.cosatu.org.za/show.php?ID=6437

Cronin, Jeremy, 2012, "Some of the Underlying Systemic Factors behind the Marikana Tragedy", *Umsebenzi Online* (30 August), www.sacp.org.za/main.php?ID=3733

Democratic Left Front, 2011, "Declaration of the Democratic Left Front" (24 January), http://tinyurl.com/ocgob2h

Democratic Left Front, 2012, "Message to the Amplats mineworkers' rally in Rustenburg (delivered by Trevor Ngwane)", (13 November), http://tinyurl.com/q2fqhpr

EFF, 2014, "Statement on NUMSA's International Symposium on Left Political Parties and Movements" (6 August), http://effighters.org.za/eff-statement-on-numsas-international-symposium-on-left-political-parties-and-movements/

Gentle, Leonard, 2014, "South Africa and the Changing Politics of Labour", *The Bullet* (Socialist Project E-Bulletin), number 1027 (27 August), www.socialistproject.ca/bullet/1027.php

Jim, Irvin, 2014, "Freedom Charter the Blueprint for a Sane Society (Ruth First Memorial Lecture)", (14 August), http://tinyurl.com/nc7bop4

Kasrils, Ronnie, 2013, "How the ANC's Faustian Pact sold out South Africa's Poorest", *Guardian* (24 June), www.theguardian.com/commentisfree/2013/jun/24/anc-faustian-pact-mandela-fatal-error

Lenin, VI, 1901, *What Is To Be Done?* www.marxists.org/archive/lenin/works/1901/witbd/iii.htm

Lenin, VI, 1918, "The Proletarian Revolution and the Renegade Kautsky", www.marxists.org/archive/lenin/works/1918/prrk/democracy.htm

Marinovich, Greg, 2013, "Conflict of Interest, Inc: Mining Unions' Leaders were Representing their Members while in Corporations' Pay", *Daily Maverick* (24 April), http://tinyurl.com/mrlnkur

NUM, 2012, "Baleni on Lonmin Killings and Violence" (20 August), www.youtube.com/watch?v=IeLzskhdYwY

Numsa, 2012, "Numsa central committee press statement" (3 September), www.numsa.org.za/article/numsa-central-committee-cc-press-statement-2012-09-02/

Numsa, 2013, "Numsa Special National Congress 17-20 December Declaration", www.numsa.org.za/wp-content/uploads/2013/12/SNC-Declaration-final-copy.pdf

Numsa, 2014, "Numsa Views on the State of Class Struggles in South Africa and the Crisis in Cosatu" (2 March), www.numsa.org.za/article/numsa-views-state-class-struggles-south-africa-crisis-cosatu/

Nzimande, Blade, 2012, "Our Condolences and Sympathies to the Marikana and Pomeroy Victims", *Umsebenzi Online* (23 August), www.sacp.org.za/main.php?ID=3724

Plaut, Martin, 2013, "South Africa: as Cosatu Divisions Increase, Remember a Quiet Voice from the Past" (28 November), http://martinplaut.wordpress.com/2013/11/28/south-africa-as-cosatu-divisions-increase-remember-a-quiet-voice-from-the-past/

Saba, Athandiwe, and Jeanne van der Merwe, 2013, "South Africa has a Protest every Two Days", *News24*, (21 January), www.news24.com/SouthAfrica/News/SA-has-a-protest-every-two-days-20130121

US Department of the Interior and US Geological Service, 2013, "Recent Strikes in South Africa's Platinum-Group Metal Mines—Effects Upon World Platinum-Group Metal Supplies" (September), http://pubs.usgs.gov/of/2012/1273/ofr2012-1273.pdf

Vavi, Zwelinzima, 2013, "Speaking notes for address to NUMSA KZN Congress", *Politicsweb* (24 November), http://tinyurl.com/p7pyqt9

Williams, Allan, 2014, "Moody's says South African strike could spook investors", *Heraldlive* (3 July), www.heraldlive.co.za/moodys-says-south-african-strike-could-spook-investors/

Lise Vogel and the politics of women's liberation
Nicola Ginsburgh

A review of Lise Vogel, **Marxism and the Oppression of Women: Toward a Unitary Theory** *(Haymarket, 2014), £19.99*

Growing anger and activism around the issue of women's oppression have seen the return of many arguments from the 1970s and 1980s regarding the usefulness or otherwise of Marxist analysis in exploring this oppression.[1] The reissuing of Lise Vogel's work, originally published in 1983, though largely neglected at that time, is a welcome contribution to current debates. At the core of Vogel's original text is an important argument that women's social position can only be made sense of through analysing the social relations of exploitation and, specifically, the unique role of women and childbirth in reproducing the conditions that enable exploitation.

Vogel presents a persuasive materialist analysis of women's oppression under capitalism, but her text suffers from a few minor faults. This review will argue that while Vogel convincingly argues against the theoretical dualism of socialist feminists and rightly sets out to construct a unitary theory of women's oppression, she fails to to fully extricate herself from the limitations of socialist feminist approaches.

The way Vogel's text is presented in the new edition is marked by

1:   Thanks to Paul Blackledge, Sally Campbell, Joseph Choonara, Sheila McGregor and Jenny Sullivan for comments on earlier drafts of this review.

the context of its reissue. In their introduction David McNally and Susan Ferguson highlight the work's newfound popularity, arguing that, partially as a consequence of various women's movements since the 1990s, postmodernism's grasp on gender theory has been gradually loosened and materialist frameworks revitalised. Their summary of Vogel's contribution is largely uncontroversial. But the new directions they suggest for developing "social reproduction theory" ultimately extend the weaker elements evident in Vogel's analysis. McNally and Ferguson attempt to identify new trends in scholarship that address oppression and exploitation, and advocate synthesising work by a number of black feminists and David Roediger's work on "whiteness" into a broader conception of social reproduction.

Ferguson and McNally's emphasis on scholars such as Roediger and Patricia Hill Collins to provide the basis for this theoretical synthesis of gender and race within a materialist framework is problematic. Both Collins and Roediger have, in different ways, argued that layers within the working class are empowered through racial identification, which proves inimical to multiracial solidarity.[2] Ferguson and McNally qualify their advocacy of Roediger by arguing that his work can be used to complement Marxist studies, such as Ted Allen's on "the invention of the white race". However, this seems bizarre, particularly as the latter has repeatedly and systematically criticised the theoretical foundations of Roediger's approach.[3] Ferguson and McNally's "new agendas" ultimately prove to be an incongruous mish-mash of currently popular theories and idioms, rather than a serious discussion of how Vogel's theory of social reproduction can be developed.

The nuts and bolts

In *Capital* Karl Marx argues that wage labour is the essence of the capitalist system: workers sell their labour power to capitalists in return for a wage. Labour power is "the aggregate of those mental and physical capabilities existing in a human being...which he sets in motion whenever he produces a use value of any kind".[4] Labour power is essential to the capitalist system and must be reproduced. Vogel's theory of social reproduction sets out to explain *how* this process occurs.

The bearers of labour power are human and as such require food and water, sleep and shelter. Vogel uses Marx's concept of "individual

---

2: For a critique of such approaches, see Choonara and Prasad, 2014.
3: Allen, 2001.
4: Marx, 1976, p270.

consumption" to refer to such processes, which are essential for the direct producer to return to work. "Supplementary labour" refers to the processes that are essential for individual consumption to proceed—chopping firewood, making beds, cooking food, repairing clothes, etc.[5] Along with the processes of recuperation and sustenance that occur on a daily basis and allow workers to return to work each day, the current workforce as a whole must also be reproduced in the long term. Supplementary labour therefore also needs to be performed in sustaining past and future workers—those too young, too old or too sick to work at a given point in time. More broadly, workers who become inactive or die need to be replaced by new workers. This can be achieved through generational replacement, the introduction of women or children into the workforce, or through acquiring outside sources of labour such as slaves or immigrants. While Vogel points to the macabre possibility that a group of workers may be worked to death and replaced by outside sources of labour—as they were in the gold mines in Roman Egypt, French Indochina's rubber plantations and Nazi Germany's *Arbeitslager*—it is more common for workers to be replaced generationally, as children are born, grow up and enter the workforce, taking the place of previous workers at the point of production.

It is this aspect of labour reproduction that lays the basis for the differential role of men and women in social reproduction:

> If generational replacement is to happen, biological reproduction must intervene. And here, it must be admitted, human beings do not reproduce themselves by parthenogenesis [virgin birth]. Women and men are different...biological differences constitute the material precondition for the social construction of gender differences, as well as a direct material factor in the differential position of the sexes in a society.[6]

Generally women have a period of time during childbearing when their capacity to labour diminishes. Other adults, historically the biological father and his kin group, provide for the women during this time. While women are clearly not all continually pregnant, this nevertheless constitutes one of the bases for the different roles that are assigned to men and women, including the fact that supplementary labour has traditionally been more likely to be performed by women. But this biological function does not, in itself, constitute a source of oppression; it is through the contradictions that

---

5:   Vogel, 2013, p149.
6:   Vogel, 2013, pp146-147.

arise from the ruling class's need to extract surplus labour and reproduce labour power that women's oppression comes into being.[7] Vogel explains:

> Class struggle over the conditions of production represents the central dynamic of social development in societies characterised by exploitation. In these societies, surplus labour is appropriated by a dominant class, and an essential condition for production is the constant presence and renewal of a subordinated class of direct producers committed to the labour process. Ordinarily, generational replacement provides most of the new workers needed to replenish this class, and women's capacity to bear children therefore plays a critical role in class society. From the point of view of social reproduction, women's oppression in class societies is rooted in their differential position with respect to generational replacement processes.[8]

Under capitalism the ruling class's need to appropriate surplus labour to create profit means the childbearing period, during which women's capacity to labour diminishes, represents a potential costly loss of production in the short term. However, capitalists need this childbearing process to occur; otherwise sources of labour would dry up (unless extracted from slave or external migrant sources). Therefore, Vogel argues, "In class societies women's childbearing capacity creates contradictions from the point of view of the dominant class's need to appropriate surplus labour. The oppression of women in the exploited class develops in the process of the class struggle over the resolution of these contradictions".[9]

Much of the argument thus far is formulated at a very general level, that of class society. But domestic labour and wage labour become increasingly polarised under capitalism as capitalists push to increase the extraction of surplus labour in the production process. The more time a wage labourer has to spend on supplementary labour, the less time can be spent working for the capitalist. The growing control over workers' lives under wage labour separates the processes of labour power and its reproduction. The character of wage labour becomes distinct from the worker's life outside of this process. This separation feeds into "powerful ideological structures, which develop a forceful life of their own".[10] Yet the division of men and women between these separate spheres is neither complete nor static:

7: Vogel, 2013, pp152-153.
8: Vogel, 2013, p135.
9: Vogel, 2013, p153.
10: Vogel, 2013, p160.

Depending on the historical situation, either the role of the family as the site of generational reproduction, or the importance of women's participation in surplus labour, or both, might be emphasised. During a period in which the ruling class's need to maximise surplus labour overwhelms long-range considerations, all individuals in the exploited class might be mobilised into surplus production, causing severe dislocations in its institutions of family life and male dominance. It is in this context that ideologies naturalising women's place in the home may come up against capital's desire for female labour, meaning these processes may proceed with challenges from both men and women.[11]

Socialist feminism

Vogel sought through her theory of social reproduction to remedy deficiencies in socialist feminist currents that began to emerge from the 1960s, particularly those arising from debate on the role of domestic labour under capitalism. Specifically, in place of dual system theories, which see "two equally powerful motors driv[ing] the development of history: the class struggle and the sex struggle",[12] Vogel set out to construct a *unitary* theory that transcended the separation of production and reproduction.

The 1960s women's movement erupted as changes in the position of women in employment and education came into conflict with supposedly archaic, but in fact relatively novel, family structures and gender roles. The Second World War had led to significant restructuring of the workforce as women flooded into wage labour to ease labour shortages. As men were demobilised after 1945 women faced pressure to leave the positions they had held during the war. But women were not successfully pushed back into pre-war work patterns, in part because the post-war boom created new labour demands. Whereas in the decades leading up to the war women in employment were usually young and unmarried, filling temporary positions, following the war many more married women and mothers worked on a semi-permanent basis. Yet these changing employment patterns were not universally welcomed, and an ideology that located women as a subservient element within the nuclear family forcefully reasserted itself.[13] Another radicalising influence on activists was the pattern of social upheavals of the 1960s—including the civil rights, anti-war and black

---

11:   Vogel, 2013, p155-156.
12:   Vogel, 1995, p35.
13:   Vogel, 2013, p3.

liberation movements and the French general strike of 1968. A layer of activists sought to root women's liberation within the wider struggle for socialism and, by the 1970s, socialist feminists had constituted themselves as a distinct layer within the women's movement.[14]

Socialist feminists immediately faced a number of questions of political orientation. Was the struggle for socialism distinct from the struggle for women's liberation? If so, how did these struggles relate to each another, and how could the goals of both be pursued without subordinating one to the other? Moreover, was an autonomous movement of women required?

Socialist feminists sought to explain women's oppression through a historical and materialist framework, while attempting to theorise a relationship between the processes of oppression and exploitation. This differentiated them from radical feminists, a section of the women's liberation movement who saw the antagonisms between men and women embedded deeply throughout human history, and who emphasised the critical importance of sexuality, and the supposed ineffectiveness and irrelevance of socialism towards the goal of women's liberation. It also differentiated them from liberal feminism, which concentrated on legal reform and political equality within the existing capitalist system. Socialist feminists tended to argue that women's oppression operates relatively autonomously from capitalist exploitation. Women's oppression was, for them, located in the sphere of reproduction, exploitation in the sphere of production. In such a dual systems perspective, the struggle against exploitation was regarded as related to but distinct from the struggle for women's liberation.

Some socialist feminists went beyond simply identifying these two relatively autonomous spheres of exploitation and oppression, attempting to theorise the relationship between them through analysing the role of women in domestic labour. Margaret Benston in 1969, followed by Peggy Morton in 1971, laid out the basic principles of a materialist analysis of domestic housework.[15] Both understood domestic labour as composed of material activities that result in products consumed within the household. The positive contribution of the domestic labour debate was the insight that the work that women did in the home sustained the household unit and enabled some of its members to go to work each day.[16] It was generally agreed by those participating in the debate that domestic labour was essential for the reproduction of labour power and that domestic labour

---

14: Vogel, 2013, pp4–6.
15: Benston, 1969; Morton, 1970.
16: Vogel, 2013, p21.

produced use values (concrete things that satisfy human needs or wants).

However, controversy arose over whether domestic labour produced surplus value, which forms the basis for profit under capitalism. Mariarosa Dalla Costa argued that women engaged in domestic work do produce surplus value because the services and products their labour creates is used to reproduce labour power—and under capitalism labour power is a commodity.[17] Women, she argued, were the slaves of male wage slaves, with this primary slavery enabling the latter. Consequently, Dalla Costa saw housewives as exploited productive workers and her work inspired a small movement that demanded wages for housework.[18]

Further debate arose over whether domestic labour should be categorised as productive or unproductive labour. The distinction between productive and unproductive labour is traditionally understood as the distinction between labour that contributes to the creation of surplus value (productive) and labour that produces use values but not surplus value (unproductive).[19] Theoretical ambiguity regarding the distinction between productive and unproductive labour plagued much Marxist scholarship in the 1970s.[20] Conceptual confusion was aggravated through particular socialist feminists giving the terms "productive" and "unproductive" moral connotations.[21] Unproductive was seen as synonymous with worthless, seemingly imbuing Marxist categories with a hidden sexist essence.

By the mid-1970s this debate had run out of steam and socialist feminists began to turn their attention to other issues. Vogel argues that, while the earliest observations made by Benston and Morton that domestic labour produced use values that are consumed within the household proved essentially correct, domestic labour does not produce exchange values, therefore neither does it produce value, nor can it be considered productive or unproductive.[22]

17: Dalla Costa and James, 1972.

18: Vogel, 2013, pp20-21. For brief critiques of the demand for wages for housework see the debates between Dallas and Hamilton, 1976, and Bruegel, 1976a; 1976b.

19: Marx, 1976, p644.

20: For instance, the Greek Eurocommunist Nicos Poulantzas not only argued that only productive workers could be considered part of the working class, but narrowed his definition of productive workers essentially to reduce it to manual, blue collar workers. See Poulantzas, 1973. For criticism see Wood, 1986, p37; McClaverty, 2005, p50; Harvey, 1982, p105.

21: Vogel, 2013, p22.

22: While making similar points to Vogel, Lindsey German puts a different slant on the argument: "Domestic labour can be seen to be *indirectly productive* of surplus value, through being directly productive of labour power. This feature is important in order to retain what is central to the domestic labour debate, and to draw the correct conclusions from it. The two dominant strands of the debate in fact lead to wrong conclusions: either to the wages for

Defective formulations?

Ultimately, despite their intentions, the socialist feminists failed organically to link gender and class, production and reproduction, exploitation and oppression.[23] Vogel attempted to theorise women's oppression while avoiding the pitfalls and limitations inherent in the domestic labour debate. In particular, she formulated her theory by taking up and extending the categories elaborated by Marx in *Capital*.

But, controversially, Vogel also argued that the limitations of socialist feminist theory derived from what has often been seen as a key Marxist work on the question of women's oppression: Frederick Engels's *The Origin of the Family, Private Property and the State*. This was, for Vogel, part of a wider set of problems in how the socialist movement engaged with women's issues from Marx and Engels onwards.

Vogel's analysis of the contribution of various 19th and 20th century socialists, which actually makes up much of the first two thirds of the book, is weak when compared to the final section elaborating her own theory of social reproduction. In particular, Vogel fails to engage with some important arguments made by Clara Zetkin and Lenin, as well as Rosa Luxemburg, Alexandra Kollontai and Leon Trotsky (the latter does not even warrant a mention), about the key role of the working class in obtaining women's liberation. Each of these revolutionaries argued vociferously that it would be necessary for working class women to fight alongside working class men to achieve their own liberation.[24] So, while Vogel criticises Zetkin's focus on women solely as *workers*, arguing that this makes the wives and daughters of the working class who do not participate in wage labour invisible, she does not engage with the key argument Zetkin was making, namely that female workers gained collective power as part of the working class as they assumed a role in capitalist production.

Likewise, Vogel's critical engagement with Marx and Engels is less impressive than her own positive contribution to the theory of women's oppression. On the one hand, Vogel defends Marx and Engels from those who argue that they were simply trapped within the chauvinistic assumptions typical of men in Victorian Britain. She asserts that Marx and Engels had much

housework campaign espoused by Selma James, or to the idea that the use values produced by the housewife have little to do with commodity production or indeed capitalism...the housewife produces only use values; but these in turn affect the value of labour power... Domestic labour exists in the form that it does precisely because of wage labour and commodity production"—German, 1989, pp72-73.

23: Vogel, 2013, p29. See also German, 1981 and 1989.

24: See Cliff, 1984, pp67-109.

more to say on the woman question than commentators have realised.[25] But, on the other hand, Vogel is particularly disdainful of Engels's *Origin*. While many of Vogel's specific criticisms of Engels's text are justified, her overall characterisation of *Origin* as a "defective text" is unnecessarily dismissive.

Engels wrote *Origin* over a period of a month in 1884, relying primarily on an anthropological text, Lewis Morgan's *Ancient Society*, and some annotations and comments made by Marx before his death in 1883. Engels sought to show how kinship patterns changed and were shaped by developments in the mode of production. Crucially, Engels argued that women's oppression came about at a particular historical juncture; the shift from subsistence to surplus-producing societies.[26] While subsistence societies might be characterised by a division of labour between men, who focused on hunting and fishing, and women, who oversaw gathering and the household, the former did not carry greater importance than the latter. The equal importance accorded to hunting *and* gathering laid the basis for both men and women's participation in collective decision making. Engels argued that oppressive relationships between men and women were absent in these societies; male supremacy only arose with the rise of class society. In primitive societies men owned the instruments necessary to hunt, fish, cultivate, etc, and therefore when production methods changed and societies began to produce a surplus, it was men who controlled that surplus. In order for men to pass on wealth to descendants, women needed to be tightly controlled. The origin of the monogamous family lay with the development of private property, and, with the advent of monogamous marriage, the nuclear family became the basic economic unit of society. Engels described this as "the world historic defeat of the female sex"; women had become "a mere instrument for the production of children" and were reduced to servitude to men.[27]

Engels located the rise of women's oppression in the economic subjugation of women in the household. Thus Engels, as well as Marx, predicted that as capitalism drew women into wage labour, the working class family and women's subjugation would be gradually eroded. Vogel is correct to point to this as an overly optimistic evaluation and she criticises Engels's optimism on three counts:

First, it misses the significance of the working class household as an essential social unit, not for the holding of property but for the reproduction of the

25: Vogel, 2013, pp36-38.
26: For a detailed defence of Engels's argument, see McGregor, 2013.
27: Engels, 1972, pp120-121.

working class itself. Second, it overlooks the ways in which a material basis for male supremacy is constituted within the proletarian household. And third, it vastly underestimates the variety of ideological and psychological factors that provide a continuing foundation for male supremacy in the working class family.[28]

Furthermore, Vogel criticises Engels's tendency to assume that "family duties" were naturally the province of women, his failure to link the development of the sphere of reproduction to the rise of capitalist society and his omission of the different character of oppression in pre-capitalist societies for women occupying different class locations.

Marx and Engels are, of course, not beyond reproach. Engels failed fully to theorise the character of women's oppression under capitalism in *Origin*—but this was not Engels's main intention in this work. Engels provides a historical account of the rise of the family as class society develops, rather than specifically setting out to theorise women's oppression under capitalism, arguing that gender roles are social and historical rather than fixed transhistorical entities. Vogel in fact fails to grapple with the historical issue of the origins of women's oppression. Thus, while she correctly argues that the family "is not a timeless universal of human society", she fails to explain why or to explain when the family arose or how its form has changed alongside changes in the mode of production.

However, Vogel's main issue with *Origin* is its supposed propagation of the dual systems perspective. Vogel accuses Engels of distinguishing between two types of production: first, the production of means of subsistence, and, second, the production of human beings. This theoretical dualism, she argues, ultimately bears responsibility for the dual systems perspectives of socialist feminism. In the offending passage Engels writes:

> According to the materialistic conception, the determining factor in history is, in the final instance, the production and reproduction of immediate life. This, again, is of twofold character: on the one side, the production of the means of existence, of food, clothing and shelter and the tools necessary for that production; on the other side, the production of human beings themselves, the propagation of the species. The social organisation under which the people of a particular historical epoch and a particular country live

---

28: Vogel, 2013, pp88-89.

is determined by both kinds of production: by the stage of development of labour on the one hand and of the family on the other.[29]

Vogel argues that, positively, this stresses the materiality of the social processes women are involved in. But:

> It implies that the production of human beings constitutes a process that has not only an autonomous character, but a theoretical weight equal to that of the production of the means of existence. In short, Engels's remarks appear to offer authoritative Marxist backing for the socialist feminist movement's focus on the family, sex-divisions of labour, and unpaid domestic work, as well as for its theoretical dualism and its strategic commitment to the autonomous organisation of women.[30]

Laying the responsibility for socialist feminists' dual-systems theory at Engels's door is unwarranted. Chris Harman has argued that, while the above passage, in truncated form, does appear to lend authority to a dual systems perspective, Engels actually went on to say that with the development of class society the two modes coexist less and less.[31] Harman writes:

> In fact, it is absolutely confusing to talk of "two modes". The mode of production in any society is a coupling together of forces of production and relations of production. The first half of the couple is continually exercising pressure for change on the second half. Every increase in the ability of human beings to control nature produces new interrelations between the human beings themselves, and therefore begins to transform the pre-existing relations of production.[32]

Vogel wrongly characterises Engels as the root cause of the socialist feminists' adherence to the dual systems perspectives. Socialist feminists' attempts to theorise the continued existence of the oppression of women in

---

29: Engels, 1972, pp71-72,
30: Vogel, 2013, pp33-34.
31: Harman, 1984, p16. The quote from Engels is followed by this passage: "The old society, built on groups based on ties of sex, bursts asunder in the collision of the newly developed social classes; in its place a new society appears, constituted in a state, the lower units of which are no longer groups based on ties of sex but territorial groups, a society in which the family system is entirely dominated by the property system, and in which the class antagonisms and class struggles, which make up the content of all hitherto written history, now freely develop."
32: Harman, 1984, pp16.

Stalinist states that were widely believed to be socialist explains their attachment to dualism much more coherently than an isolated, decontextualised passage in *Origin*.

Vogel's incomplete task

Vogel's shared belief that such states were indeed socialist ultimately weakens her analysis of the capitalist form which is central to her book, and consequently she is unable fully to overcome the dualism of socialist feminists. These weaknesses are most evident in her discussion of strategy. Vogel poses the question by looking at the gap between women's formal equality and social equality. Under capitalism a particular conception of equality emerged. In a famous passage from *Capital* Marx put it thus:

> The sphere of circulation or commodity exchange, within whose boundaries the sale and purchase of labour power goes on, is in fact a very Eden of the innate rights of man. It is the exclusive realm of Freedom, Equality, Property and Bentham. Freedom, because both buyer and seller of a commodity, let us say of labour power, are determined by their own free will. They contract as free persons who are equal before the law. Their contract is the final result in which their joint will finds a common legal expression. Equality, because each enters into relation with the other, as with a simple owner of commodities, and they exchange equivalent for equivalent.[33]

Value, determined by abstract human labour, eschews the differences between types of labour; labour is abstracted within the commodity. Capitalism equalises human labour through the exchange of commodities. However, behind this formal equality, which characterises the sphere of circulation, stands the deep economic and social *inequality* of class exploitation in the sphere of production. Yet, because this conception of equality has material roots in capitalism, Vogel writes that "equality of persons is not...simply an abstract political principle or a false ideology...far from a useless exercise in bourgeois reformism, the battle for democratic rights can point beyond capitalism".[34]

Vogel argues that the tensions between demands for formal equality and real social inequality form the "basis for the development of a woman's movement oriented toward socialism",[35] and goes on to argue that the

---

33: Marx, 1976, p280.
34: Vogel, 2013, pp171-172.
35: Vogel, 2013, p175.

left has failed to intervene in these struggles successfully. She argues that this is because socialist and socialist feminist approaches have focused on women at work and domestic labour, which has produced an economistic and reductive analysis. This orientation, she argues, "fails to account for the oppression of women not in the working class, and cannot explain the potential for building progressive women's organisations that cross class divisions, nor the possible obstacles to uniting women from distinct racial or national groups into a single women's movement".[36]

The answer to this conundrum for Vogel is "analysing how a broad based women's liberation movement may represent an essential component in the fight for socialism". Vogel understands that women's liberation is tied up with the fight for socialism, postulating that "so long as capitalism survives, domestic labour will be required for its reproduction, disproportionately performed by women and most likely accompanied by a system of male supremacy".[37]

Vogel's preference for cross-class alliances of women is informed both by her experience of the women's movement in the US and by her understanding of women's oppression in "actually existing" socialist societies. First, in the US the women's movement was largely composed of such cross-class alliances. It had a decidedly different character from the British women's movement, which had a greater orientation on the working class and trade unions. Second, Vogel's classification of countries such as China, Cuba and the Soviet Union as socialist hamstrings some of her best insights. She argues that while supposedly socialist societies have made important advances with regard to women's participation in production and political life, they have not been able to shift the burden of housework or systematically alleviate women's subordination. For Vogel, "socialism" has not precipitated the erosion, and eventual abolition, of women's oppression in such societies and, consequently, a distinct movement for women's liberation becomes necessary. Therefore, while repeatedly criticising the tendency of socialist feminists to treat the fight for socialism and women's liberation as autonomous spheres, Vogel ends up advocating a strategy that tacitly replicates this dualism.

The IS tradition

Tony Cliff's theory of state capitalism allowed the International Socialist tradition to explain quite simply how women's oppression could exist in socialist countries: it doesn't. By identifying the countries in question as

---

36: Vogel, 2013, p176.
37: Vogel, 2013, p176.

state capitalist, this tradition was able to avoid the theoretical quagmire entered by those defending the socialist credentials of the Soviet Union and similar Stalinist states. Moreover, the importance of women becoming workers and the impact this would have on the family and the relationships between men, women and children is a key insight of Marx and Engels that Vogel misses, but which was taken up by this tradition.

The general trends reveal growing employment rates for women throughout the century (see table). While the number of women in part-time employment has hovered around 42 to 45 percent for the past 30 years, the number of women in full-time employment has increased. The growth of service industries, typically staffed by women, and the decline of manufacturing, dominated by men in the 20th century, contributed to these trends.

Employment rates for men and women aged 16 to 64, 1971 to 2013, UK (includes part and full time work)
Source: Labour Force Survey, ONS

	Percentage (seasonally adjusted)	
	Men	**Women**
Jan–Mar 1973	91.8	54.2
Jan–Mar 1983	77.8	53.8
Jan–Mar 1993	75.2	61.6
Jan–Mar 2003	79.0	66.4
Apr–Jun 2013	76.2	66.7

Women, therefore, have increasingly become an important part of the workforce, eroding the atomisation of women in individual households. This experience in the workplace has changed women's expectations, feeding into demands for greater equality. Thus, while Vogel advocates cross-class alliances and criticises the left's focus on women at work, in our tradition we have defended a focus on women as workers, recognising both the importance of women becoming social beings outside of the household and the central role of the working class in achieving real liberation *for all women*. That does not mean abstaining from other, limited and partial, struggles against women's oppression or failing to engage with feminist currents. But it is only through men and women acting together as part of the working class that oppression can ultimately be smashed.

Whether working class men could ever be part of the struggle to emancipate women informed the debate over "male benefits" (a debate magnified out of all proportion by critics of the International Socialist tradition) in which Lindsey German, Sheila McGregor and Chris Harman argued against the position held by feminists and socialist feminists that all men benefit from women's oppression and therefore have an interest in defending the system of male supremacy.[38] It was argued that the main beneficiary of women's oppression was not men, but capital. This claim did not involve a denial that men have advantages over women in society, but rather involved recognising that these divisions work against the class interests of both men and women. As German put it:

> Whatever advantages working class men might have, their interests, just like those of working class women, lie in joining the fight against women's oppression. This is because the roots of women's oppression lie in class society in general and capitalist society in particular... The capitalist system rests on the exploitation of workers, both men and women. Women workers also suffer a specific oppression which is located in the continuing privatised reproduction of labour power. This points to a solution which involves collective working class action.[39]

We cannot rid the world of women's oppression without also ridding it of the capitalist system that sustains it. Divisions in the ranks of labour, whether through gender, race or nationality, strengthen capital's power over us. It is only through collective working class action across these divisions that exploitation, and the oppression it gives rise to, can be eradicated.

Despite the criticisms of *Marxism and the Oppression of Women* set out here, the book does present a sophisticated theoretical basis for understanding women's oppression under capitalism. Ultimately Vogel's softness towards Stalinism, the high level of abstraction at which she develops her arguments, and her dismissive attitude towards certain key insights made by the socialist tradition undermine her ability to explore the origin of, or changes to, women's oppression, and lead her to orientate on cross-class alliances of women. Nonetheless, Vogel deserves to be read and critically utilised by all those seeking to understand and challenge women's oppression.

38: See German 1981, 1986; Harman, 1984, and McGregor, 1985.
39: German, 1986, p138.

References

Allen, Theodore W, 2001, "On Roediger's Wages of Whiteness", *Cultural Logic*, volume 4, number 2, http://clogic.eserver.org/4-2/allen.html

Benston, Margaret, 1969, "The Political Economy of Women's Liberation", *Monthly Review*, volume 21, number 4.

Bruegel, Irene, 1976a, "Wages for Housework", *International Socialism 89* (first series), www.marxists.org/history/etol/newspape/isj/1976/no089/bruegel.htm

Bruegel, Irene, 1976b, "Once More on Wages for Housework: A Reply to Elana Dallas and Judith Hamilton", *International Socialism 91* (first series), http://tinyurl.com/n8jaqfl

Choonara, Esme, and Yuri Prasad, 2014, "What's Wrong with Privilege Theory", *International Socialism 142* (spring 2014), www.isj.org.uk/?id=971

Cliff, Tony, 1984, *Class Struggle and Women's Liberation* (Bookmarks), http://tinyurl.com/nc9bcsr

Dalla Costa, Mariarosa, and Selma James, 1972, "Women and the Subversion of the Community", in Mariarosa Dalla Costa and Selma James (eds), *The Power of Women and the Subversion of the Community* (Falling Wall Press).

Dallas, Elana, and Judith Hamilton, 1976, "We Come to Bury Housework...Not to Pay for It", *International Socialism 90* (first series), http://tinyurl.com/n7hrs5f

Engels, Frederick, 1972 [1884], *The Origin of the Family, Private Property and the State* (Lawrence and Wishart), www.marxists.org/archive/marx/works/1884/origin-family/preface.htm

German, Lindsey, 1981, "Theories of Patriarchy", *International Socialism 12* (spring),www.isj.org.uk/?id=240

German, Lindsey, 1986, "Oppression, Individuals and Classes: A Rejoinder to John Molyneux", *International Socialism 32* (summer),http://tinyurl.com/n3qyux7

German, Lindsey, 1989, *Sex, Class and Socialism* (Bookmarks).

Harman, Chris, 1984, "Women's Liberation and Revolutionary Socialism", *International Socialism 23* (spring), www.marxists.org/archive/harman/1984/xx/women.html

Harvey, David, 1982, *The Limits to Capital* (Basil Blackwell).

Marx, Karl, 1976, *Capital*, Volume I (Penguin).

McClaverty, Peter, 2005, "Class", in Georgina Blakely and Valerie Bryson (eds), *Marx and Other Four-Letter Words* (Pluto).

McGregor, Sheila, 1985, "A Reply to John Molyneux on Women's Oppression", *International Socialism 30* (autumn), http://tinyurl.com/kam7bjy

McGregor, Sheila, 2013, "Marxism and Woman's Oppression Today", *International Socialism 138* (spring), www.isj.org.uk/?id=885

Morton, Peggy, 1970, "A Woman's Work is Never Done", in, Edith Altbach (ed), *From Feminism to Liberation* (Schenkman Publishing).

Poulantzas, Nicos, 1973, "Marxism and Social Classes", *New Left Review*, number 78.

Vogel, Lise, 1995, "Questions on the Woman Question", in *Women Questions: Essays for a Materialist Feminism* (Pluto).

Vogel, Lise, 2013, *Marxism and the Oppression of Women: Toward a Unitary Theory* (Haymarket).

Wood, Ellen Meiksins, 1986, *The Retreat from Class: A New "True" Socialism* (Verso).

Good sense on global warming
Andreas Ytterstad

Good sense, for Antonio Gramsci, was the "healthy nucleus of common sense".[1] This article tries to make sense of what Gramsci meant by good sense, and seeks to develop his understanding of good sense into a resource we can use to stop runaway global warming in time. Although I conclude by briefly outlining the politics of good sense on global warming, the article is not primarily concerned with *how* we use good sense on global warming. Before using something we must know what that something is. The something here is the potential we—as human beings, as most people, as working class people across the world—have in our heads to solve the climate crisis. I shall argue in the first most general part of the article that good sense is a conception of necessity, an interest in truth and a relational, emergent morality among those who do *not* rule our planet. More concretely, the second part of the article will find good sense on global warming in the shape of use value rationality and anti-capitalism, in climate justice and in changing livelihoods prompted by the climate change already under way.

This is not an article about what Gramsci said about global warming. I agree with John Bellamy Foster[2] who claims Gramsci did not sufficiently connect his Marxism to nature and physical realities. Some of the recent

---

1:    Gramsci, 1971, p327.
2:    Foster, Clark and York, 2011, pp215–247; Foster, 1999, pvii.

scholarship on the "ecological Gramsci"[3] is too anthropocentric, focused on human beings, and the way we "frame" nature.[4] By contrast, the "philosophy of praxis" we need for the age of global warming needs to be much more in tune with nature, and the natural sciences themselves: "In a slight revision of Marx's principle of historical materialism, we can say human beings make their own history, not entirely under conditions of their choosing but rather on the basis of natural-environmental and social conditions inherited from the past".[5]

Nature is not all in our heads. However, Gramsci's democratic understanding of popular consciousness remains very important for anybody who wants to build a mass movement to stop global warming. In his *Prison Notebooks* he repeatedly insisted that everybody—not just a privileged few—was a philosopher and an intellectual, with the capacity to grasp "advanced science".[6]

The resources of good sense on global warming, in other words, are the consciousness resources of the many. They are not reserved to the few who have read the eloquent writings on nature of Marx and Engels themselves, refined by contemporary ecological Marxists.[7] But Gramsci says different things about good sense. This is fine, because good sense really does consist of multiple resources. But I am dubious of some passages where Gramsci seems to equate good sense with Marxism, or with his particular take on Marxism, the "philosophy of praxis".[8] Some interpreters of Gramsci even suggest that the role of Marxism is to create "good sense" in place of "common sense".[9] I disagree and I will stick with the idea that good sense on global warming is a resource that Marxists may or may not learn from and develop further. As Stuart Hall put it: "The 'good sense' of the people exists, but it is just the beginning, not the end of politics. It doesn't *guarantee* anything".[10]

Unfortunately, as I have shown elsewhere,[11] Stuart Hall and most readers of Gramsci do not even try to address what a good beginning good sense really is, for anybody who wants to change the world. That is what I

3:   See Ekers and others, 2013.
4:   Ytterstad, 2014.
5:   Foster, Clark and York, 2011, p291.
6:   Gramsci, 1971, pp9, 323, 347, 424.
7:   Foster, Clark and York, 2011; Foster, 1999; Malm, 2007.
8:   Coben, 2002, p269; Gramsci, 1971, pp345–346, 386–387, 423, 462.
9:   Boggs, 1976, p71.
10: Hall, 1991, p125
11: Ytterstad, 2012, pp25–26, 68–71.

intend to do, with examples and illustrations, in what follows.

Some of these examples and illustrations come from my experience of trying to build a popular climate movement in Norway. As deputy leader of Concerned Scientists Norway I have been involved in building two alliances. The broadest one, the Climate Election Alliance, was originally set up in 2011 by Grandparents Climate Action. By the time of the last general election in Norway, more than 100 organisations had joined the Alliance, including the biggest single union, the Norwegian Union of Municipal and General Employees (NUMGE). Together with two other unions, most of the environmental organisations and even the Norwegian Church, NUMGE supported a short book I wrote last year, demanding 100,000 new climate jobs in offshore wind and in transport, while cooling down the drive for Norwegian oil.[12]

The other alliance emerged from the sponsors of that book. This year we were able to host a magnificent conference called "Bridge to the Future—A Climate Solution from Below". Attended by 350 people in the House of Literature in Oslo, it was also watched via streaming by more than 1,000 people elsewhere in Norway.[13] For parts of that day, the hashtag climate jobs (#klimajobber14), a non-existent word in Norwegian public debate, traded as second only to Ukraine in Norway on Twitter. I have written elsewhere on how the alliance experienced it: "To varying degrees of course, but nonetheless: it was a day we felt that almost impossible feeling of popular empowerment over the present and pending nightmare called global warming".[14]

Tempting as it is, I am not going to explain success stories from Norway as a product of good sense on global warming. To detect and strengthen good sense is a question of art, not just of science. But having a scientific understanding of good sense as a resource helps, and it has at least given me some confidence to act upon the statement by climate author and activist Bill McKibben: "Climate change is the single biggest thing humans have ever done on this planet. The only thing that needs to be bigger is our movement to stop it".[15]

12: Ytterstad, 2013. The book was followed by a sequel on how to cool down Norwegian oil (Ryggvik, 2013), also financed by NUMGE, together with the Norwegian Civil Service Union.
13: Videos from the Conference, two of them in English, can be seen at our website http://klimakonferanse2014.no
14: Ytterstad, forthcoming.
15: McKibben won the 2013 Sophie Prize for environment and sustainable development in Norway, which further popularised this quote—go to www.sofieprisen.no/Prize_Winners/2013/index.html

Conception of necessity—the human being resource

So what then, according to Gramsci, is good sense? Longstanding readers of this journal, like myself, will have seen this description of contradictory consciousness many times before:

> The active man-in-the-mass has a practical activity, but has no clear theoretical consciousness of his practical activity, which nonetheless involves understanding the world in so far as it transforms it. His theoretical consciousness can indeed be historically in opposition to his activity. One might almost say that he has two theoretical consciousnesses (or one contradictory consciousness); one which is implicit in his activity and which in reality unites him with all of his fellow workers in the practical transformation of the real world; and one, superficially explicit or verbal, which he has inherited from the past and uncritically absorbed.[16]

This quote is from a note called "Relation between science, religion and common sense", and it is indeed one of the richest notes on good sense in the prison notebooks. But it is not in this passage, but a few pages earlier, that Gramsci explicitly attempts to define good sense as "a conception of necessity which gives a conscious direction to one's activity".[17]

There are differences between this definition of good sense and the consciousness "implicit in his activity and which in reality unites him with all of his fellow workers". The latter description suggests that good sense is something local that belongs to the working class.[18] For example, Alf Nilsen proposes, following Raymond Williams, "that we consider the nature and origins of good sense as a *local rationality*".[19] Such local rationality is often a very useful resource for combating racism inside the workplace, for example.[20] It is not so useful in the case of global warming. Local experience can certainly help prompt working class engagement on global warming, as I will show when I discuss livelihood below, but to understand why people choose to fight against global warming, Gramsci's actual definition of good sense is much more relevant. Elsewhere, Gramsci elaborates on this definition. By necessity he means *perceived* necessity for most people, that

---

16: Gramsci, 1971, p333.
17: Gramsci, 1971, p327.
18: It also seems to suggest that good sense belongs to men, but I see such masculine connotations as a product of conventions of Gramsci's time. When I cite "man" in this article, I mean human beings.
19: Nilsen, 2009, p124.
20: Hall, 1996, p432.

"necessity exists when there exists an effective and active *premiss*, conscious-ness of which in people's minds has become operative, proposing concrete goals to the collective consciousness and constituting a complex of convic-tions and beliefs which act powerfully in the form of 'popular beliefs'".[21]

Such a conception of necessity on global warming has to do with the amount of greenhouse gases we can emit into the atmosphere. The necessity to act on global warming is developing fast and becoming ever more concrete for people. It used to be about the concentration of carbon dioxide (in parts per million, ppm) a livable atmosphere could endure. In 2006 the UN Intergovernmental Panel on Climate Change (IPCC) esti-mated the threshold for dangerous climate change at 450ppm. Prompted by climate scientists like James Hansen, who argued in 2007 that 450ppm was too risky, activists soon began to perceive this necessity more radi-cally. McKibben set up 350.org, insisting that the limit should be 350ppm, 50ppm *lower* than current levels, and spends the first two terrifying chapters of his book *Eaarth* making sure that we know "in our bones" that "Eaarth is an uphill planet now", and that "you have to work harder to get where you're going".[22] More recently McKibben has helped clarify and popularise the idea of a carbon budget. To understand the threshold nowadays, you just have to "do the math". We have 565 gigatonnes of carbon dioxide left to burn if we are to have a reasonable chance of avoiding runaway climate change. Stock markets, however, have already priced in 2,795 gigatonnes worth of fossil fuel reserves. In other words, investors have already made a bet that the world will fail to curb emissions. Climate activists, by contrast, now know that: "We'd have to keep 80 percent of those reserves locked away underground".[23]

The conception of necessity is thus a resource that is not restricted to workers. It is simply part of human rationality. We are essentially better equipped to fathom, and hence potentially to stop, global warming than snails. No simplification of the climate sciences and no metaphor for the carbon cycle will ever convince intelligent animals, like dolphins, of the perils ahead. You can free Willy, but you cannot make him into a philoso-pher. As Gramsci puts it: "Thought is proper to man as such".[24]

21: Nilsen, 2009, pp412-413.
22: McKibben, 2010, p86.
23: McKibben's "Do the Math" article, originally in *Rolling Stone*, was also published as a foreword to another book with some good sense on global warming, written by Mike Berners-Lee and Duncan Clark called *The Burning Question: We can't Burn Half the World's Oil, Coal and Gas: so How do we Quit?*" (Berners-Lee and Clark, 2013).
24: Gramsci, 1971, p347.

The interest in truth—the radical Enlightenment resource

The human capacity to think, however, is also a historical achievement. Gramsci could not have displayed such faith in the good sense of the people without the heritage of the scientific revolution and the Enlightenment. This heritage is, contrary to what some postmodern readings of Gramsci imply,[25] a good thing. When the bourgeoisie was a revolutionary class, its best thinkers were passionate about seeking the truth.[26] A whole range of thinkers on the environment were much more honest and radical 200 years ago. John Bellamy Foster has drawn our attention to the "Lauderdale Paradox"—that an increase in private riches decreases public wealth, after the eighth Earl of Lauderdale. "'The common sense of mankind', Lauderdale contended, 'would revolt' at any proposal to augment private riches 'by creating a scarcity of any commodity generally useful and necessary to man'".[27] This revolting state of affairs is now part and parcel of neoliberal hegemony in the shape of carbon trading.[28]

The conception of necessity, indeed the natural necessity for emancipation, runs through Thomas Paine's 1776 pamphlet *Common Sense*, for example: "However our eyes may be dazzled with show, or our ears deceived by sound; however prejudice may warp our wills, or interest darken our understanding, the simple voice of nature and reason will say, 'tis right." But the bourgeois versions of universal ideals were always incomplete, even hypocritical. Slavery was rampant in the US when The Declaration of Independence stated that we are created equals, that we should all have the right to pursue happiness, and that "whenever any form of government becomes destructive of these ends, it is the right of the people to alter or to abolish it".

Because of this hypocrisy the workers' movement took up such ideals and tried to deepen them, well before Marx and Engels did so explicitly. Paul Blackledge shows that the demand for equality had a double meaning for Marx and Engels. Part of it arose spontaneously from the bodily experience of "crying social inequalities", but the other part consisted in the radicalisation of the bourgeois universal demands. To Marx, Engels and Gramsci, arguments for universal human freedom did not thus simply break down into the bread and butter issues connected to social inequalities, typically fought over by trade unions. Rather the working class were seen "as

---

25: For example Nun and Cartier, 1986.
26: Harman, 1998; 1999.
27: Foster, Clark and York, 2011, p55.
28: Lohman, 2011.

potential agents, not only of their own liberation, but also of the universal liberation of humanity".[29]

But for politicians and capitalists today the conception of necessity is more rhetorical than real. Another resource of good sense, alluded to by Gramsci, largely explains why. Although many of our rulers understand the danger of global warming, the system they rule—or that rules them—puts severe limits on their actions. Therefore, they are not interested in all the truths about global warming. Good sense is something that needs to be fought for, not something we can passively await:

> The philosophy of praxis...does not aim at the peaceful resolution of existing contradictions in history and society but is rather the very theory of these contradictions. It is not the instrument of government of the dominant groups in order to gain the consent of and exercise hegemony over the subaltern classes; it is the expression of these subaltern classes who want to educate themselves in the art of government and who *have an interest in knowing all truths*.[30]

Three examples will suffice to show that the interest in knowing "all truths" about global warming, the second part of good sense in my reading of Gramsci, is not evenly distributed among human beings.

First, the deniers. They are a motley crew. Many who doubt or belittle the danger of global warming may just be ignorant of, or perhaps psychologically predisposed against, the warming and warning signs. But the "merchants of doubt", especially in the US,[31] come from the fossil fuel industry or are extreme free marketeers. Before the Norwegian Progress Party was elected into government, as—horror of horrors—they are now, their climate spokesperson tried to have their national congress vote that they did not believe in the science behind global warming. He has also publicly said that CO_2 is something the left has chosen as a substitute for Karl Marx, echoing the conservative and famous denier James Dellingpole, who calls greens watermelons—red on the inside.[32] Moronic as this appears, there is a kernel of truth hidden in the campaigns against natural scientists as communists in disguise. They deny global warming not because they have better scientific arguments, but because they realise or half guess that

29: Blackledge, 2012, pp52–53.
30: Gramsci, quoted in Thomas, 2009, p452, my emphasis.
31: Hoggan, 2009; Klein, 2011; Oreskes and Conway, 2010.
32: See Lynas, 2012, for a critique.

in order to stop it you would need massive government intervention into the economy. This intervention is not just a socialist argument,[33] but something famous environmentalists like Lester Brown[34] and leading American energy researchers also call for.[35] This, of course, is anathema to neoliberals so hard core neoliberalism is not at all interested in knowing "all truths" about global warming.

My second example concerns not only the current "blue-blue" Norwegian government, but the previous "red-green" one as well. Part state-owned, part privatised Statoil have put substantial efforts into convincing the public that Norwegian oil and gas are the cleanest in the world, sustainable, and therefore climate friendly in their own right.[36] Former leader of the Norwegian Labour Party, now head of NATO, Jens Stoltenberg has been instrumental in pushing this message across. As Yngve Nilsen has shown, Stoltenberg has, for more than 20 years, been heavily and personally involved in ensuring that Norwegian climate change policy has converged around the notion of "unilateral common implementation". This means that Norway does not require the signature of international partners, but reserves the right to credit itself for what it has defined as global mitigative measures: "Norwegian export of oil, gas, and gaspower (gasskraft) were defined as such measures, and Norwegian climate change policy consequently came to equal the facilitation of production and marketing of petroleum from the Norwegian continental shelf".[37]

More than ten years after Nilsen's important dissertation, "Don't mention the oil" is still part and parcel of the hegemony of Norwegian climate change policy. When research challenged this absurdity in the summer of 2013, demonstrating that a limit on Norwegian oil would indeed reduce world emissions,[38] climate spokespersons from the Tory Party, the Progress Party and the Labour Party quite simply said they did not "believe" it. Again it is the lack of a real interest in knowing all truths, the lack of good sense, that best explains this other, more specifically Norwegian stripe of denialism.

My third example, the most challenging one perhaps for revolutionary socialists, is how the unions in Norway have responded to the proposed campaign for climate jobs. Do the workers really want to

33: Neale, 2008.
34: Brown, 2009.
35: Jacobsen and Delucci, 2011.
36: Ihlen, 2007; Nilsen, 2001; Ryggvik, 2013; Skjærseth and Skodvin, 2003.
37: Nilsen, 2001, p195.
38: Fæhn, 2013.

"educate themselves" and challenge the oil-industrial complex[39] underpinning Norwegian climate change policies? It is no coincidence, nor very surprising, that so far the unions most solidly behind the idea of a transition away from oil have organised public sector workers. There is less of a conflict between their immediate job interests and the long-term universal interest in curbing emissions than in parts of the private sector. It is more difficult with the Industry and Energy Union, who organise members both in renewable industries *and* in fossil fuels. Their leader is concerned about the breakneck speed of Norwegian oil exploration at the moment, but refers to our call for climate jobs as a "desktop project".[40] It is even more difficult with the largest private sector union within the Norwegian TUC, Fellesforbundet, with more of their members in and around the oil industry. The union has persuaded the TUC as a whole to be positive towards more oil drilling off the coast of northern Norway.

The various degrees of support in the unions for a worker-led transition to a low carbon economy speak of varying degrees of success by activists and environmentalists in winning the concrete arguments. But they also illustrate what an important new book launching the field of environmental labour studies[41] fleshes out more generally: that there are both structural constraints and opportunities for good sense on environmental issues in trade unions. The international working class may objectively have "radical chains", in the sense implied by Marx.[42] *If* they shook them off, they could pave the way for universal emancipation. But the interest in knowing all truths only exists as a potential resource within the actually existing trade union movement. Climate jobs in Norway at the moment are a little like the demand for an eight-hour day, or even socialism, used to be: A good idea, but could it really work in practice?

The morality of good sense—evaluative realism

Locating an interest in truth at the core of common sense helps us to understand what is *good*, ie in the obvious moral connotation of the word, in good sense. If we look closer at the moral content of good sense we can see how Gramsci moves easily from "is" to "ought".[43] The *Silent Spring*

39: Ryggvik, 2010, 2013.
40: www.abcnyheter.no/penger/oekonomi/2013/10/06/norge-kan-ga-fra-oljenasjon-til-miljoenasjon-hvis-vi-vil
41: Räthzel and Uzzell, 2012.
42: Marx, 2000, p256.
43: I write much more about this in my dissertation. See Ytterstad, 2012, pp45–47, 204–229.

described by Rachel Carson,[44] a spring where birds no longer sing, is a sorry state of affairs—and so it is speaking objectively, not just as a bird-watcher. The extinction of the golden toad due to loss of mist in Costa Rica is rightfully also, as Tim Flannery shows in his bestseller *The Weather Makers*, seen as a "warning" of global warming.[45] With the projected rate of extinctions detailed in Mark Lynas's *Six Degrees*, global warming is an existential question—not in a philosophically elaborated sense but in a mundane self-evident sense. Confronted by the likelihood that up to half of the world species may die out if global warming exceeds two degrees by 2050,[46] we need only minimally paraphrase Thomas Paine: "The simple voice of nature and reason will say, 'tis not right."

This is often more difficult for scientists, who tend to have an idea of objectivity that excludes norms and values. I often tell a story of Knut Alfsen, Director of Norwegian climate change research centre CICERO, to illustrate this point. He spoke at the Grandparents meeting in 2011 that kicked off the Climate Election Alliance, as did I. After his talk, which included terrifying graphs of projected warming trends in the 21st century, one of the grandparents, very worried from the sound of her voice, asked Alfsen what we could do to prevent all of this. His reply began by saying that in order to answer that question, he had to "switch hats" from being a researcher to a grandfather himself. Alfsen, an economist and social scientist himself, was in this talk primarily relaying findings from the natural sciences, where hard facts are rightfully often separated from morality or politics, "subatomic particles and natural selection are just facts, and that is all there is to say on the matter".[47] Emissions of greenhouse gases, and the need to curb such emissions, by contrast, are both natural and social facts. Values and morals therefore creep into most lines of research relevant to global warming. The process of adaptation to sea level rise in the Nile Delta, for instance, has been shown to be highly skewed by class. Rich farmers can afford to build sea walls; poor ones cannot, and are therefore forced to make do with fences made of reeds and sand.[48]

Most people are like grandparents—not like scientists. Andrew Sayer has written a book with the excellent title *Why Things Matter to People*,[49] that explains why, whereas social scientists prefer cold rational description,

---

44: Carson, 1962.
45: Flannery, 2005, pp114–122.
46: Lynas, 2007, p168.
47: Creaven, 2007, p16.
48: Malm, 2013.
49: Sayer, 2011.

and tend to see values and morals as things that exist beyond reason, most people do not. In their practical reasoning, and in the ethical dimension of their everyday life, rationality and values, is and ought, tend to merge. That is part and parcel of their good sense, I would add. We do not need to switch hats to care about global warming. Arguably, they incline towards what Sean Creaven calls evaluative realism. If our conception of necessity tells us that we cannot emit greenhouse gases beyond 450 or 350ppm, that is in itself a fact that "provides us with moral obligations by force of logical necessity".[50] Until the *is* of global warming leads to the *ought* of slashing emissions from fossil fuels humanity, to repeat the ending of *Common Sense* by Thomas Paine "will feel itself like a man who continues putting off some unpleasant business from day to day, yet knows it must be done, hates to set about it, wishes it over, and is continually haunted with the thoughts of its necessity".[51]

Put differently, the strongest moral convictions come from our deepest held understanding of the facts.[52] Gramsci is onto this same point in his note on "Moral Science and Historical Materialism":

> The scientific base for a morality of historical materialism is to be looked for, in my opinion, in the affirmation that "society does not pose for itself tasks the conditions for whose resolution do not already exist". Where these conditions exist "the solution of the tasks *becomes* duty, "will" *becomes* free". Morality would then become a search for the conditions necessary for the freedom of the will…and the demonstration that these conditions exist.[53]

Now, how you interpret the good sense conception of necessity, specified further by "a search for the conditions necessary for the freedom of the will", depends on behalf of which class you are acting. In terms of climate change, you could argue—as our rulers do—that the necessary conditions for solving the task of cutting greenhouse gase emissions already exist, in the shape of market mechanisms. Or you could issue governmental reports for offshore wind, where the idea that wind turbines could replace the oil rigs is not even part of the "mandate".

But when an environmental representative of NUMGE prepared a note for our book, on the potential for climate jobs in offshore wind, he

50: Creaven, 2007, p17.
51: Paine, 1997.
52: Collier, 2003, is also very good on this point.
53: Gramsci, 1971, pp409–410, 432.

found that 50,000 jobs were a completely realistic number. To have the world, including Norway, run on clean energy is realistic technically and economically—given sufficient state intervention. The problem is social and political.[54] When our leaders appeal to political realism, based on oil and market hegemony, we must respond with what I call natural realism in our book on climate jobs. The foreword to that book by James Hansen is also a good example of evaluative realism; facts prompt morals:

> We have, as concerned scientists and citizens of planet Earth, a moral responsibility to widen the sense of what is practical and possible in climate change policy across the world. We cannot simply report the facts to our governments, and then hope for the best. It is now 25 years since I reported some of the early findings of global warming to the US Congress. It is safe to conclude that facts alone will not make them move. Social forces need to be mobilised who can make them do what they claim cannot "realistically" be done.[55]

Good sense as an emergent and relational resource

James Hansen is very interesting. To have one of the most famous climate scientists in the world resign as Director of NASA to become an activist[56] is astonishing, and brings to light the failure of the climate change politics of our rulers. His personal trajectory and his comments above illustrate how good sense, so to speak, becomes visible. In the *Prison Notebooks* Gramsci usually speaks of good sense as emergent, latent or embryonic. It is only through mass action that good sense becomes manifest: "The social group in question may indeed have its own conception of the world, even if only embryonic; a conception which manifests itself in action, but occasionally, and in flashes—when, that is, the group is acting as an organic totality".[57] This does not happen in "normal times", says Gramsci, but as the translators of the English *Selections from the Prison Notebooks* point out in a footnote on the same page, in "the exceptional (and hence potentially revolutionary) moments in history in which a class or a group discovers its objective and subjective unity in action".

This *emergent* dimension[58] often depends, in turn, on the *relational*

54: Jacobsen and Delucci, 2011.
55: Ytterstad, 2013, pp11–12, 21–27.
56: Gillis, 2013.
57: Gramsci, 1971, p327.
58: Ytterstad and Russell, 2012; Ytterstad, 2012, pp50–52.

dimension[59] of good sense. James Hansen makes no secret of the very bad relations that have developed between him and the US Congress over the years. Gramsci refers to good sense in the note entitled "Subversive" in the *Prison Notebooks* adding that the Italian word for subversive contains in it a critical first phase of class consciousness against "officialdom". Politically this consciousness can be mobilised by the right as well as on the left.[60] However, as Gramsci goes on to write, "the lower classes, historically on the defensive, can only achieve self-awareness via a series of negations, via their consciousness of the identity and class limits of their enemy".[61] Although global warming in the abstract concerns all living life, a "spirit of cleavage"[62] between those who rule and those who do not, is necessary to put good sense in motion. The blue-blue government we just elected in Norway is a horrible symptom of bourgeois hegemony. Seven of its ministers come from the denialist, racist Progress Party. As I write these lines, it is opening a cleavage the climate movement will need to sharpen even further in the coming period.

Use value rationality and anti-capitalism

The second part of this exposition of good sense on global warming is more concrete. All aspects of good sense must always be understood in particular contexts, but this is especially so for the relational and emergent resources of good sense briefly described above. The emergence of protest movements by definition happens in certain times and places. In this section I will look at how use value rationality and anti-capitalism emerged as elements of good sense, and in the next one I look at climate justice and livelihood.

Gramsci did not write that good sense was the healthy nucleus of common sense until late in his life in prison, in 1932.[63] His emphasis on truth, though, is detectable in his much earlier political writings. In June 1919, in the midst of the emergence of factory councils in Turin, he wrote that: "To tell the truth, to arrive together at the truth, is to achieve a communist and revolutionary act".[64] In my dissertation I propose that Gramsci discovered good sense during this period of workers' struggle,[65] and then

---

59: Ytterstad, 2012, pp47-50.
60: Ytterstad, 2012, see also Robinson, 2005.
61: Gramsci, 1971, pp272–273.
62: Thomas, 2009, p438.
63: According to Peter D Thomas this was a crucial year, for the coming together of Gramsci's philosophical "moments" (Thomas, 2009, ppxix, 39).
64: Gramsci, 1977, p68.
65: Ytterstad, 2012, pp46–47.

wrote about what he learnt more abstractly in the *Prison Notebooks* many years later. Here he writes of how the newspaper he edited, *L'Ordine Nuovo,* discovered how the workers developed "certain kinds of new intellectualism" and tried to "determine its new concepts".[66] As workers began to run the factories themselves, their perception of the purposes of that production began to change. Through seeing the factory "as a producer of real objects and not of profit", the worker gave "an external, political demonstration of the consciousness he has acquired".[67]

Put in the terms of Andrew Collier,[68] the truth that workers began to arrive at was a *use value rationality* on the brink of replacing the exchange value rationality that penetrates not just the economy but the entire social life of capitalism.

One illustration of use value rationality is the Norwegian biodiversity law, according to the Environmental Ministry among the most ambitious and far-reaching in the world. In its declaration of principles it lines up three fundamental ways we value nature. We have intrinsic value (*egenverdi*), use value (*nytteverdi*) and experiental value (*opplevelsesverdi*). All three sets of values can be subsumed under use value rationality because all of them primarily involve qualitative reasoning of the sort we would understand by practical sound judgment, which—incidentally—is also how good sense is referred to in English lexicons. Any interference in nature should negotiate between all these fundamentals, said the chief developer of the biodiversity law at a seminar I attended a few years ago. But while the authorities (pretend to) negotiate these values, exchange value continues to be fundamental to the metabolic relationship between capitalism and the environment.

Indeed, it is easier to grasp the generality (and variety) in use value rationality by way of its negation through exchange value rationality.[69] Paul Burkett has shown how respondents behave in surveys made within the discipline of "contingent valuation analysis", which is specifically aimed at setting a price on environmental goods, including those related to global warming. Burkett finds "common sense resistance" against price setting across cultural divides.[70] Joan Martinez-Alier contends that a great many of today's environmental conflicts are rooted in opposition to the commodity fetishism of capitalism "that sees only one way to value the world".[71] Indeed,

---

66: Gramsci, 1971, pp9–10.
67: Gramsci, 1971, p202.
68: Collier, 2003, pp23–36.
69: Foster, Clark and York, 2011, p39.
70: Burkett, 2009, p73.
71: Martinez-Alier, 2006, p274.

it is not difficult to find use value rationality and climate justice as both latent and emergent examples of good sense on global warming. This particular bit of anti-capitalism runs through environmental history. From the British poets responsible for the impulse called "back to the land" to Rachel Carson's *Silent Spring* in the US in the early 1960s; from the "wilderness idea" to the deep ecology of Arne Næss; from the workers in Manchester in the 1840s to Chico Mendez and the rubber tappers in Amazonia in the 1980s[72], there is opposition to a system that values everything in money, and ignores the intrinsic value of life, of human beings and of nature.

I remember reading intricate discussions in this journal,[73] of whether Marx's theory of commodity fetishism was too perfect an explanation to be accepted. I perceived it as a very abstract thing that explained too much. How can you ever break free, if—as Raymond Williams put it so wonderfully—capitalism reduces us to consumers, "stomachs or furnaces... being a very specialised variety of human being with no brain, no eyes, no senses, but who can gulp".[74] But it becomes more plausible if we perceive commodification not as an abstract theoretical category, but as "the historical development of the tension between the requirements of money-making and monetary valuation on the one hand, and the needs of human beings, of sustainable human development, on the other".[75] Such a view might explain why "Our world is not for sale!" was such a potent message in Seattle in 1999. As Naomi Klein and social movement academics have noted,[76] some of those sentiments hibernated after 9/11 and resurfaced in the climate justice movement with the slogan "Our climate is not your business" used outside venues of carbon trading. Klein, author of *No Logo*,[77] was the chief speaker at the opening rally of the "people's assembly" in Copenhagen in 2009. Her concluding words express the opposition to exchange value rationality on global warming rather eloquently: "Life may be coming to an end, because of too much obedience. We need a global mass movement. Think of it as the mother of all carbon offsets".[78]

72: Guha, 1999, brings out use value rationality within environmental movements and thinkers very well.

73: Some of it was occasioned by Alex Callinicos's book *Marxism and Philosophy* (Callinicos, 1983a); see also Callinicos, 1983b, for a glimpse of that debate.

74: Williams, 1989, p216.

75: http://mrzine.monthlyreview.org/2007/aguiar240407p.html

76: Reitan, 2012; Ytterstad and Russell, 2012.

77: Klein, 2000.

78: Ytterstad and Russell, 2012; Ytterstad, 2010.

Climate justice and livelihood

Use value rationality and anti-capitalism are fairly long-standing features of good sense, very relevant for the fight against global warming. The call for climate justice, by contrast, is more recent. It more clearly illustrates the *emergent* dimension of good sense, and is also more regional and culturally specific, emanating primarily from the Global South towards the Global North. Formally it is enshrined in principle 7 of the 1992 Rio Declaration on Environment and Development, which states: "In view of the different contributions to global environmental degradation, states have common but differentiated responsibilities." At the UN climate summits, some of the strongest moral appeals for radical global cuts in emissions have come from small island states such as the Maldives, who even brought in Mark Lynas as an adviser to their negotiating team in Copenhagen. The conception of necessity has driven Maldivians to take an uncompromising position, insisting, based on scientific projections, that the country "will disappear into the sea" if targets are not set at 350ppm, that is at 1.5 degrees global warming.[79] An even more radical climate justice perspective has emerged from Bolivia, echoing the important Cochabamba Conference in April 2010. Pointing not only to the historical debt of the Global North, but to the right for future atmospheric space for development, the demands of the climate justice activists in Cochabamba included a target to stabilise temperatures to one degree of warming and 300ppm, a full rejection of carbon markets and a "Universal Declaration on the rights of Mother Earth to ensure harmony with nature".[80]

The language of Mother Earth, Pachamama, reminds us of the importance of indigenous communities and cosmologies to the development of the climate movement. Some of the more principled rejections of exchange value rationality come precisely from the indigenous organisations present at such summits. Slogans against the green economy, because it was seen as a *greed* economy, were everywhere to be heard at the 50,000 strong demonstration against the sequel to the Rio Summit in 2012. "La Tierra no se Vende, La Tierra se Defiende!" (The Earth is not for Sale, the Earth is for Defending!)[81] No wonder that quite a few authors highlight agency from the Global South, and indigenous communities in particular, when they look for alternatives to neoliberal hegemony.[82]

79: Alstadheim and Stoltenberg, 2010, pp29–30. Although, as Patrick Bond (2012) has documented, outright bribery of the Maldives by Western countries, particularly the US, has contributed to stifle some of its good sense at international summits of late.
80: Bond, 2012, p198.
81: Personal observation (20.6.2012) and translation.
82: Carroll, 2010; Foster, 2009, pp52–53; Vetlesen, 2008.

Yet environmental justice has a history in the Global North as well, among anti-racists, (eco)feminists and among the poor in US cities.[83] Good sense is *relational*, not only between North and South, but between classes within countries as well.[84] And although some cosmologies may be better at expressing outrage in their good sense, the emergence of climate justice can be explained by more material factors. It is when global warming begins to be experienced and perceived as a human, social and political problem in its own right that climate justice may come to appear as the healthy core of common sense rather than a lofty ethical command. The class rage after Hurricane Katrina in New Orleans was well captured by the television series *Treme*. J Timmons Roberts suggests that:

> a high-water mark of the infant climate justice movement so far may have been when on 28 October 2002 thousands of activists marched for "climate justice" in the streets of Dehli, India, during the [UN conference of the parties to] the Kyoto treaty. In their Dehli Declaration, they affirmed that "climate change is a human rights issue—it affects our livelihoods, our health, our children and our natural resources".[85]

This idea of livelihood, encapsulating both the natural and social conditions of a decent life, seems to me a promising way of anchoring, and perhaps globalising, environmental justice. At the heart of a host of environmental concerns there is a profound experience of conflict. The other side have gone *too* far now; they have industrialised, polluted and emitted too much. They have chopped down too many trees, killed too many wild animals or meddled too much with the gene pool. It is the sensation that *some limit has been crossed that puts our livelihoods at risk*, which gives room for all the reflection and moral outrage, all the repentance and utopian visions, competing for good sense on global warming, and a host of other environmental issues as well.

Although Raymond Williams did not speak of good sense, livelihood was a concept he did develop in his ecological writings. This idea steers clear of two faultlines, "the received and dominant concept of the Earth and its life forms as raw material for generalised production" on the one hand and on the other hand the idea of "an apparently unmediated nature". Williams wants to "avoid a crude contrast between 'nature' and 'production', and to seek the practical terms of the idea which should supersede both: the idea

---

83: Bond, 2012, p167; Guha, 1999.
84: Wilkinson and Pickett, 2010; Ytterstad, 2012, pp47–50.
85: Roberts, 2007, p296.

of 'livelihood', within and yet active within, a better understood physical world and all truly necessary physical processes".[86] Livelihood is good sense for how we depend both on each other and on nature. When people speak of their livelihood, it is therefore a good place to look for good sense on global warming. Indeed, it is the rift in the metabolism between the eco-system and modern capitalism[87] that makes so many people in so many places worry for their livelihoods.

Summary and a few conclusions

As this article went to press, popular climate movements were on the rise again. On 21 September there were protests around the world against global warming with many of those involved raising radical anti-capitalist demands. The demonstration in New York was the largest ever on the issue. Just a few days before, the alliance between unions, environmentalists and the Norwegian church launched a campaign for 100,000 signatures demanding: "Put a brake on Norwegian oil extraction—100,000 climate jobs now!". These signatures will be collected up until 13 March 2015, when the next "Bridge to the Future" conference will be held in Oslo, where big national and international trade union leaders, bishops and environmentalists will be on the platform.[88]

The burning need to cut emissions fast has united many different people to put pressure on their leaders. I have called this "conception of necessity" the first resource of good sense on global warming, a resource every sane thinking person on this planet can have, but something Barack Obama and most leaders of this planet merely pretend they have. In reality they are not so interested in the truths of global warming as they are in pro-tecting business and national interests. Such an interest in truth, the second resource of good sense on global warming, is greater among the oppressed and among the best parts of the trade union movement. That is why it is so crucial to develop climate change solutions from below.

Facts alone seldom move scientists, but two facts are becoming clearer, and have started to move people, and encourage "labour movement participa-tion in global warming activism".[89] Fact one: Emissions are going up, up, up. Fact two: They need to come down, down, down. One reason why people and trade unions are beginning to move is due to evaluative realism, the third

86: Williams, 1989, p237

87: The metabolic rift is the key Marxist insight on the relationship between humans and nature, according to Foster, Clark and York, 2011.

88: http://broentilframtiden.com

89: www.labornotes.org/2014/07/climate-campaign-tipping-point-unions-get-board

part of the "healthy nucleus" of common sense in this article. The growth of protests, and in the case of Norway at least, of popular alliances, also illustrates the fourth and fifth resources, the relational and the emergent dimensions of good sense on global warming. Put simply, more people are getting angrier.

In the second part of this article, I have shown how movements themselves, working class movements and environmental movements, past and present, have developed good sense relevant to the fight against global warming. We have seen the spread of use value rationality and anti-capitalism, and the emergent feeling of climate (in)justice, prompted by changes in the climate that are already destroying the livelihoods of people. None of these consciousness resources are conclusive of good sense on global warming. Indeed, the full meaning and potential of good sense on global warming will only be disclosed in future mass struggles.

Finally, the most difficult question: What is the politics of good sense on global warming? The short answer is, I fear, that there is none. Or perhaps better: good sense on global warming facilitates a great variety of political strategies precisely because it consists of multiple resources, and because good sense on global warming is being developed—fast—by climate movements themselves. Autonomists may grab hold of one resource, and fight for the appropriate protest tactic accordingly. That is what seems to have happened with the radical wing of the climate justice movement.[90] Social democracy may incorporate snippets of another resource to renew and regreen itself and the capitalist hegemony it has come to terms with long ago.[91] That is what is happening now in Norway.

A revolutionary Gramscian politics of good sense on global warming must, by contrast, be both all-embracing *and* interventionist in character. It must be all-embracing because all the resources of good sense on global warming must be strengthened if we are to create truly great mass movements. We need to strengthen our understanding of the science and seriously explore all the uncomfortable truths of global warming, not just the ones Al Gore tells us about. We need to fight for climate jobs for workers in the rich North but we also have to build climate justice solidarity with people who have nothing in the Global South. One of the things I have learnt through the building of climate alliances in Norway is the need to tolerate, indeed encourage, all kinds of climate solutions from below.

90: Lahn, 2013; Reitan, 2012.
91: Jens Stoltenberg is surprisingly candid about how Norwegian social democracy is using capitalism to solve "the greatest challenge of our time", in an interview book on Norwegian climate change policy he himself asked for (Alstadheim and Stoltenberg, 2010).

Part of the interventionism, Leninism if you prefer, must be not just to strengthen each and every resource of good sense, but to bring them together to the best of our capability. Lenin argued for expanding trade union consciousness, which tends to be locally based, into a socialist consciousness. Socialists need to be "tribunes of the people" reacting with moral outrage on behalf of all oppressed groups. In the age of global warming, we must take this even further, to include everything that breathes in our common biosphere.

Jonathan Neale is, I think, onto the same interventionist approach when he writes: "In most cases we are talking to people who have green ideas in their heads about climate change and socialist ideas about economics. Our job is usually to bring the two sides of their heads together".[92] A revolutionary Gramscian and Leninist perspective is about trying to give coherence to the resources of good sense, in a way that opens the door to a different, working class led solution. In a revolution this strategy may be as concrete as the demands of the Russian one, for land, bread and peace. As global warming runs apace, such concrete demands may arise as the appropriate ones again, especially if the wager on working class leadership turns out to pay off again in the fight against environmental destruction. The ecological Marxist Paul Burkett believes, as does the present author, that it will, seeing the working class as:

> the only systemically essential group that directly experiences the limitations of purely economic struggles over wages and working conditions as ways of achieving human development, given the increasingly communal and global character of the environmental problems produced by capitalist production.[93]

If the global working class fights in earnest, for jobs, for the climate and for the planet, there is a chance that we can win a sustainable world. That is my bet, and the reason why my main focus as an activist in Norway is on the climate jobs solution. If I am right about the existence of the healthy consciousness resources outlined in this article, it is a reasonable bet. At the very least, good sense on global warming should help power the optimism of the will that socialists need to have, when we join and build climate movements wherever we are.

92: Neale, 2010.
93: Burkett, 2009, p300.

References

Alstadheim, Kjetil Bragli, and Jens Stoltenberg, 2010, *Klimaparadokset: Jens Stoltenberg om vår tids største utfordring*. (Aschehoug).

Berners-Lee, Mike, and Duncan Clark, 2013, *The Burning Question: We Can't Burn Half the World's Oil, Coal and Gas: so How do we Quit?* (Profile Books).

Blackledge, Paul, 2012, *Marxism and Ethics* (State University of New York Press).

Boggs, Carl, 1976, *Gramsci's Marxism* (Pluto Press).

Bond, Patrick, 2012, *Politics of Climate Justice: Paralysis Above, Movement Below* (University of KwaZulu-Natal Press).

Brown, Lester R, 2009, *Plan B 4.0: Mobilising to Save Civilisation* (Substantially Revised), (W W Norton & Company).

Burkett, Paul, 2009, *Marxism and Ecological Economics* (Haymarket).

Callinicos, Alex, 1983a, *Marxism and Philosophy* (Clarendon).

Callinicos, Alex, 1983b, "Marxism and Philosophy: a Reply to Peter Binns", *International Socialism* 19 (spring), www.marxists.org/history/etol/writers/callinicos/1983/xx/binns.html

Carroll, William K, 2010, "Crisis, Movements, Counter-hegemony: in Search of the New", *Interface Journal*, volume 2, number 2.

Carson, Rachel, 1962, *Silent Spring* (Penguin).

Coben, Diana, 2002, "Metaphors for an Educative Politics: 'Common Sense', 'Good Sense' and Educating Adults", in Carmel Borg, Joseph Buttigieg, and Peter Mayo (eds), *Gramsci and Education* (Rowman & Littlefield).

Collier, Andrew, 2003, *In Defence of Objectivity and Other Essays: on Realism, Existentialism and Politics* (Routledge).

Creaven, Sean, 2007, *Emergentist Marxism: Dialectical Philosophy and Social Theory* (Routledge).

Ekers, Michael, Hart, Gillian, Kipfer, Stefan, and Alex Loftus, 2013, *Gramsci: Space, Nature, Politics* (Wiley-Blackwell).

Flannery, Tim, 2005, *The Weather Makers: the History and Future Impact of Climate Change* (Atlantic Monthly Press).

Foster, John Bellamy, 1999, *Marx's Ecology: Materialism and Nature* (Monthly Review Press).

Foster, John Bellamy, 2009, *The Ecological Revolution: Making Peace with the Planet* (New York University Press).

Foster, John Bellamy, Brett Clark, and Richard York, 2011, *The Ecological Rift: Capitalism's War on the Earth* (Monthly Review).

Fæhn, Taran, 2013, "Climate Policies in a Fossil Fuel Producing Country: Demand versus Supply Side Policies", Discussion paper number 747 (17 June), *Statistics Norway*, www.ssb.no/en/forskning/discussion-papers/climate-policies-in-a-fossil-fuel-producing-country

Gillis, Justin, 2013, "Climate Maverick to Retire From NASA", *New York Times* (1 April), www.nytimes.com/2013/04/02/science/james-e-hansen-retiring-from-nasa-to-fight-global-warming.html?_r=0

Gramsci, Antonio, 1971, *Selections from the Prison Notebooks* (Lawrence and Wishart).

Gramsci, Antonio, 1977, *Selections from Political Writings: 1910-1920* (Lawrence and Wishart),

Guha, Ramachandra, 1999, *Environmentalism: A Global History* (Longman).

Hall, Stuart, 1991, "Postscript: Gramsci and Us", in Roger Simon, *Gramsci's Political Thought: An Introduction* (Lawrence And Wishart).

Hall, Stuart, 1996 [1986], "Gramsci's Relevance for the Study of Race and Ethnicity", in Morley, David, and Kuan-Hsing Chen (eds), *Stuart Hall: Critical Dialogues in Cultural Studies* (Routledge).

Harman, Chris, 1998, *Marxism and History* (Bookmarks).

Harman, Chris, 1999, *A People's History of the World: From the Stone Age to the New Millennium* (Bookmarks).

Hoggan, James, 2009, *Climate Cover-up: The Crusade to Deny Global Warming* (Greystone Books).

Ihlen, Øyvind, 2007, *Petroleumsparadiset: norsk oljeindustris strategiske kommunikasjon og omdømmebygging* (Unipub).

Jacobsen, Mark Z, and Mark A Delucci, 2011, "Providing all global energy with wind, water, and solar power, Part I: Technologies, energy resources, quantities and areas of infrastructure, and materials", *Energy Policy*, volume 39, issue 3.

Klein, Naomi, 2000, *No Logo: No Space. No Choice. No Jobs* (Flamingo).

Klein, Naomi, 2011, "Capitalism vs the Climate", *The Nation* (28 November), www.thenation.com/article/164497/capitalism-vs-climate

Lahn, Bård, 2013, *Klimaspillet: en fortelling fra innsiden av FNs klimatoppmøter* (Flamme).

Lohman, Larry, 2011, "Finalisation, Commodification and Carbon: the Contradictions of Neoliberal Climate Policy", *Socialist Register 2012: Crisis and the Left*.

Lynas, Mark, 2007, *Six degrees: Our Future on a Hotter Planet* (Fourth Estate).

Lynas, Mark, 2012, "Watermelons: How Environmentalists Are Killing the Planet, Destroying the Economy and Stealing Your Children's Future", *New Statesman* (16 February), www.newstatesman.com/node/183906

Malm, Andreas, 2007, *Det är vår bestämda uppfattning att om ingenting görs nu kommer det att vara för sent* (Atlas).

Malm, Andreas, 2013, "Sea Wall Politics: Uneven and Combined Protection of the Nile Delta Coastline in the Face of Sea Level Rise", *Critical Sociology*, volume 39, number 6.

Martinez-Alier, Joan, 2006, "Social Metabolism and Environmental Conflicts", *Socialist Register 2007: Coming to Terms with Nature*.

Marx, Karl, 2000, *Early Writings* (Prentice Hall).

McKibben, Bill, 2010, *Eaarth: Making a Life on a Tough New Planet* (Times Books).

Neale, Jonathan, 2008, *Stop Global Warming: Change the World* (Bookmarks).

Neale, Jonathan, 2010, "Climate politics after Copenhagen", *International Socialism* 126 (spring), www.isj.org.uk/?id=637

Nilsen, Alf Gunvald, 2009, "'The Authors and the Actors of their Own Drama': Towards a Marxist Theory of Social Movements", *Capital & Class*, volume 33, number 3.

Nilsen, Yngve, 2001, *En felles plattform?: norsk oljeindustri og klimadebatten i Norge fram til 1998* (Det humanistiske fakultet, Universitetet i Oslo).

Nun, José, and William Cartier, 1986, "Elements for a Theory of Democracy: Gramsci and Common Sense", *Boundary 2*, volume 14, number 3.

Oreskes, Naomi, and Erik M Conway, 2010, *Merchants of Doubt: How a Handful of Scientists Obscured the Truth on issues from Tobacco Smoke to Global Warming* (Bloomsbury).

Paine, Thomas, 1997 [1776], *Common Sense* (Dover Publications Inc), http://pinkmonkey.com/dl/library1/sense.pdf

Räthzel, Nora, and David Uzzell (eds), 2012, *Trade Unions in the Green Economy: Working for the Environment* (Routledge).

Reitan, Ruth (ed), 2012, *Global Movement (Rethinking Globalizations)* (Routledge).

Roberts, J Timmons, 2007, "Globalising Environmental Justice", in Phaedra Pezzullo and Ronald Sandler (eds), *Environmental Justice and Environmentalism: the Social Justice Challenge to the Environmental Movement* (MIT Press).

Robinson, Andrew, 2005, "Towards an Intellectual Reformation: The Critique of Common Sense and the Forgotten Revolutionary Project of Gramscian Theory", *Critical Review of International Social and Political Philosophy*, volume 8, number 4.

Ryggvik, Helge, 2010, *Til Siste Dråpe: om Oljens Politiske Økonomi* (Aschehoug).

Ryggvik, Helge, 2013, *Norsk Olje og Klima* (Gyldendal akademisk).

Sayer, Andrew, 2011, *Why Things Matter to People: Social Science, Values and Ethical Life* (Cambridge University Press).

Skjærseth, Jon Birger, and Tora Skodvin, 2003, *Climate Change and the Oil Industry: Common Problem, Varying Strategies* (Manchester University Press).

Thomas, Peter D, 2009, *The Gramscian Moment: Philosophy, Hegemony and Marxism* (Brill).

Vetlesen, Arne Johan, 2008, *Nytt klima: miljøkrisen i samfunnskritisk lys* (Gyldendal).

Wilkinson, Richard G, and Kate Pickett, 2010, *The Spirit Level: Why Equality Is Better for Everyone* (Penguin).

Williams, Raymond, 1989, *Resources of Hope: Culture, Democracy, Socialism* (Verso).

Ytterstad, Andreas, 2010, "Alle i samme båt?" in Kristin Skare Orgeret and Anne Hege Simonsen (eds), *Elisabeth Eide: det utålmodige mennesket* (Unipub).

Ytterstad, Andreas, 2012, *Norwegian Climate Change Policy in the Media: Between Hegemony and Good Sense* (PhD dissertation, Oslo University).

Ytterstad, Andreas, 2013, *100,000 klimajobber og grønne arbeidsplasser nå!* (Gyldendal).

Ytterstad, Andreas, 2014, "Framing Global Warming: Is That Really the Question? A Realist, Gramscian Critique of the Framing Paradigm in Media and Communication Research", *Environmental Communication: A Journal of Nature and Culture* (published online 21 May).

Ytterstad, Andreas, forthcoming, "Climate jobs as tipping point—Norwegian grassroots challenging the oil and climate change hegemony", in Kajsa Borgnäs, Teppo Eskelinen, Johanna Perkiö and Rikard Warlenius (eds), *The Politics of Eco Socialism—Transforming Welfare* (Routledge).

Ytterstad, Andreas, and Adrienne Russell, 2012, "Pessimism of the Intellect and Optimism of the Will: A Gramscian Analysis of Climate Justice in Summit Coverage", in Elisabeth Eide and Richard Kunelius (eds), *Media meets Climate: the Global Challenge for Journalism* (Nordicom).

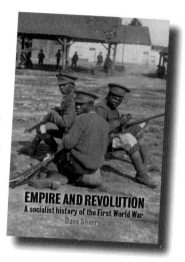

Theories of difference:
the Subaltern project examined

Talat Ahmed

A review of Vivek Chibber, **Postcolonial Theory and the Specter of Capital** *(Verso, 2013), £19.99*

Postcolonial theory has been the dominant intellectual trend within academia relating to studies of imperialism, decolonisation and the legacy of empire for the last two decades. Its central attractive feature has been to posit the non-Western world and its peoples as the subject of history and central agents shaping their own destiny. Postcolonial thinking has aimed to challenge the notion that the only way to understand the non-Western world is through its interaction and relationship with Europe and instead puts forward an intellectual agenda that seeks to "provincialise" Europe. The traditional Eurocentric framework assumes that non-Western societies essentially had no history worthy of the name until the impact of European colonialism as the dynamic for change. It was thought that progress in such societies could only come through a Western "civilising mission". For many scholars, students and anti-imperialist activists, postcolonialism represents a radical critique of all existing thinking about race and imperial power and, within this, the Subaltern Studies project stands out as a particularly inspirational framework for 21st century theorising about these questions.

The Subaltern project began life as a collective around the *Subaltern Studies* journal, published from Delhi in 1982 and focusing on South Asia. Over the next two decades 11 volumes emerged and several monographs, as scholars went beyond the limitations of traditional colonial narratives but more fundamentally also sought to challenge the nationalist historiography that had emerged during the struggle for colonial freedom. National liberation movements had rightly sought to overthrow conservative colonialist interpretations of their region's history, but they tended to replace one "Whiggish" story of progress with another, and though the authors of this narrative had brown and black skins, this often resulted in a rather narrow and elitist hagiography of "great men" as heroic figures of the anti-colonial struggle.

Taking their cue from Antonio Gramsci, who had written about "subaltern classes", as well as the English Marxist historian E P Thompson, who had visited India in 1976-7 and inspired a focus on "history from below", a group of historians of South Asia came together as part of the New Left that had emerged in India in the late 1970s. They consciously sought to offer a new theory of modernity for the Global South and posed this as a fundamental review of all existing theoretical paradigms. The whole raison d'être of Subaltern Studies had been to uncover the hidden histories of forgotten subjects such as peasants, workers, low caste and untouchable groups that traditional historical frameworks had neglected. Classic works like Ranajit Guha's *Elementary Aspects of Peasant Insurgency in Colonial India* and Dipesh Chakrabarty's essay, "Trade Unions in a Hierarchical Culture: The Jute Workers of Calcutta, 1920-50", showed the potentialities of this new historical approach.[1] Focusing on popular consciousness and subaltern agency, the merit of Guha's work was to locate peasant identity and consciousness within the conditions of rural India in terms of the relationship of the peasantry to dominant economic and political groups of landlords and moneylenders.[2] He questioned the use of colonial data, informed as it was by the categories of scientific racism stemming from the colonial sciences. Both the policies of the Raj and elitist national historiography utilised official data and followed its logic of defining peasant mass action as "criminal" and "pre-political" because it was seen as "unstructured movements of the masses".[3] Guha rightly condemns the selective use of these sources and the interpretations they advance for their denial of agency to peasant insurgency.[4] Similarly, Chakrabarty, an eminent labour historian, raises important questions on ideology and culture in his essay; particularly those concerning militant strike action alongside poor trade union organisation and the

---

1:    Guha, 1983; Chakrabarty, 1984.
2:    Guha, 1983, p8.
3:    Guha, 1983, p5.
4:    Guha, 1983, pp106-107.

continuing presence of a middle class syndicalist cadre—"the outsider-in".[5] Again he argues that the autonomy of jute workers was underplayed if the focus was primarily on workers' leadership and therefore ignored the hierarchical manner in which some forms of this intellectual leadership treated workers as a passive entity to be led. These earlier works were empirically informed, historically specific and thus carried an intellectual weight.

Locating itself within Gramscian and Thompsonian categories, the radical claims of Subaltern Studies would appear on the surface to lend itself to a broad Marxist analysis. Instead, as Vivek Chibber notes in his impressive new study of the Subaltern Studies collective, the group worked to overcome what they assumed were "the blinders imposed by Marxist theory".[6] Subalternism as a "discipline" has had limited scrutiny from left leaning academics or political activists. This makes Chibber's analysis extremely welcome as an important and pioneering Marxist critique that is the first thoroughgoing and comprehensive assessment of this project. Chibber excavates the foundational basis of the theoretical framework provided by the key figures of the collective: Ranajit Guha and Dipesh Chakrabarty, but also examines the much hyped and influential work of another collective stalwart, Partha Chatterjee.

Initially the founders of the Subaltern Studies project aimed to offer a distinct explanation for non-Western economic and political development. So for Guha, a key issue was why the path of non-Western societies differed so dramatically from those in Europe. For him with respect to India, the answer lay in the failure of the nationalist bourgeoisie to realise the universalising principle of capitalism. Whereas in Europe the rising bourgeoisie was able to refashion society in its own image, and completely destroy feudal relations, the Indian bourgeoisie achieved "dominance without hegemony" over the rest of society.[7] According to Guha, classic bourgeois revolutions in Europe saw a new revolutionary class take power that was then able—through the establishment of liberal bourgeois democracy—to integrate the interests of non-elite and subaltern groups within their own project, and so win these groups to identifying with the bourgeois revolutions. Capitalist modernity in India, by contrast, evolved with the "coexistence" of semi-feudal social relations with bourgeois property rights. This in turn created two separate spheres of discourse existing independently of each other—an elite arena comprising

---

5: Chakrabarty, 1984, p135.

6: Chibber, 2013, p10.

7: Guha, 1997, pp16; 19; 65; 102. This book was a seminal work that underpinned and continues to shape non-materialist explanations of development in the Global South.

a rich minority and a subaltern space inhabited by the vast majority of those excluded from the nationalist project.

Guha maintains that the English and French bourgeoisie were able to rule with consent as they succeeded in wedding subaltern groups—labouring classes, industrial workers, small artisanal groups, peasantry—to identify with liberal reforms, democratic order and elective assemblies. No such "universalising" took place in India. In India the national bourgeoisie could not speak for the majority of society; this is identified as the "structural fault" of the Indian bourgeoisie's lack of political ambitions. Chibber quite rightly takes Guha to task over his analysis and interpretation of the English and French Revolutions of 1640 and 1789 respectively stating that the revolutionary periods in Europe witnessed attempts by the new bourgeois class to "contain and suppress subaltern demands for representation" and to use "a significant dose of coercion" when necessary.[8] Thus it is demonstrated that the European experience of bourgeois revolutions was not as straightforward and linear as Guha implies. These revolutions took decades to unfurl and were fraught with contradictions and violent class struggles. At the end of this process the most radical element of the bourgeoisie lost its revolutionary character, as it sought to entrench its rule over the lower orders.

Chibber reminds the reader that capitalism does not universalise social organisation based on the consent of the governed. Rather, what is universalised is "the compulsion to produce in order to sell—production for exchange value, not for use". Capitalists, contrary to Guha's belief that the bourgeoisie will attempt to enact the will of the subaltern classes in a cross-class alliance, will fight for "a narrower, more exclusionary regime".[9] In fact the rising European bourgeoisie was focused on capitalist production but quite willing to allow earlier relations of power to remain so long as they could capitalise on newly developing methods of production. There was no mission to improve the quality of life of peasants and urban workers or promote democratic reforms and equality. These reforms, when they did appear, were the result not of bourgeois benevolence, but of agitation from below against the bourgeoisie; "capitalism has always striven not just for economic domination but also for political domination, inasmuch as the latter helps secure the viability of the former".[10]

Subaltern scholars use this flawed model of European transformation to move away from empirically informed research and to criticise the

---

8:   Chibber, 2013, p99.
9:   Chibber, 2013, p125.
10: Chibber, 2013, p152.

"methodological Eurocentricism" at the heart of historical writing. By the end of the 1980s Dipesh Chakrabarty, building on Guha's analysis, applies it to his detailed work on the jute industry in Calcutta. Here he concludes that jute mill workers of the period were "pre-individualist", inhabiting a "pre-capitalist culture" where community—not class—determined their consciousness.[11] Consequently, jute workers were incapable of participating consistently in modern forms of politics because the concept of trade unions as "bourgeois democratic organisation" was alien to this cultural space.[12] Even their relationship with trade union leaders was locked in a "*babu-coolie*" hierarchical structure.[13] Again colonial capitalism differed from "original" capitalism in the West because the former did not produce "bourgeois forms of power" as the nationalist ruling class did not penetrate popular domains. Instead what was produced was a "capitalism but without capitalist hierarchies, a capitalist dominance without a hegemonic capitalist culture, or in Guha's phrase 'dominance without hegemony'".[14]

Chakrabarty goes further to identify different types of authority being exercised by employers in Europe as compared to India. Under "proper" capitalism, power is exercised "through an articulated body of rules and legislation",[15] making this transparent, predictable and clearly demarcated. Conversely, Bengali jute mill employers exercised power in an arbitrary, personal and often violent manner.[16] This leads Chakrabarty to characterise labour relations in India as essentially paternalistic based on workers seeing managers in the role of *loco parentis* and accepting punishment as "parental" justice.[17] Chibber again takes issue over this simplified and mechanical interpretation of capitalist class relations. Using Marx's writings in *Capital*, he shows how capitalism is the most dynamic system that "can sustain a broad gamut of power relations and social identities", where "traditional institutions and identities can find new life within capitalism".[18]

Guha's conflation of liberal, nationalist historiography with Marxist theory is key to his weak postulations. Along the way he is dismissive of Marxist concepts and explanations of bourgeois revolutions as basically part of the same Western liberal ideological framework that does not apply to

---

11: Chakrabarty, 1989, p218.
12: Chakrabarty, 1989, p132.
13: Chakrabarty, 1989, p145.
14: Chakrabarty, 2000, p15.
15: Chakrabarty, 1989, p172.
16: Chakrabarty, 1989, pp170-177.
17: Chakrabarty, 1989, p163.
18: Chibber, 2013, p151.

India. The language used by Chakrabarty lays emphasis on religion, caste and village ties. Both emphasise cultural specificity, the uniqueness and exceptional character of Indian society. The assertion of divergence leads Guha and Chakrabarty to reify the very subaltern groups they set out to rescue from the "enormous condescension of posterity".[19]

Such ideas were initially seen as innovations within Marxism but Chibber argues that at each juncture the authors of Subaltern Studies moved further away from classical Marxism and linked their project to the most "dynamic trend in post-Marxist theorising"—postcolonial studies.[20] This trajectory is most pronounced in the widely quoted and super-trendy subaltern scholar Partha Chatterjee. He too emphasises the power of community consciousness for poor Bengali peasants where "alliances are not seen as the result of contracts based on common interests; rather, they are believed to be the necessary duty of groups bound together by mutual bonds of kinship".[21] Chatterjee insists there is an entirely different *psychology* in Western subalterns than Eastern. In the West political psychology revolves around secular conceptions of the individual and their rights; whereas in the East agency is motivated by the concept of duty or obligation, resulting in a religious orientation.[22] For Chatterjee peasant communitarian identity is central to rural politics which will generate "a project to write an *Indian history* of peasant struggles", not a "history of peasant struggles *in India*".[23] This theory of divergence is located in Chatterjee's analysis of anti-colonial nationalism, which he chastises for its adherence to the modernising agenda of the nation-state. He in fact refers to it as colonial nationalism because it is derivative of colonial forms of thought, at the heart of which are reason, science and the individual, notions associated with Enlightenment thinking.[24] Consequently, the Enlightenment is dismissed as a Western European mode of thinking every bit as nasty as colonialism because it perpetuates Western dominance, even after decolonisation. To underline this cultural variance Chatterjee makes a distinction between the "spiritual greatness of the East and the material advantage of the West".[25]

Chibber is quite rightly scathing about the nonsense this is predicated on and charges Chatterjee with reviving orientalist notions of Eastern

---

19: Thompson, 1980, p12.
20: Chibber, 2013, p8.
21: Chatterjee, 1993, p165.
22: Chibber, 2013, p153.
23: Chatterjee, 1993, p167, Chibber's emphasis.
24: Chatterjee, 1986, p43.
25: Chatterjee, 1986, p51.

culture in which actors lack individuality and are instead "other-oriented".[26] In his careful deconstruction of Chatterjee's *The Nation and Its Fragments*, Chibber demonstrates, with devastating panache, how the ostensible radical scholar ends up making the case for India's exceptional difference with the West as inevitable, the result of some age-old cultural traits. Chibber notes how in this framework there is an abandonment of historicism and its substitution with some timeless, inexplicable values. Chatterjee's grasp of nationalism is weak, superficial and impressionistic, and fused with an "inflated assessment of the role of ideas",[27] where capitalism is written out of the history of modern nation-states and the rise of nationalism. Not only are Marxist categories out of the window but for Chibber this is evidence not of radicalism but of its antithesis.

Another weakness of Subaltern Studies was how the early desire to focus on industrial workers and peasant agency quickly gave way to a looser and more eclectic definition of "subalterneity". This encompassed more fashionable concerns based on Michel Foucault's approach to power and knowledge and the weaknesses of Edward Said's *Orientalism* and hence an obsession with linguistic deconstruction and theorising for the sake of theorising, a method more suited to cultural and literary approaches than one based on a critical examination of historical evidence. Rather than trying to identify broad historical patterns and examining the relationship between exploitation and oppression, there was a celebration of "the fragment" which offered disconnected stories about the past. The rejection of "grand narratives" as "hierarchical" and "oppressive" resulted in conclusions based on voguish social theory and an increasingly turgid style of writing incomprehensible to most workers, peasants and low caste communities—those the group ostensibly championed—and, in reality, to many academics.

One example of this is the seminal but highly abstract essay by Gayatri Chakravorty Spivak, "Can the Subaltern Speak?".[28] Tantalisingly subversive as the title suggests, Spivak attempts to recover the voices of women about the practice of *sati* (widow self-immolation), which have been ignored in both Western and Hindu nationalist explanations. However, Spivak's method here is not particularly helpful or insightful, based as it is on a convoluted philosophical, existential discussion of what it means to be subaltern and with a puzzling conclusion that "the subaltern cannot speak". The explanation is that Western thought and knowledge denigrate non-Western forms of

---

26: Chibber, 2013, pp160-161.
27: Chibber, 2013, p281.
28: Spivak, 1988, pp281-283.

knowing by labelling these mythical and folkloric. So in order to be "heard" the subaltern has to mimic, learn and adapt to Western forms of knowledge, thereby dismissing their own reasoning processes, language and thought as folklore. Hence the subaltern cannot speak! This mode of thought legitimises the very object of what it seeks to dispute: it gives credence to the idea of exceptionalism in non-Western societies, that there is something intrinsically different in them, some unknown and un-quantifiable entity that is uniquely "indigenous". The notion of what constitutes indigenous is vague and, one suspects, deliberately so, to avoid the difficult question of how these non-Western societies have themselves been the product of change, conflict and a mass of contradictory phenomena.

Some critics have argued that Chibber conflates Subaltern Studies into postcolonial theory. There is some truth to this. Chibber's own Marxist understanding has been influenced by the intellectual framework of "Political Marxism" which has sought to place history at the heart of Marxist analysis, partly also under Thompson's inspiration. This was a necessary corrective to the plethora of ahistorical, intellectually unanchored and politically flawed types of research that dominate so much of academia, including regrettably what passes for Marxist, radical studies. Postcolonial theory's chief concern was the cultural legacy of the colonial project and the ongoing impact of imperialism in post-independent societies. Hence its focus on knowledge production and reproduction, cultural and social control and the power to represent, define and interpret colonial societies. Though a perfectly valid response to colonial experience, the analytical tools became Foucauldian, psychoanalytical, critical theory, and lately, gender-sex theory and an obsession with linguistic categories. As such it borrows heavily from postmodernist techniques and its intellectual heritage is firmly rooted in the poststructuralist school. Though it castigates colonial powers for "essentialising" the non-Western world as the "other" with fixed cultural traits, postcolonial theory nevertheless sees categories of "West" and "non-West" as given entities that have a timeless essence.

The distinction between Subaltern Studies and postcolonialism is that postcolonial theory expressly rejected Marxist analysis as every bit as Western and European as the colonial project. Their criticism is predicated on the well-worn shibboleths of Marxism being "Eurocentric, reductive, determinist" and consequently incapable of explaining the non-Western world. It is interesting to note how Foucault, feminist analysis of patriarchy and psychoanalytical studies are not seen as Western! Subalternist thinking began life on a more promising premise—to challenge nationalist interpretations of the postcolonial world as the only narrative that could explain pre-colonial, colonial and postcolonial history. It sought to interrogate a version of history that told the national story in a linear fashion and took a reductionist approach to exploitative and oppressive social relations among and within the "colonial" peoples. Through its championing of "subaltern" subjects it led an offensive against "essentialising" approaches based on notions of fixed cultural traits. But, as Chibber so ably demonstrates, the radical posturing of subaltern authors would target Marxism as much as colonial and nationalist interpretations.

Subaltern Studies did not aim to go down this route but Guha's understanding of Marxism was rooted in Stalinist orthodoxy encapsulated in the Communist Party of India (CPI), a tradition that held a stageist version of historical developments whereby colonial societies had to enter capitalism first before building for socialism. As such national movements were to be supported uncritically and independent working class politics from below suppressed in the "national" interest. This is the antithesis of classical Marxism as a theoretical tool and lies at the heart of the methodological and political flaws of the Subalternists. Guha was a member of the CPI and schooled within its Stalinist orthodoxy. In the post-1956 era after the Soviet invasion of Hungary many people resigned their membership of Communist parties—including E P Thompson. The courageous questioning of their political heritage sadly did not lead to a renewed effort to return to the tradition of Russia in 1917, of genuine revolution from below. Similarly in India the Subaltern collective did not try to reforge a new explicitly anti-Stalinist Marxist historiography, in part because of the growing intellectual fashion for poststructuralism internationally but more fundamentally due to the bastardised version of Marxism they had been taught. As Guha and others moved away from what they perceived as the "real" Marxist tradition, they abandoned Marxism altogether and their intellectual moorings became more fluid and unanchored.

Chibber is not claiming that all societies are identical or that there are not specificities that need explaining. This has been the charge against Marxism by postcolonial and subalternist thinkers. But this is based on a vulgar interpretation of Marxism that is a million miles from the deeply rich and creative tradition of classical Marxism, a tradition sadly closed to most Indian Marxists because of their Stalinist heritage. And if they challenged it in any way it was forms of Maoism, Guevarian politics and other Third Worldist notions that became the mainstays of Indian Marxism. The political practice has been dominated by a top-down version of socialism, and the CPI's entry into electoral politics resulted in corrupt parliamentary cretinism and a deep compromise with local and international capital.

Chibber's understanding of bourgeois revolutions and their outcomes owes much to the scholarship of Ellen Meiksins Woods and Robert Brenner, with which this journal differs on some major questions. Nevertheless, Chibber's careful dissection of early Subaltern thought exposes the simplified, mechanical and mistaken interpretation at the heart of their explanation for the rise of the bourgeoisie and capitalist class relations.

Chibber is at pains to defend Enlightenment values as universal, particularly against charges of "Eurocentrism". This is all the more reason to point out that the Enlightenment was not the sole preserve of European thinking. Notions of scientific rationality, reason and political rights were deeply influenced by ideas emanating from across the Eurasian landmass, and in this produced a cultural fusion entailing Islamic, African and Asiatic civilisations. Marx himself was a child of the Enlightenment but he went way beyond its bourgeois constraints towards a truly global universalism of working class self-emancipation.

Although Subaltern scholars claim to offer a new theory of global modernity of the South, and to stand in the great radical traditions of the 20th century "shorn of their analytical and critical infirmities",[29] regrettably, Subaltern Studies has demonstrated through its embrace of the postcolonial theoretical paradigm that it is beholden to many of the analytical and critical infirmities of the poststructuralist and postmodernist template.

Chibber recognises that scholars and students are open to questioning the orthodoxies of classical liberalism, nationalism and the limitations of postcolonial theory and with that predisposed to a healthier scepticism of the previously unquestioned authority of the Subaltern Studies project. In spite of the deep disfigurement of Stalinism there has been some good historical writing on South Asia using a Marxist framework with the aim of trying to present an integrated and whole picture of historical phenomena. Damodar Dharmananda Kosambi's pioneering *An Introduction to the Study of Indian History*; Irfan Habib's *The Agrarian System of Mughal India 1556-1707* and his *A People's History of India* volumes; Ram Sharan Sharma's book *Indian Feudalism*; Romila Thapar's work on the social history of Ancient India and Sumit Sarkar's seminal work on the Swadeshi Movement and his theoretical work *Writing Social History* are all exemplars of how to write history: historically informed, intellectually rigorous, theoretically coherent, methodically researched and politically committed.[30] With the exception of

---

29: Chibber, 2013, p284.
30: Kosambi, 1956; Habib, 1963; Habib, 2001-4; Sharma, 2005; Thapar, 1966; 2003; Sarkar, 1973; 1998.

Thapar, who is not a Marxist, all the above have operated under a clear Marxist framework that is not characterised by reductionism or determinism. Paradoxically, despite their schooling in the Indian Communist tradition, the scholarship of this generation of historians has been marked by sensitivity to the creative and powerful impulses of classical Marxism as a method to understand historical developments in the Global South.

Chibber is correct to point to the limitations and flaws of both postcolonial studies and the Subaltern Studies project and to the general hostility towards Marxism that these schools of thought have encouraged. Rather than illuminating how capitalism has impacted on Indian society, Subaltern Studies ends up obscuring and, worse still, resurrecting Orientalist categories. One key question that the book hints at but does not fully develop is why these ideas have come to such prominence in the last three decades or more. Chibber notes that the path taken by Subaltern Studies was simply keeping pace with "broader shifts".[31] And these shifts demonstrate how scholastic techniques do not exist in a vacuum. Interest in Marxist ideas could rise in the late 1960s and early 1970s, set as they were against a backdrop of momentous struggles initially on the part of students but taking a more militant organised working class orientation into the 1970s. Likewise we need to locate the intellectual moorings of postcolonial theory in the lack of sustained, combative onslaught by the organised working class—subordinate groups—to shift the balance of class forces back in our direction irreversibly. Postmodernism and postcolonial studies have evolved from poststructuralist theoretical paradigms, where class is a thing of the past and if it has any relevancy it is only in so far as it is one of several categories alongside gender, ethnicity, "tribal" identity, caste, region, religion, and so on. There is a material basis for why certain intellectual trends develop and take root among radical scholars and students. Postcolonial theory has been a product of retreat, in spite of its radical posturing. Its supposed "chicness" is more evidence of a lack of rigour and shallowness than serious intellectual labour.

Sadly, Subaltern Studies, for the reasons mentioned above, has not challenged but accommodated to the whole gamut of post/anti-Marxist theoretical agendas so beloved by the academic establishment. Chibber has provided a valuable historical survey of the Subaltern intellectual agenda from its promising beginning to this ignoble endpoint, and it deserves to be widely read and critically discussed by all those seeking a way out of the theoretical impasse represented by postcolonial theory.

31: Chibber, 2013, p7.

References

Chakrabarty, Dipesh, 1984, "Trade Unions in a Hierarchical Culture: The Jute Workers of Calcutta, 1920-50", in Ranajit Guha (ed) *Subaltern Studies*, volume 3 (Oxford University Press).

Chakrabarty, Dipesh, 1989, *Rethinking Working-Class History: Bengal 1890-1940* (Princeton University Press).

Chakrabarty, Dipesh, 2000, *Provincialising Europe: Postcolonial Thought and Historical Difference* (Princeton University Press).

Chatterjee, Partha, 1986, *Nationalist Thought in the Colonial World: A Derivative Discourse* (Zed Books).

Chatterjee, Partha, 1993, *The Nation and its Fragments: Colonial and Postcolonial Histories* (Princeton University Press).

Chibber, Vivek, 2013, *Postcolonial Theory and the Specter of Capital* (Verso).

Guha, Ranajit, 1983, *Elementary Aspects of Peasant Insurgency in Colonial India* (Oxford University Press).

Guha, Ranajit, 1997, *Dominance without Hegemony: History and Power in Colonial India* (Harvard University Press).

Habib, Irfan, 1963, *The Agrarian System of Mughal India 1556-1707* (Asia Publishing House).

Habib, Irfan, 2001-4, *A People's History of India* (4 volumes) (Tulika).

Kosambi, Damodar Dharmananda, 1956, *An Introduction to the Study of Indian History* (Popular Book Depot).

Sarkar, Sumit, 1973, *The Swadeshi Movement in Bengal, 1903-1908* (People's Publishing House).

Sarkar, Sumit, 1998, *Writing Social History* (Oxford University Press).

Sharma, Ram Sharan, 2005, *Indian Feudalism* (Macmillan India).

Spivak, Gayatri Chakravorty, 1988, "Can the Subaltern Speak?", in Cary Nelson and Lawrence Grossberg, *Marxism and the Interpretation of Culture* (Macmillan).

Thapar, Romila, 1966, *A History of India: Volume 1* (Penguin).

Thapar, Romila, 2003, *Early India: From the Origins to AD 1300* (Penguin).

Thompson, E P, 1980, *The Making of the English Working Class* (Penguin).

Debating imperialism

Adrian Budd

A review of Leo Panitch and Sam Gindin, **The Making of Global Capitalism: The Political Economy of American Empire** *(Verso, 2012), £20*

As the world commemorates the centenary of the First World War (with limited awareness of its meaning) a book by two leading Marxists that explores contemporary imperialism demands our careful assessment.

A century ago there were two broad Marxist approaches to imperialism. Firstly, there was Karl Kautsky's theory of "ultra-imperialism" which suggested the potential for the replacement of rivalry by an alliance of the imperialist countries against subordinate parts of the world. The second approach, the classical Marxist perspective of inter-imperialist rivalry developed by Lenin and Bukharin, argued that competitive capital accumulation produced giant firms that operated increasingly internationally and enlisted their home states in their conflicts with other nations' capitals. The bloodshed and horrors of the war and subsequent decades showed that rivalry provided a superior explanation of international capitalist dynamics.

By 1971 Bob Rowthorn noted the emergence of an additional perspective. He argued that a new US super-imperialism had developed in which the US dominated other capitalist powers and had become the "organiser of world capitalism", able to contain such antagonisms as did appear.[1]

1:    Rowthorn, 1971, p31. Rowthorn refers only to the West since, unlike the tradition of this journal, he did not see the USSR as capitalist or the Cold War as a form of inter-imperialism.

Panitch's and Gindin's work sits squarely in this camp, with occasional nods towards ultra-imperialism.

Based on earlier collaborative work and an impressive amount of research, *The Making of Global Capitalism* (henceforth *TMGC*) provides a comprehensive history of US capitalism and the economic statecraft mobilised to open the global economy to US influence over the last century or so.[2] *TMGC*'s focus is captured in its first two sentences:

> This book is about globalisation and the state. It shows that the spread of capitalist markets, values and social relationships around the world, far from being an inevitable outcome of inherently expansionist economic tendencies, has depended on the agency of states—and of one state in particular: America.[3]

What has emerged from the US state's role in the development of globalised capitalism, including the imposition of US-designed rules for the global economy, is "the American informal empire, which succeeded in integrating all the other capitalist powers into an effective system of coordination under its aegis".[4] This is not Michael Hardt's and Toni Negri's *Empire*, within whose post-national space the idea of rival national imperialisms is outdated.[5] Nor does it neatly correspond to the transnationalist perspective developed by Marxists like William Robinson, because neither a transnational capitalist class nor a global state based on the International Financial Institutions (IFIs) is emerging. In the first place, *TMGC* notes that capital's national roots and institutional linkages remain important, and that US multinational corporations, however international, remain American rather than transnational.[6] Meanwhile, the IFIs were an expression of US post-war power and remain sites of negotiation and coordination between separate "national systems of regulation among the advanced capitalist states".[7] Nevertheless, *TMGC* shares with these perspectives the view that US hegemony has so successfully contained conflicts within the West that the idea of inter-imperialist rivalry is no longer helpful.

2: See Panitch and Gindin, 2004, 2005a, 2005b, 2005c.

3: Panitch and Gindin, 2012, pvii.

4: Panitch and Gindin, 2012, p8.

5: Hardt and Negri, 2000.

6: Panitch and Gindin, 2012, p345, footnote 26. See also Jones, 2006.

7: Panitch and Gindin, 2012, p235. On transnationalism see Robinson, 2004. For a critique, see Budd, 2007.

Appearance and essence

Most of this review concerns Panitch's and Gindin's understanding of imperialism, but other aspects are worthy of comment. Their argument that states, particularly the US state, remain central to globalised capitalism is a welcome riposte to wilder claims about the retreat of the state before the power of capital. But the relation of states to capitalism's wider social relations and the underlying dynamics of capitalist relations of production are somewhat under-explored, and certainly under-theorised. Therefore the US state appears relatively unconstrained in its ability to oversee and transform other states and the world system. While the US has been very successful in orchestrating other states, globalised capitalism is not simply the product of US state planning.

The overestimation of agency over deeper structural determinations is repeated in the analysis of economic crisis. Marxism explains capitalist crises (for all that each has specific features and immediate causes) by reference to underlying social relations, particularly by the competition between capitals that helps to generate the tendency of the rate of profit to fall. Panitch and Gindin, by contrast, highlight the actions of social forces. While they register a decline in profit rates from the late 1960s, they explain the 1970s economic crisis chiefly by reference to workers' rising confidence and ability to increase wages in the advanced capitalist states after over two decades of the long post-war boom.[8] Similarly they contend that the post-2007 crisis was caused by financial volatility rather than "a profit squeeze or collapse of investment due to general overaccumulation", since "profits and investments had recovered strongly since 1982".[9] The danger of this focus on agency is that it carries the possibly unintended message that capitalism can stay healthy, and profit rates high, if the working class share of national income remains subdued and better policies or regulations are pursued.

A focus on immediate agency not adequately rooted in underlying relations may also explain *TMGC*'s over-estimation of the incorporation of the working class into US capitalism. Given workers' experience of exploitation, the argument that neoliberalism has "materially integrated" US workers via debt-driven consumerism that renders them dependent

---

8:    For critiques of this theory of crisis see Brenner, 1998, and Harman, 1984.

9:    Panitch and Gindin, 2012, p20. This is part of their wider claim that neoliberalism has "resolved" US capitalism's 1970s profitability crisis, which "came to an end" after 1982 (p164). This is hardly supported by their own table (pp182-183), which shows a recovery in after-tax profits in 1982-3 but further declines in five of the next nine years. More generally, many leading Marxist economists demonstrate that profit rates have barely risen over recent decades—see Choonara, 2012.

on rising stock markets and asset values (if they own property) tells only part of the story. Workers may indeed be fatalistically resigned to consumerist fantasies to some extent, particularly after the defeats for the unions that preceded (and enabled) the neoliberal turn. In the short term this may have "had a profoundly negative impact on working class organisation and culture" but it is hard to see that "individualised consumerism rather than collective services and a democratised state and economy became the main legacy of working class struggles in the 20th century".[10] Aside from its pessimism, this perspective underplays the persistence of, and popular support for, welfare states and suggests that consumerism can provide more than a mere short-lived smoothing of capitalism's antagonistic class relations. A better and more dialectical starting point in explaining the relative lack of labour-movement resistance to neoliberalism is Gramsci's concept of contradictory consciousness. A similarly dialectical and many-sided appreciation of the antagonisms and contradictions at its heart would also greatly help Panitch's and Gindin's analysis of the American empire.

Contemporary imperialism

Panitch and Gindin argue that the US that has successfully organised other capitalist powers behind its globalising project has not suffered relative decline, as many others claim. This argument has some powerful elements. The US still has the world's largest economy, continues to account for roughly half the world's research and development, and US corporations remain leaders in most strategically important high-tech industrial sectors.[11] The US state remains strategically vital to the rest of the world, capable of influencing the decisions of and imposing rules (on banking and accountancy, etc) on all others, and the US dollar is central to the world's financial and trading systems.

A key part of the construction of the American empire that *TMGC* highlights has been the US's ability to "internationalise" other states, which thereby "accept some responsibility for promoting the accumulation of capital in a manner that contributed to the US-led management of the international capitalist order".[12] This sometimes demonstrates US structural power—setting domestic rules (on tax, banking regulation, etc) that others feel compelled to accept—and sometimes the use of a disciplinary power designed to send a message to other states, as when the US mobilised the IMF against Britain's

---

10: Panitch and Gindin, 2012, p339.
11: Starrs, 2014, updates this argument.
12: Panitch and Gindin, 2012, p8.

Labour government in 1975-6. In internationalising other states, *TMGC* argues, the US managed to "largely efface the interest and capacity of each 'national bourgeoisie' to act as the kind of coherent force that might have supported challenges to the informal American empire".[13]

Many of Panitch's and Gindin's arguments about relative decline and internationalisation challenge received wisdom and methods of measurement. If the US is in decline, how can its capitals dominate virtually all key industrial sectors? Why, if China is on course to displace the US as the world's major power, as many argue, does Chinese capital barely register in these key sectors? How is hegemonic decline squared with the US ability to set rules for the global trade and financial systems? These questions suggest that we need nuanced thinking on decline, but they do not demand that we simply deny it: the US economy does account for a slowly declining share of world output (the EU is declining far more rapidly), which imposes pressures on the US state in terms of its domestic legitimacy and ability to mobilise resources to maintain its global primacy. For all that the US has managed to slow its decline in the quarter century since Paul Kennedy warned of "imperial overstretch", and although US primacy seems likely to persist for many years, the world is increasingly multi-polar.[14] This is barely registered in *TMGC*.

TMGC's account of internationalisation also tells only part of the story. In a world of plural states, underpinned by the economics of competitive accumulation, each state seeks to influence others, their economic and strategic environment, the world's major powers, and the rules governing international relations of various kinds. This lies behind US attempts to internationalise other states, but they too have their interests. Subordinate states do not passively accommodate superpower demands and even among strategic allies there is negotiation, consultation, compromise and occasional resistance.[15] These various forms of conflict are under-played in *TMGC*'s account of internationalisation. They are not equally significant, and perhaps too much is made of minor intra-Western squabbles over trade or state support for the capitals operating on particular national territories.[16]

13: Panitch and Gindin, 2012, p11.

14: See Kennedy, 1989.

15: Hannes Lacher's concept of the national/global dialectic, whereby all states defend their interests by projecting their powers into the international system while being simultaneously subject to the pressures of that system, provides a useful way of understanding the limits of "globalisation" and the context within which all states operate. See Lacher, 2003.

16: In one sense the 2014 spat between Germany and the US over electronic espionage was a minor issue. But imagine how we might feel on discovering that someone we had a shared interest with—say a partner or work colleague (let alone a manager!)—was intercepting our emails.

But these conflicts of interest point to a structured competitive rivalry, albeit within limits, that is quite marginal in the image *TMGC* presents of a relatively smoothly and consensually integrated American empire. That competitive rivalry is the basis for the persistence of inter-imperialist rivalry.

Geopolitics

Having successfully internationalised other states, and facing no "coherent challenge" to its informal empire, Panitch and Gindin see the US as "the ultimate guarantor of capitalist interests globally".[17] Consequently, they argue, the West's ruling classes are now so integrated under the US empire that they no longer have antagonistic interests and the classical Marxist perspective of inter-imperialist rivalry is outdated.[18]

The continued defence of the classical Marxist theory of imperialism is disparagingly labelled "economism". Logically, therefore, the superiority of Panitch's and Gindin's approach would be spelled out, but there is a significant omission in their work, which offers no developed theorisation of why politics should be prioritised in the analysis of empire, or of the relationship between capital and states, economics and politics.[19] Indeed, the focus on US financial power, albeit aided by the actions of the US state, gives *TMGC* an economistic flavour of its own. This is underlined by the neglect of the area of geopolitics, and specifically that most political of acts—war. This in turn means that *TMGC* is almost silent on one key (and in recent years very visible) aspect of the US state that is at the heart of its enquiry, namely its military power projection and strategic planning.

It is unclear from *TMGC*'s analysis of the apparently pacifying power of the US informal empire why the US accounts for approaching half the world's military spending. Nor does it address the shared commitments of US geostrategists: there are certainly tactical differences between, say, Zbigniew Brzezinski, one of Barack Obama's key advisers, and the neoconservatives who shaped the foreign policy of Bush junior, but there is a bipartisan commitment to the strategic goal of securing American global primacy and deterring the emergence of peer competitors. A key aspect of that primacy, for Brzezinski, is US control of Eurasia (including its "enormous concentration of natural gas and oil reserves") in order to prolong political fragmentation

---

17: Panitch and Gindin, 2012, p11.
18: Indeed, they suggest that past inter-imperialist rivalry resulted from "the role of pre-capitalist ruling classes", thereby absolving capitalism of responsibility for the horrors of war—Panitch and Gindin, 2012, p5.
19: For important attempts at such theorisation by writers in the tradition of this journal see Callinicos, 2009, and Harman, 1991.

and "prevent the emergence of a hostile coalition that would eventually seek to challenge America's primacy".[20] That others shared Brzezinski's perspective was demonstrated by the almost complete elite consensus around the Iraq war of 2003, albeit that it eroded slightly once the occupation began to face Iraqi opposition. Yet *TMGC* contains only four entries on Iraq, none of them dealing with the war and its significance, which was to assert US leverage over energy supplies to other major powers, including its allies, and demonstrate that it is the rule-enforcer of last resort.

Also missing in *TMGC* is any discussion of the geopolitical aspects of China's rise. But, as recent and continuing events around China's land and sea borders (with Japan, Taiwan, North and South Korea, India, Vietnam, in the South China Seas, etc) indicate, China has not simply been internationalised to support the US informal empire but defends and projects its own interests. It does so within a structured framework of rivalries, and it is an awkward fact for *TMGC* that China's increasing articulation with the global economy has been accompanied by its own military modernisation and aggrandisement on the one hand, and Obama's "pivot to Asia", which entails a military reorientation towards the Asia-Pacific region to contain China, on the other. The perspective of inter-imperialist rivalry seems best suited to explaining this.

The geopolitical and military dimensions of world order remain significant because capitalism's fundamentally anarchic and competitive nature ensures that it can never be anything other than uneven and uncontrollable. As the size and market power of separate capitals constantly rise and fall, the pecking order of capitalist states is subject to constant change, even within the most integrated Western core of the system. Who, for instance, could have predicted after the USSR's collapse, the deepening of US-led globalisation and, in 2003, the rapid destruction of Saddam Hussein's regime, that the US would later suffer the debacle in Iraq that contributed to its relative powerlessness over Crimea, Syria, Israel's attack on Gaza, and the rise of the Islamic State in 2014? But states do not react passively to unevenness and setbacks, and it is inconceivable that US strategists are not planning their response to these vicissitudes. As the astute transnationalist theorist Kees van der Pijl argues (against Kautsky but also applicable to a lesser extent to Panitch and Gindin), "the argument against the idea of a stable, collectively managed capitalist world order remains valid".[21]

20: Brzezinski, 1997, p198.
21: Van der Pijl, 2006, pxi.

Conclusion

TMGC is an important book. It contains a wealth of illuminating material and perceptive arguments and repays careful reading. I have criticised it not to score points but because those who would change the world must look reality in the face, comprehend it as accurately as possible and fashion appropriate methods to transform it. Much of *TMGC* helps us to do that, but its core argument is one-sided and lacks a dialectical appreciation of how inter-imperialist rivalry has been both transformed and preserved as the US has risen to a position of primacy.[22]

The inter-imperialist rivalry of a century ago was modified by the mid-20th century by one of its own consequences, namely the emergence of superpower imperialism during the Cold War. Today the global economic integration and primacy of a single superpower that *TMGC* explores signal a further modification. But, while US power contributes to the satisfaction of the world's ruling classes' common interest in the stability and reproduction of global capitalism, and helps to keep conflicts between them in check, competition between national ruling classes has not disappeared, and the US is a participant in that competition. The US, then, is subject to what Doug Stokes calls "dual national and transnational logics", promoting its own interests while simultaneously seeking to secure a world order safe for capitalism as a whole.[23] Thus the contemporary world order is best understood as an inter-imperialist system modified and conditioned by the primacy of a pre-eminent (but not always dominant) superpower. Within this framework there is a persistent dialectic of cooperation and competition, accommodation and rivalry.

To understand the contemporary world order in this way is not to underestimate capitalism's capacity to contain conflict and absorb shocks, but neither is it to overestimate its coherence and strength. The latter error, which I believe Panitch and Gindin fall into, risks missing opportunities to present a socialist alternative to the horrors of empire that they too would like to see consigned to the history books.

22: There is a parallel with monopoly—a consequence of competition that formally transcends but simultaneously preserves it.
23: Stokes, 2005, p230.

References

Brenner, Robert, 1998, "The Economics of Global Turbulence", *New Left Review* I/228, http://newleftreview.org/I/229

Brzezinski, Zbigniew, 1997, *The Grand Chessboard: American Primacy and its Geostrategic Imperatives* (Basic Books).

Budd, Adrian, 2007, "Transnational Marxism: a Critique", *Contemporary Politics*, volume 13, number 4.

Callinicos, Alex, 2009, *Imperialism and Global Political Economy* (Polity).

Choonara, Joseph, 2012, "Round-up on political economy", *International Socialism 136* (autumn), www.isj.org.uk/?id=853

Hardt, Michael, and Antonio Negri, 2000, *Empire* (Harvard University Press).

Harman, Chris, 1984, *Explaining the Crisis* (Bookmarks).

Harman, Chris, 1991, "The State and Capitalism Today", *International Socialism 51* (summer), www.isj.org.uk/?id=234

Jones, Geoffrey G, 2006, "The Rise of Corporate Nationality", *Harvard Business Review* (October), http://hbr.org/2006/10/the-rise-of-corporate-nationality/ar/1

Kennedy, Paul, 1989, *The Rise and Fall of the Great Powers* (Vintage).

Lacher, Hannes, 2003, "Putting the State in its Place: the Critique of State-Centrism and its Limits", *Review of International Studies*, volume 29, number 4.

Panitch, Leo, and Sam Gindin, 2004, "Global Capitalism and American Empire", *Socialist Register 2004: The New Imperial Challenge*.

Panitch, Leo, and Sam Gindin, 2005a, "Finance and American Empire", *Socialist Register 2005: The Empire Reloaded*.

Panitch, Leo, and Sam Gindin, 2005b, "Euro-Capitalism and American Empire", in David Coates (ed), *Varieties of Capitalism, Varieties of Approach* (Palgrave Macmillan).

Panitch, Leo, and Sam Gindin, 2005c, "Superintending Global Capital", *New Left Review* II/35, http://newleftreview.org/II/35/leo-panitch-sam-gindin-superintending-global-capital

Panitch, Leo, and Sam Gindin, 2012, *The Making of Global Capitalism* (Verso).

Robinson, William I, 2004, *A Theory of Global Capitalism: Production, Class, and State in a Transnational World* (John Hopkins University Press).

Rowthorn, Bob, 1971, "Imperialism in the Seventies—Unity or Rivalry?", *New Left Review* I/69, http://newleftreview.org/I/69/bob-rowthorn-imperialism-in-the-seventies-unity-or-rivalry

Starrs, Sean, 2014, "The Chimera of Global Convergence", *New Left Review*, II/87, http://newleftreview.org/II/87/sean-starrs-the-chimera-of-global-convergence

Stokes, Doug, 2005, "The Heart of Empire? Theorising US Empire in an Era of Transnational Capitalism", *Third World Quarterly*, volume 26, number 2.

Van der Pijl, Kees, 2006, *Global Rivalries from the Cold War to Iraq* (Pluto Press).

Psychopolitics in the Twenty First Century: Peter Sedgwick and radical movements in mental health

The work of Peter Sedgwick and in particular his classic text PsychoPolitics (1982) has a renewed relevance in the context of 'austerity', the privatisation of welfare provision and emergent forms of radical activism in mental health. This conference will provide an opportunity to explore Sedgwick's ideas and assess his legacy in light of these contemporary developments. The organisers welcome proposals for papers/workshops from academics, service users/survivors and mental health practitioners.

Venue: Liverpool Hope University,
Taggart Avenue, Liverpool L16 9JD

Date: Wednesday 10th June 2015

For more information on the conference contact
Rich Moth: **mothr@hope.ac.uk**or Helen Spandler: **HSpandler@uclan.ac.uk**.

To join the mailing list or submit a paper proposal email:
sedgwickconf2015@hope.ac.uk

Organised by Department of Social Work, Care and Justice, Liverpool Hope University and **supported by**: Social Work Action Network (SWAN), Asylum: the Magazine for Democratic Psychiatry, UCLan Schools of Social Work and Health, Journal of Critical and Radical Social Work

"Anti-politics" and the return of the social: A reply to Alex Callinicos

Tad Tietze and Elizabeth Humphrys

> The concrete analysis of the concrete situation is not an opposite of "pure" theory, but—on the contrary—it is the culmination of genuine theory, its consummation—the point where it breaks into practice.

> Lukács: *Lenin: A Study in the Unity of his Thought.*[1]

In his diagnosis of the causes of the crisis of the radical left in the last issue of this journal,[2] Alex Callinicos criticised the "anti-politics" analysis that we have developed over recent years, in particular at our blog Left Flank.[3] Surveying the current context we stand by our delineation of three distinct but interrelated types of "anti-politics": A widespread popular mood; the emergence of political projects that attempt to capitalise on this mood; and a revolutionary socialist strategy to overcome the state (and, therefore, the practice of politics centred on it) once and for all. We contend that Callinicos's objections rest on two errors: theoretical confusion about the relationship between society and politics, and a muddled "concrete analysis of the concrete situation".

1: Lukács, 1970, p43.
2: Callinicos, 2014.
3: http://left-flank.org/

A generalised crisis of politics

The comparative strength of bourgeois politics throughout most of the 20th century led to confusion among Marxists about the relationship between society and politics. Mass parties and related organisations like trade unions drew millions of people into direct political activity and into seeing the state as a site where their social interests could be represented. The era of mass democracy obscured the reality that the state's primary interest was the maintenance of capitalist social relations against the interests of the vast majority of people. Social power was represented within the state only in a distorted, debased, or estranged way via political parties associated with classes, other social groups or policies. Further, the practice of politics—in both parliamentary and more "radical" forms—tended to channel the social weight of the organised working class into the limits set by the state. Rather than going onto enemy terrain to disrupt its logic, such engagement with politics more often adapted to its rules, leading to the diffusion, derailment and disorganisation of social resistance.

As we argued in the article Callinicos directly addresses, our starting point was to locate the popular reception to Russell Brand's attack on the political system in "the crisis of representation that leads most people to see politics as completely detached from their lives. Crucially, this detachment is not caused by the political class being less 'representative' of their social base than in some previous era; rather, its lack of a social base makes the political class's actual role in representing the interests of the state within civil society more apparent." Further, it is the separation of the state from civil society that "creates the appearance of representation, one that masks the underlying social relations of domination. It is this appearance that is now breaking down".[4]

Australia provides a useful case study. Labourism was the pivot around which Australian politics was organised during the 20th century, and popular detachment from politics since then has been driven by the decline of the Labor Party's social base in the unions, whose membership and strength have collapsed in the last 30 years. This was in part because the unions actively participated in a social contract with the Labor governments of 1983-96 that drove through "neoliberal" restructuring. At the time the union left around the Communist Party argued this "accord" represented the apex of working class political action.[5]

By the time of the most recent Labor government (2010-13) the party was suffering state election results and national opinion polling comparable

---

4:   Humphrys and Tietze, 2013.
5:   Tietze, 2012; Humphrys, 2012; Humphrys and Tietze, 2014.

to lows not seen since the Great Depression. Up to a third of its former base has defected to the Greens Party, which itself underwent a serious setback after entering an alliance with Labor.[6] And in case people thought this was just a crisis of one side of politics, the right wing Tony Abbott government has experienced the worst first 12 months of a new government since regular polling began, with its austerity agenda under serious threat. These are just the latest instalments in a protracted political derailment, and the dysfunction is sufficiently bad that elite commentators publicly fret that the system is no longer capable of delivering pro-business "reform". Meanwhile media discussion of the anti-political mood among voters is everywhere. Importantly, this is happening despite Australia avoiding a serious economic downturn after 2008, alongside a very low level of social struggle since the mid-2000s.

While the specifics vary in different countries, similar patterns emerge. The late Peter Mair's *Ruling The Void* details the hollowing out of the political system in Europe in the decades leading up to the crisis of 2008, measured in terms of collapsing party memberships, declining voter allegiance, growing electoral volatility, the deterioration of associated organisations and increasingly negative social attitudes towards politics and politicians.[7] This has taken place in countries like Greece, Spain and Portugal where dictatorships collapsed in the 1970s, even though the resultant democratic settlements initially seemed to rest on solid institutional roots in civil society for their stability and cohesion.[8] While recent economic chaos has accelerated these processes of decline, they long predate the current era of "austerity".

Under capitalism *all* politics is *necessarily* "capitalist politics" precisely because "the political" only exists as a separate—and alienated—sphere in modern, bourgeois society. This is why we say that a consistent strategy of social revolution must be "anti-political": because by ending the capitalist state and moving to replace capitalist social relations with an organisation of freely associated producers, the social revolution will remove the material basis of a separate politics. Our position is not that intervention into politics or "taking power" is unimportant. On the contrary, we think that understanding the precise nature of the relationship between the social and political—and how this plays out concretely in the present—is an essential precondition of knowing how to intervene in the sphere of politics so as to maximise the chance that social struggles can defeat the limits constantly being imposed by the political.

6:   Tietze, 2013.

7:   Mair, 2013.

8:   See, for example, Kampagiannis, 2013 on Greece.

Anti-political social movements?

Unless we start with the capitalist nature of previously robust political structures we can fall into a one-sided view that their decay necessarily limits social progress. It is true that in recent times minority sections of the right such as UKIP and the French National Front have taken advantage of popular revulsion with the political class, but Callinicos is wrong to imply that the prevailing anti-political mood tends to lead to regressive outcomes. By way of contrast, the example of Spain is one that raises questions about where the crisis of politics might lead and what kinds of social struggles may emerge as a result. Callinicos only touches on the 15-M ("Indignados") movement, despite it being the largest and most radical social movement of the last 15 years in the West, perhaps because it so clearly contradicts his narrative.[9]

While 15-M was similar in form to other movements originating in square occupations, such as "Occupy", Syntagma and Gezi, it reached far deeper into Spanish society than these, and at its height some 6 million people were directly involved. Yet the movement was also characterised by a high level of antipathy to politics, including an initial refusal to allow trade unions, political parties and even the revolutionary left to participate in openly organised form. One of 15-M's central slogans was *"No nos representan"* ("They don't represent us") and the movement erupted in the lead-up to the 2011 general election at a time when the traditional left was seen as part of the problem, quite understandably, given the unions' deal with the Socialist government to wind down resistance to austerity in 2010. The recent meteoric rise of Podemos—an electoral intervention expressing both a sharp critique of "the political caste" and the social demands of 15-M that won 8 percent of the vote in European elections within months of being formed—further poses the question of how anti-politics might relate to radical struggle.[10]

The disdain for political parties within 15-M and other recent movements is more acute than that within the anti-capitalist movement over a decade ago. Yet the Marxist left tends to dismiss the growing antagonism of social movement participants towards existing politics as a kind of infantile disorder to be corrected. This reminds us of the kind of incomprehension at social change Bob Dylan was referring to when he sang: "Something is happening here/But you don't know what it is/Do you, Mr Jones?"

Nevertheless, Podemos—a left political project relating to the anti-political mood—is not without contradictions, in particular its ambiguous position regarding the state. As its campaign chief Íñigo Errejón made clear

---

9: Stobart, 2014a; 2014b.
10: Stobart, 2014c.

in a recent essay, he does not see the party's relentless attacks on "the political caste" as a critique of politics or the state *per se*. In his view Podemos's version of social change would occur through the radical reshaping of existing state structures, not a revolution against the state. Quite brazenly in the light of the struggles that dominated the three years preceding Podemos's breakthrough, Errejón claims:

> We dared to criticise the rigidity of the concept of "social", which constitutes a separate entity that precedes politics, and which needed first to accumulate forces, and only then could translate electorally. Contrary to the argument claiming that there is "no shortcut", defended by "movementist" currents and the extreme left, Podemos—born from "above" and not "from below"—argues that election time is also a time of articulation and construction of political identities. [11]

This argument for subordinating social interests to the primacy of politics finds its echo in the approach of much of the Marxist left, depending as it does on the kind of inverted view of society that Marx criticised in Hegel and others in the 1840s. For Marx, on the other hand, the basis of politics is to be found in the social relations that constitute bourgeois civil society.[12]

The struggle inside Podemos, which has drawn thousands of activists into a more centralised and focused national body, is therefore one between those like Errejón whose focus is on delivering change from above (with the movements acting as a prop for this) and those who want to make it a vehicle for progressive social transformation from below. Because Podemos was born of radical social struggles, its fate is not pre-determined. But it ultimately depends on whether it is content to become another player on the existing terrain of politics or whether it tries to mobilise what Marx and Engels called "the real movement" against the state.[13] The panic induced by Podemos in Spain's elites is tied up with the threat of the latter and not the former.

Theoretical confusion and weaknesses of analysis

In his article Callinicos writes, "The trouble is that the state, the broader political process of which it is the focus, and the parties that struggle over it remain fundamental determinants of the social, whatever autonomists

---

11: Errejón, 2014.
12: Marx 1975a; 1977.
13: Marx and Engels, 1968.

and neoliberals fondly claim".[14] As with Errejón this represents a reversal of Marx's argument. Callinicos also quotes Daniel Bensaïd's suggestive formulation that politics involves "transfigured social antagonisms".[15] Bensaïd seems to us to be saying much more than politics simply being the "concentration" of capitalist social relations, yet whenever Callinicos returns to the relationship between social and political contradictions he either conflates them or implies a fairly direct connection. It is the specific nature of this relationship, of politics and the state being estranged or abstracted expressions of capitalist society, that is crucial. It's not for nothing that Marx sometimes called the capitalist state an "abstract state" and even "this supernaturalist abortion of society".[16]

Further, when Callinicos writes that "the state operates in the interests of capital, but this does not mean that struggles over the state are all versions of bourgeois politics"[17] he conflates two types of struggle: those that are social and those that are merely political. That is, he confuses struggles where ordinary people take action to change society in their own interests—including in relation to the state—with political activities that merely seek a change in the policies, personnel or form of the state. Of course, there are many struggles that contain both types of activity, but by definition communism is the result of a struggle for social emancipation that ends the state, not a struggle that stops at political emancipation in relation to the state, a distinction Marx drew most famously in "On the Jewish Question".[18]

We believe that Callinicos's theoretical confusion on the relationship between society and politics, one shared by most of the radical left, also lies at the core of our disagreement over the nature of the current period and the problems of the left.

Callinicos charges us with "worse still", making "the present situation seem better than it is" by associating the anti-capitalist left with "anti-politics".[19] We presume this reflects his desire to paint the rise of anti-politics as a negative development. Instead, when he writes that "capital is economically weak, but much stronger politically, less because of mass ideological commitment to the system than because of the weakness of credible anti-capitalist alternatives",[20] he gets things completely upside-down. The social

---

14: Callinicos, 2014, p115.
15: Bensaïd, 2013, quoted in Callinicos, 2014, p118.
16: Marx, 1975a; 1966.
17: Callinicos, 2014, p118.
18: Marx, 1975b.
19: Callinicos, 2014, p119.
20: Callinicos, 2014, p111.

and economic dominance of capital over labour is much greater than 30 or 40 years ago, in large part because the defeats of the 1970s and 1980s undermined workers' collective social strength. The ability of capitalists to push the costs of the current crisis onto workers through job losses, wage cuts and productivity drives is evidence that this has not been reversed. On the other hand, organised politics has been undergoing all kinds of convulsions and meltdowns despite the relative absence of powerful "from below" organisations and struggles like those of the last "upturn".

Clarifying the roots of a crisis that spans the entire political spectrum, one which the radical left has found itself caught up in despite relating to explosive mass struggles over the last 15 years, is therefore at the centre of our analysis.

Callinicos claims that, "In equating 'communism' with anti-politics, Humphrys and Tietze make concessions to the autonomist myth that it is possible to change the world without taking power and thereby to renounce strategy".[21] While many will read his labelling of our argument "autonomist" as an insult—in particular because the term was used to attack dissident members in the SWP's recent crises—we think Callinicos's characterisation also emerges from his theoretical confusion. Furthermore, it seems to be designed to distract from how, far from renouncing strategy, we make an argument about the nature of the period that has profound strategic implications.

Callinicos, meanwhile, splits the journey of the European radical left into two phases: an "era of good feelings" up to mid-2005 where it "began to have an impact on the bourgeois political scene" on the back of mass movements; and an era of fragmentation once the movements receded. We find his account unpersuasive.

Firstly, of the "radical left" parties Callinicos mentions, only the SSP (Scottish Socialist Party) and Respect actually fit his periodisation in terms of measures like electoral results, let alone their relationship to patterns of struggle. In the absence of a more empirically-based argument it's hard to avoid the conclusion that Callinicos is projecting the SWP's experience onto quite different circumstances elsewhere.

Secondly, he treats the radical left in relative isolation from the general malaise of bourgeois politics, in particular the openings thereby created. Attention to such factors would, for example, explain Die Linke's 2009 *increase* in vote over its 2005 breakthrough during relative social quiescence—on the basis it was underpinned by the worsening of the SPD's fortunes through its coalition with Angela Merkel.

21: Callinicos, 2014, p119.

Finally, we think Callinicos gives a one-sided account that focuses too much on the power of "objective" factors in the left's problems, at the expense of lending his analytical skills to a much-needed critique of radical left strategy. He sees the progress of the radical left as limited much more by the lack of sustained "economic class struggle" than any subjective errors. Even the disastrous decision by Rifondazione Comunista to join a centre-left governing coalition that betrayed its supporters in the social movements is given short shrift in order to sustain an overarching narrative of circumstances beyond any political actor's control. This strikes us as class struggle fatalism. We fail to see how such fatalism will develop the political clarity needed to avoid repeating the cycle of hope and despair Callinicos depicts.

Conclusion

The rise of "anti-politics" in the current period is a product of the breakdown of the political order that prevailed in many rich capitalist countries for much of the 20th century. While this has created space for some political projects of the left and right to take advantage of popular disdain for political elites, it has also thrown light on the relationship between the social and political spheres of modern capitalism. The Spanish experience, discussed above, most sharply poses the question of how the interests of the great mass of people can be won—through relatively uncritical participation within the logic of capitalist politics or through social struggles that seek to challenge that logic? It is possible that this wave of anti-politics will end with "the political" reasserting itself in a new form on some quite different social basis, but without overturning capitalism—that is, if there is no social emancipatory movement that can come out on top instead.

Recognising "anti-politics" is not the same as negating intervention in the political sphere. But it means that the goal of such interventions is to surpass the alienated sphere of the political instead of perpetuating it. We cannot conjure social struggles out of thin air, but neither do we do ourselves any favours by pre-empting them with the demand they conform to the rules of the political game.

References

Bensaïd, Daniel, 2013 [2004], *An Impatient Life: A Political Memoir* (Verso).

Callinicos, Alex, 2014, "Thunder on the Left", *International Socialism* 143 (summer), www.isj. org.uk/?id=994

Errejón, Íñigo, 2014, "Spain's Podemos: Inside View of a Radical Left Sensation" (15 July), *Revolting Europe*, http://revolting-europe.com/2014/07/15/spains-podemos-inside-view-of-a-radical-left-sensation/

Humphrys, Elizabeth, 2012, "Still Stuck in the 1980s? The Unions and the Accord", *Overland*, https://overland.org.au/2012/08/still-stuck-in-the-1980s-the-unions-and-the-accord/

Humphrys, Elizabeth, and Tad Tietze, 2013, "Anti-Politics: Elephant in the Room" (31 October), *Left Flank*, http://left-flank.org/2013/10/31/anti-politics-elephant-room/

Humphrys, Elizabeth, and Tad Tietze, 2014, "Qantas and Job Losses: the Reality of Union Decline must be Faced" (5 March), *The Guardian*, www.theguardian.com/commentisfree/2014/mar/05/how-relevant-are-australian-unions

Kampagiannis, Thanasis, 2013, "The Greek Crisis: Between Democracy & Dictatorship?" (20 November), *Left Flank*, http://left-flank.org/2013/11/20/greek-crisis-democracy-dictatorship/ (Original in Greek in *Σοσιαλισμός από τα κάτω*, journal of SEK: the Greek Socialist Workers Party)

Lukács, Georg, 1970, *Lenin: A Study on the Unity of His Thought* (NLB), www.marxists.org/archive/lukacs/works/1924/lenin/

Mair, Peter, 2013, *Ruling the Void: The Hollowing of Western Democracy* (Verso).

Marx, Karl, 1966 [1871], "First Draft", in *The Civil War in France* (Foreign Languages Press), www.marxists.org/archive/marx/works/1871/civil-war-france/drafts/ch01.htm

Marx, Karl, 1975a [1843], "Critique of Hegel's Doctrine of the State", in: Marx, Karl, 1975, *Early Writings* (Penguin).

Marx, Karl, 1975b [1843], "On the Jewish Question", in Marx, Karl, 1975, *Early Writings* (Penguin), www.marxists.org/archive/marx/works/1844/jewish-question/

Marx, Karl, 1977 [1859], "Preface", in *A Contribution to the Critique of Political Economy* (Progress Publishers), www.marxists.org/archive/marx/works/1859/critique-pol-economy/preface.htm

Marx, Karl, and Frederick Engels, 1968 [1845], "Chapter I", in *The German Ideology* (Progress Publishers), www.marxists.org/archive/marx/works/1845/german-ideology/ch01a.htm

Stobart, Luke, 2014a, "Whatever happened to the Indignados? 1: Radical Struggle" (17 March), *Left Flank*, http://left-flank.org/2014/03/17/whatever-happened-indignados-part-1/

Stobart, Luke, 2014b, "Whatever happened to the Indignados? 2: Regime Crisis" (24 March), *Left Flank*, http://left-flank.org/2014/03/24/whatever-happened-indignados-2-regime-crisis-uprisings/

Stobart, Luke, 2014c, "Spain shows that the 'Anti-Politics' Vote is not a Monopoly of the Right" (28 May), *Guardian*, www.theguardian.com/commentisfree/2014/may/28/spain-podemos-anti-politics-not-monopoly-right

Tietze, Tad, 2012, "ALP's Condition Terminal? A Crisis of Social Democracy" (12 March), *The Drum*, www.abc.net.au/news/2012-03-12/tietze-alp-condition-terminal-crisis-of-social-democra/3883978

Tietze, Tad, 2013, "A Change in the Order of Things? The Left, the Greens and the Crisis", *Overland* 212 (spring), https://overland.org.au/previous-issues/issue-212/feature-tad-tietze/

SAY IT LOUD!
Marxism and the fight against racism

Brian Richardson (ed)

£9.99

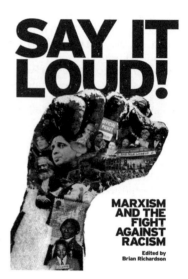

This major new book seeks to challenge the idea that racism is inevitable by taking a critical look at the origins and history of racism in Britain and abroad.

It looks in particular at the experience of the last 30 years in Britain, from the 1981 riots through Stephen Lawrence and the war on terror.

Highlighting key examples of black and white unity, resistance and struggle in the US and Britain, it intervenes in current debates about racism and how we fight it.

Out now from Bookmarks.

Bookmarks the socialist bookshop
1 Bloomsbury Street, London WC1B 3QE
020 7637 1848   www.bookmarksbookshop.co.uk
publications@bookmarks.uk.com

BOOKMARKS
PUBLICATIONS

Marxism, psychology and genocide: a reply to Andy Ridley

Sabby Sagall

A ndy Ridley's review of my book on genocide, *Final Solutions: Human Nature, Capitalism and Genocide*, charges me with two principal errors: psychologism and, less centrally, a mistaken analysis of the social basis of Nazism. Taking the second one first, Ridley asks: "Was it just the German middle classes that harboured such murderous potential?"[1] Numerous studies by sociologists and social theorists such as Hans Gerth, Arthur Schweitzer, Seymour Martin Lipset, Michael Kater, as well as Marxists, have identified the middle class as the section of society that experienced the kind of oppression that made them most prone to crisis and consequent membership of and support for the Nazi party.

Ridley makes an additional error in describing Adolf Hitler as Austrian. Hitler was born in Austria, but into a German family, members of a minority German community. As such, Hitler resembled other famous ultra-nationalist outsiders: Napoleon, born in Corsica, and Joseph Stalin, born in Georgia.

However, Ridley's main criticism of my book is that its attempt to analyse the motivation of the perpetrators of the Holocaust is psychologistic. He backs this up by arguing that my use of psychoanalysis is wrong:

> The psychology of the perpetrators is made over-determinant in the historical process... The Holocaust can only be fully understood in the

---

1:   Ridley, 2014, p208.

complex, dynamic and changing context of imperialism, German military expediency and defeat…tensions between the Nazi leadership and German capital, profound economic crisis, a fractured German state and a weak and opportunistic ruling class.[2]

Ridley, furthermore, criticises the Marxist psychoanalysts Erich Fromm and Wilhelm Reich for failing "to give enough weight to the class conflict and the changing material, social and political conditions underlying the rise of fascism and the road to the Holocaust".[3] Ridley thus rejects the contribution of the Frankfurt School (though Reich was not a member) who sought to reconcile Marxism with the insights provided by the psychoanalytical tradition.

My reply is threefold. Firstly, Ridley ignores the extensive historical, sociological and political analyses I provide as the main context within which Nazism arose: from the manner in which German capitalism developed at the end of the 19th century to the social and economic crises of the different sections of the German middle class following Germany's defeat in the First World War and the economic impact of the Great Depression.[4]

Secondly, as I make clear, both Reich and Fromm locate the Nazification of the German middle classes in the context of the development and crisis of German capitalism. I quote Reich's analysis: "The rapid development of the capitalist economy…the continuous and rapid mechanisation of production, the amalgamation of the various branches of production in monopolistic syndicates and trusts, form the basis of the pauperisation of the lower middle class merchants and tradesmen." Fromm, moreover, writes: "Nazism resurrected the lower middle class psychologically while participating in the destruction of its old socio-economic position. It mobilised its emotional energies to become an important force for the economic and political aims of German imperialism".[5] Therefore, for both Reich and Fromm, class, and capitalist development and crisis, must be at the heart of any analysis of Nazism and the Holocaust.

Ridley argues, further, that Fromm and Reich fail to give enough weight to the "delusional and deranged" nature of Nazi ideology. This is certainly a feature of the Holocaust that I deal with in my book: "The adoption of the Final Solution reflected Nazism's delusional notion of the Jews as

---

2: Ridley, 2014, pp207, 208.
3: Ridley, 2014, p207.
4: Sagall, 2013, pp186-200.
5: Sagall, 2013, pp201, 200.

the all-powerful masters of the world, a belief that was pathological in virtually a clinical sense." I quote here the American psychoanalyst Heinz Kohut who described Hitler's "grandiose fantasy [which] contains elements of a magical-sadistic control over the world".[6]

Thirdly, and most importantly, I reject Ridley's claim that my analysis is psychologistic. Indeed, he sets up a straw man: "Bad parenting was not the root cause or driving force of Nazi atrocity, nor was a supposed German middle class 'authoritarian personality'".[7] My argument was never that family life and an authoritarian social character were the be-all and end-all of Nazism and the Holocaust, merely that they formed one link in the chain of explanation, that they played a role, one that psychoanalysis helps us understand and that Marxists should not ignore.

Are Reich's notion of "character structure" and Fromm's concept of "social character" psychologistic? According to Fromm, social character is "the essential nucleus shared by members of a group which has developed as the result of the basic experiences and mode of life common to that group...the specific form in which human energy is shaped by the dynamic adaptation of human needs to the mode of existence of a given society".[8] Ridley argues for concentration on a "materialist" analysis of the Holocaust. Surely it is clear that Fromm's and Reich's concepts are firmly rooted in material, social and historical conditions. They are useful tools enabling us to mediate between the external structures of exploitation and oppression and the minds of individuals and social classes.

I would, therefore, reject Ridley's claim that my approach to the psychology of fascism is "abstract, essentialist and static". It would possess those features if I had described a mentality that always remained the same, irrespective of the historical circumstances, and which had no historical referent. But it is precisely the concept of social character—with its corollary of predisposition and precipitation—that enables me to avoid those pitfalls.

But Ridley ignores this distinction between a psychological predisposition, consisting of an inner tendency, a set of emotional features such as anger, hatred, anxiety, depression, rooted in the historical experience of an individual or a class, which, however, is not active at all times, and the specific precipitating conditions that activate it. It is indeed a major social, economic or military crisis that precipitates such a predisposition into actual murderous acts. Both predisposing and precipitating factors are necessary if we are to provide a

---

6:    Sagall, 2013, p220.
7:    Ridley, 2014, p208.
8:    Sagall, 2013, p67.

fully rounded explanation, one that is both theoretically valid and empirically plausible. As regards precipitating factors, in *Final Solutions* I argue that the Nazis came to power because of the deep crisis of German capitalism ushered in by the Great Depression, and that the decision to carry out the Holocaust was probably triggered by defeat on the Russian front.

My description of the German middle class authoritarian social character means that this group broadly shared a set of personal character-istics that made them, because of their history, and under certain historical circumstances, more predisposed to respond in a destructive manner than was the case with other social classes, eg the German working class. This also answers the question Ridley poses: "Why hadn't the German middle classes acted on these impulses earlier?"[9]

Hence my analysis of the psychology of fascism is not "static" or "essentialist" since I show how it changed under changing historical condi-tions. Nor is it "abstract" since it is backed by empirical data. Psychoanalyst Henry Dicks undertook a chilling study of the mentality of a group of SS killers. Klaus Theweleit provided a fascinating analysis of middle class pathology in his analysis of the writings of members of the Freikorps fol-lowing Germany's defeat in the First World War. And I quote the psychiatric tests on Adolf Eichmann carried out by I S and S Kulcsar and L Szondi.[10]

The logic of Ridley's position is that the only valid approach to the subjective aspect of Nazism is at the level of ideology, ie conscious ideas. Feelings, conscious and unconscious, shared by large numbers of the German middle class in the 1920s and 1930s, which later culminated in the enormous destructiveness on the part of a minority, are not part of a legiti-mate analysis of Hitler's support.

Nor is my analysis "deterministic". I argue that "the concept of social character, in both social theory and psychoanalysis, was developed in an attempt to bridge the gap between structure and agency, between society and individuals or groups, to see human behaviour as both determined by and in turn determining social structures".[11]

Moreover, I reject Ridley's charge that I give "class conflict and changing social and political conditions" secondary importance.[12] At the heart of my analysis is the notion that it was the historical crisis of the German middle classes that was, potentially, the root of their Nazification,

---

9: Ridley, 2014, p208.
10: Sagall, 2013, p204.
11: Sagall, 2013, p64.
12: Ridley, 2014, p207.

and that it was the crisis of German capitalism that activated this potential. I also make it clear that "the disastrous failure of the left to unite against Hitler abandoned Germany to the Nazis".[13]

Ridley seems not to accept that a multi-dimensional analysis is required—one that attempts to identify the many facets of a highly complex set of historical phenomena, including the subjective elements, and to link them in an organic whole. This is surely what a dialectical approach involves. He concedes that "psychology has its part to play in any Marxist historical analysis",[14] but he offers no clue as to what this might be, so it seems more formal deference than real commitment to understanding the mentality of the perpetrators.

In contrast, my argument is that:

> psychoanalysis—because of its dynamic approach, its appreciation of the way the past casts its shadow over the present, its materialist focus on the family and hence on society, and because of its understanding of unconscious sources of motivation—is the psychological theory best equipped to dealing with the subjective factors at the heart of political and social action, in this case genocide.[15]

We cannot comprehend psychic or emotional phenomena such as feelings and motives through the application solely of economic, political or even ideological concepts. This is true both at the individual and the collective level. In other words, there is an area of human existence that is irreducibly subjective, that cannot be flattened out by the weight of our objective social relations or understood simply as their mirror image. Some of the greatest Marxist historical writers such as Edward Thompson and Leon Trotsky showed a very good understanding of this.

The attempt to unite the objective socio-economic historical processes with their subjective emotional aspect is the essence of the Frankfurt School. But the subjective dimension is one link in the chain, not the whole explanation. Ridley argues that "the deranged views and violent fantasies of the Nazis were born of irrational and racist ideology".[16] Now, does he believe that "deranged views and violent fantasies" are solely an ideological or intellectual phenomenon? Are they not, in addition and more

---

13: Sagall, 2013, p200.
14: Ridley, 2014, p208.
15: Sagall, 2013, p5.
16: Ridley, 2014, p208.

precisely, expressions of a pathological emotional life? In other words, are they not expressions of feelings, many unconscious, factors to be explained in the first instance by psychological rather than purely ideological factors? If so, then again we need a psychology, albeit one that fits into a Marxist analysis of history and society, that explains how large groups of people, perhaps the majority of the members of a social class, came to share such feelings of hatred and anger towards other groups.

The logic of Ridley's position seems to be that we can develop an analysis of Nazism and the Holocaust without a psychological element in the explanation. He charges me with psychologism but does he not risk slipping into economic determinism, implying that we can proceed directly from socio-economic crisis to racism and genocide without a mediating link such as "social character"? In my view, British Marxism has often mistakenly tended to ignore the subjective, psychological element in the historical process. Sadly, Ridley's review perpetuates this error.

References

Ridley, Andy, 2014, "Dark Thoughts: Psychology and Genocide", *International Socialism* 143 (summer), www.isj.org.uk/?id=985
Sagall, Sabby, 2013, *Final Solutions: Human Nature, Capitalism, and Genocide* (Pluto).

Book reviews

An episode from the end of empire
John Newsinger

Aaron Edwards, **Mad Mitch's Tribal Law: Aden and the End of Empire** (Mainstream Publishing, 2014), £20

On 3 July 1967 the Argyll and Sutherland Highlanders, under the command of Colonel Colin "Mad" Mitchell, reoccupied the town of Crater in Aden. The town had been in the hands of the insurgent National Liberation Front since the mutiny and uprising of 20 June that had left 22 British soldiers dead and 31 wounded. The reoccupation was accompanied by a great press celebration of British prowess and the lionisation of Mitchell himself. He became a media favourite as the hero who had restored British prestige and pride and put the Arabs in their place. Once back in control, the Argylls set about dominating the town by a policy of "no-nonsense toughness" that once again had the enthusiastic support of the right wing press for whom Mitchell could do no wrong. Accusations of brutality were routinely dismissed.

Mitchell, however, was a loose cannon. Harold Wilson's Labour government was absolutely committed to withdrawal from South Arabia whereas Mitchell clearly believed that his "robust" methods could have turned the tide against the insurgency and that this outpost of empire could have been held if the political will

had been there. Elements within the military and the intelligence agencies were never to forgive Wilson for this retreat. At the time, however, Mitchell was a continual embarrassment for both his military and political superiors, particularly as the retreat from South Arabia turned into a humiliating rout. The scale of the disaster in Aden was not to be repeated until the British were driven out of Basra in 2007 and had to be rescued by the Americans in Helmand.

Despite the Aden fiasco, the British military had long boasted of its counter-insurgency prowess and this celebration was replicated in the academic literature. Malaya and Northern Ireland, in particular, were held up as models of how to fight insurgencies, showing other countries how such campaigns should be fought. This reputation was effectively demolished by the British performance in Iraq and Afghanistan. These defeats have prompted a reassessment of earlier campaigns by a number of historians and certainly the academic consensus today is that the British army's reputation was undeserved, that its successes were exaggerated, its defeats minimised and its commitment to the use of minimum force and to "hearts and minds" a myth. An attempt to restore the army's reputation was inevitable and leading the charge is Aaron Edwards, a senior lecturer at the Royal Military Academy, Sandhurst.

His *Mad Mitch* is, however, fatally compromised by imperial nostalgia and hero worship. These faults distort its arguments and leave the reader somewhat unsure about the nature of the beast. One is left feeling that Edwards would have preferred writing a eulogistic biography of Colin Mitchell rather than attempting what must in the end be judged a failed effort at evaluating his part in the Aden fiasco. Edwards clearly regrets the passing of empire, of the days when Britain had an empire "over which the sun famously never set" and "Britannia really did rule the waves". The loss of this empire, he blames, at least in part, on "the policies of post-war Labour governments that embraced decolonisation as a point of principle". And he recommends his account of the Aden Emergency as chronicling "the last battles of a once-great empire". Into the breach stepped the hero of his story, Colin Mitchell, who saved at least some of Britain's honour by the manner of his retaking and holding of Crater in July 1967. What we have here is military history written very much from the perspective of the right of the Conservative Party. Views and opinions, that one thought were confined to the afternoon musings of particularly reactionary retired officers and very right wing Tory MPs, and even then only after they'd had a few drinks, regularly manifest themselves in Edwards's pages.

Although he does not make it explicit, Edwards clearly believes in his heart that there was an alternative to the loss of the empire and that South Arabia could have been saved. This is the implicit assumption of the book. His reluctance to make this absolutely explicit suggests that, however reluctantly, he is actually aware that this is so much romantic wishful thinking. The reality is that after Suez, British retreat was inevitable, regardless of which party was in power and who was prime minister. Having "betrayed" the white settlers, their "kith and kin", in Kenya, are we seriously expected to believe that even a Conservative government would have stood by the sheikhs of South Arabia? It

might have been different if there had been oil there, but there wasn't. His eyes blinded by the glare of the imperial sunset, Edwards refuses to recognise this. Instead he places the blame for this final retreat on, of all people, Denis Healey! We are seriously told that it is hard "to think of a Labour politician more decidedly anti-colonialist than Denis Healey". He predictably mentions that Healey had once been a member of the Communist Party, but not that by the 1960s he was one of the stalwarts of the right wing of the Labour Party, a hard-nosed pragmatist, wholly committed to the NATO alliance. It is, of course, complete nonsense, indeed a right wing myth, to blame the loss of empire on post-war Labour governments. Indeed, Healey went on to preside over the early stages of British involvement in the suppression of the Dhofar insurgency against the Sultan of Oman, a conflict that saw a Labour government supporting an oil-rich slave-owning absolute monarch against popular rebellion, once again pitting Islamism against a secular revolutionary movement. Edwards fails even to acknowledge this campaign, presumably because it so starkly contradicts his particular right wing critique of a supposed Labour anti-colonialism.

What of his account of the actual conflict? Edwards does acknowledge that there were abuses: troops "kicking in doors, verbally abusing civilians and destroying the homes of the people they arrested". This sort of behaviour was "a self-inflicted wound" that only strengthened the rebels. He even acknowledges the use of torture by the British: "A preferred technique was apparently to place the detainee in a chair...then slap both his eardrums." Medical records "frequently noted" that detainees had burst eardrums. The Fort Morbut Interrogation Centre was apparently known to the Adenis as "the fingernail factory". Such methods have been used in every British counter-insurgency campaign to a greater or lesser degree.

But what of the Argylls? In January 1981 a number of Argyll soldiers were convicted of involvement in the brutal killing of two Catholic civilians in Northern Ireland, the so-called "Pitchfork Murders". This led to ex-soldiers coming forward to tell the Glasgow *Sunday Mail* of similar conduct in Crater. Eventually a dozen men signed statements detailing the shooting of unarmed civilians, the shooting of prisoners, the killing of wounded prisoners by morphine injection, the unprovoked bayoneting to death of a teenager and widespread theft and looting. When these revelations appeared in print, more ex-soldiers came forward to corroborate the stories, including some who had originally denied any such conduct. How does Edwards deal with this? He writes that none of these accusations were "ever substantiated", there was a "lack of corroborating evidence" and there was nothing in "the regimental and public archives", which is hardly surprising. His defence of the Argylls is somewhat undermined, it has to be said, when he goes on to conclude "that there are no grounds for suggesting that murders took place on anything like the scale alleged".

One of Edwards's complaints about the allegations is that they smeared Mitchell, creating the suspicion that he encouraged this sort of behaviour. But his own account of Mitchell's proposed solution to the Northern Ireland conflict, which the latter advocated in 1972, when he was a Tory MP, rather undermines this complaint. In an interview Mitchell urged the introduction of capital punishment for the possession of firearms, selective assassination and inviting the IRA leadership to peace talks and then shooting them out of hand!

One last point: Edwards suggests that "the violence unleashed by Islamist terrorists has roots in Britain's forgotten war on terror". The implication is, of course, that if Britain had stood firm in Aden, today's Islamist terrorists would not exist. This is impossible to take seriously. Indeed, if one wanted to make this sort of point, today's Islamists surely owe less to the secular rebels Britain was fighting in Aden than to the royalist Islamist rebels that Britain, together with Saudi Arabia and Israel, were covertly aiding at this time against a secularist republican government in neighbouring Yemen. But, of course, the staunchest advocates of the Yemen intervention were various individuals on the far right of the Conservative Party, the likes of Julian Amery, whose strategic fantasies Edwards takes much too seriously. With the British army still licking its wounds after Basra and Helmand and reeling from the coalition's cuts, it will take more than Edwards's fantasy history to restore its reputation for waging counter-insurgency warfare.

Land and freedom
Martin Empson

Andro Linklater, **Owning the Earth: The Transforming History of Land Ownership** *(Bloomsbury, 2014),* £20

Throughout our history humans have had many different ways of using land. Alongside this, the question of ownership has also changed dramatically. For the vast majority of human history humans lived as hunter-gatherers—ownership of land was a transient concept which meant nothing when the group moved on elsewhere. A lingering sense of this can be seen in feudal times, when land was measured very differently from today. In 1602 William Shakespeare paid £320 to purchase four "yardlands of arable land and 20 acres more of meadow". A yardland was an area "large enough to support a family". On good arable land, this might be 25 acres but the same measure of poorer quality "rough pasture" could be more than 40 acres.

Andro Linklater notes that wherever "individually owned landed property" has become the dominant form of land ownership it has been associated with new ways of measuring land. Parcelling up land into exact physical sizes meant that owners could sell it to a buyer "without local knowledge". This systematic approach to carving up the land can be seen in the way that every major city founded in the 19th century, from North America to South Africa and Australia, uses the British Empire's unit of measurement, the chain, as the basis for everything from street widths to the area of public squares. Alongside this, Linklater argues, comes a change to mortgage law. Instead of a borrower losing everything if they failed to keep up repayments, they now had "equity in the land". This meant that should land be foreclosed on they still retained some value once the debt had been paid off.

From the mid-1500s onwards a raft of new rules were introduced helping to undermine the old feudal relationships. In 1450 some 60 percent of England's 12 million acres of farmland was held by the crown, the church or the nobility. By 1700 their share had fallen to less than 30 percent. The rise of a new group of landowning families came to dominate the political scene. Linklater argues that the adult males of 200,000 landowning families now decided who went to parliament and who enforced the rules. While Linklater sees this as a "land revolution" in terms of the changing ownership of land, he fails to identify that what has taken place is a revolution in property relations that has helped end the old feudal order.

Linklater discusses how the English Civil War gave rise to new—revolutionary—ideas. Groups like Gerrard Winstanley and the Diggers who argued that "the Earth with all her Fruits of Corn, Cattle, and such like, was made to be a common Store-house of Livelihood to all Mankinde". Linklater points to the

"Putney debates and scores of Leveller-inspired pamphlets [that] not only imagined the possibility of the king being subject to the will of the people, but made the breathtaking claim that every free person was entitled to the unique array of privileges won by property owners" (p53).

But having mobilised a parliamentary army against the king on the basis of challenging the old order, victory in the civil war meant that Oliver Cromwell also turned on the radical elements on his own side.

Linklater fails to understand the revolutionary dynamic that takes place over the course of the civil war. He argues that:

"as the landowners monopolised power and entrenched their privileges after 1653, the balance of opinion would tip away from the Levellers and towards Cromwell, so that by the end of the century English freedom was once more seen to be a privilege of property" (p54).

When Cromwell's son in law, General Ireton, argued at the Putney debates that only those "with a permanent fixed interest in this kingdom" could have a say in how it was run he was declaring the limits of the political and economic change that his class was prepared to condone.

By only seeing the outcome of the civil war in terms of the question of private property and its relationship to political freedom, Linklater misses the revolutionary nature of the transformation that has taken place. Parliamentary victory in the English Civil War was simultaneously a defeat for the old feudal order and, at least temporarily, for any dream of radical agrarian change. It opened England up to a new capitalist order.

Karl Marx argued that for capitalism to become the dominant form of production required "divorcing the producer from the means of production" by turning "the immediate producers into wage labourers". This meant forcefully evicting the majority of the rural population from the land.

The process of enclosures that resulted from this need allowed landowners to massively improve their wealth. "The reason whereof is that in pasture he [the landlord] hath the whole profit, there being required neither men nor charge worth speaking of", explained one 17th century historian.

While similar processes took place in a number of places in Europe, Linklater argues that "only in England and North America did 17th century land become capital". In other countries private ownership of land did not pass "outside the nobility", which in Poland, for instance, "made it impossible to use the land as security to raise loans from the wealthy city burghers". This had the effect of entrenching serfdom throughout most of Europe. Linklater suggests that this is why societies governed by property relations introduced from Britain came to dominate the world.

"The land revolution that linked property interests to capital creation brought into being a modern system which archaic

societies organised on half-feudal, half-tribal lines were powerless to resist. The disparity was apparent in Ireland where Cromwell and Ireton could keep a professional army in the field for four years and finance the £10 million cost of the campaign with London loans, fully covered by the sale of Irish land. The history of the next two centuries would make it universally obvious that a private property society could harness resources that were not available to societies organised in other ways" (p108).

Later he continues:

"The difference between peasant Europe and capitalist Britain was not one of production but of ownership. While the common law concentrated ownership of land and produce in one person, peasant ownership was always held by the family, and however clearly its use belonged to the peasant, the land itself ultimately belonged to a lord. This divided ownership gave peasant society a particular quality that prized endurance over enterprise" (p127).

Capitalism did transform land ownership and much else. This is clearest in the Americas, where Senator Henry Dawes could say in 1877 that the problem with the Cherokee practice of owning land in common was that there was "no enterprise to make your home any better than that of your neighbour's. There is no selfishness, which is at the bottom of civilisation."

The Enlightenment philosopher John Locke had a different view of the New World. Linklater writes that Locke saw America as a place of "limitless possibility where people lived in perfect freedom surrounded by empty land". From this state, "private property spontaneously, naturally and inevitably occurred". Linklater is taken by Locke's approach, continuing that while the land had been held in common ownership before government, "By working a piece of the earth and improving it...a person separated it from what had been shared and thereby acquired exclusive ownership." Thus the "natural rights of ownership" come from the labour expended in working the land.

For Linklater this is a key part of the development of property relations under capitalism. But it can only work if those that don't have property are looked after, either through the provision of common land or other social assistance. But this approach comes unstuck when he tries to understand later developments. For instance, writing about the history of Germany he suggests that:

"The failure of Prussia's landowners to force property rights onto the political agenda of the united Germany...was exacerbated by the simultaneous absence of any statement of innate human rights... The lack of any concept of natural rights for individuals, either through their possession of property or by being built into the constitutional foundation of the state, proved to be of fatal significance" (pp303-304).

This leads, in Linklater's view, to a weak German legal constitution. The landowning Junker class lacked authority and any philosophy of individual rights and thus failed to gain popular appeal. To deal with this, they founded the Agrarian League which resorted to scapegoating the Jews. So for Linklater, "Germany's democracy failed [with the rise of the Nazis] because no system of individual rights was established before the country was industrialised" (p305).

But this is to ignore the fact that fascism could have been triumphant in countries that did develop individual rights. The success of Hitler had less to do with Germany's legal framework than with the

failure of the left to defeat the Nazis. By ignoring the revolutionary struggles of the period after the First World War, and the failings of the anti-fascist movement in the 1920s and 1930s, Linklater ignores the real forces that shape history.

This is also a failing when Linklater discusses the Russian Revolution. The Bolsheviks put enormous emphasis on the importance of redistributing land in order to build an alliance of the peasantry and the working class. Linklater ignores this, instead focusing on Stalin's forced collectivisation, which he sees as a direct continuation of Lenin's policies, rather than as a consequence of the defeat of the revolution.

Consequently Linklater develops a critique of capitalism and how land is owned and used, but cannot see any alternative. Linklater gives a potted history of attempts to redistribute land from the top down. But as he points out, no government that represents those who benefit from an unequal distribution of land would seriously consider altering the status quo in the interest of "fairness".

Despite this, Linklater hopes that corporate interests will solve the problem:

"Most corporate investors will sooner or later realise that property based on state-enforced law looks less secure than the kind based on natural right. The basic Lockean premise is that such a right arises out of an innate sense of justice. On that basis a corporate owner's claim to property in land must ultimately depend on finding a way to make good the loss to those deprived of its use" (p397).

Capitalism doesn't have any such innate sense of justice. But Linklater himself shows that those who work the land tend to create more communal communities. A strength of this book is the sweeping discussion of how the question of land has been central to how different societies have organised themselves through time. The question of how we use land today and in the future will remain an important issue. But because Linklater ends up concluding that "how the land is owned" is the "key to solving" all these problems he fails to systematically challenge the real barrier to "feeding nine billion people".

The problem is the existence of the capitalist system. Unfortunately, Linklater does not examine any of the contemporary movements that fight to redistribute land and organise for the rights of landless workers and peasants. It is these people, together with the working class, who have the potential to transform society and solve the question of land ownership in the interest of everyone. But because Linklater dismisses the revolutionary transformation of society, he ends up putting faith in a system that has failed those that work the land for 400 years.

50 years of theorising class
Xanthe Rose

Leo Panitch, Greg Albo and Vivek Chibber (eds), **Socialist Register 2014: Registering Class** *(Merlin Press, 2013),* £16.95

Discussion of classes, how they form, their composition and how they can act consciously have featured on the left since the time of Karl Marx. Such debates were among those leading to the formation in 1964 of the journal *Socialist Register*, which

has been published annually since. This, the 50th edition, returns to an examination of class in the light of changing capitalist productive and social relations.

There is much within this year's issue that is worth reading and engaging with. Many of the discussions touch on debates taking place not just within left academia, but also among those involved in organising against crisis and austerity. Arun Gupta has contributed a very readable piece on unionisation drives within the US retailer Walmart, detailing the scale of this corporate giant and the consequences for the labour market in general of its strategy of turning labour into what he calls "another just in time commodity". He provides an overview of campaigns such as the Service Employees International Union's "Campaign for 15", which has successfully organised fast food workers and gave the impetus for a $15 an hour wage campaign that continues to gather pace across the US.

A number of contributions engage with theoretical approaches to class. Ursula Huws revisits classical Marxist categories in the light of challenges she sees as posed by digital labour. She identifies some key concerns about the commodification of everyday life, and "consumptive" and reproductive labour, in a critical engagement with the widely used but highly problematic concept of "immaterial labour". She is particularly interested in integrating these changes into a new labour theory of value.

Bryan Palmer's excellent discussion of precariousness challenges the notion that this condition constitutes a separate class formation. Palmer rejects the idea that precarious labour requires an entirely novel approach to a Marxist understanding of class, or the notion that class necessarily involves complete uniformity of experience.

Postcolonial theory, together with feminist theory, has offered some of the most consistent challenges to the centrality of class in Marxist theory. Vivek Chibber attempts to revitalise a Marxist conception of universalism in response to postcolonialist charges that universalising concepts are themselves part of the colonial project. He aims his critique at Dipesh Chakrabarty, author of *Provincializing Europe*, but his target is the trajectory of postcolonial theory more generally, whose fragmentary approach he views as inhibiting and weakening the radical left.

A hefty central section of the *Register* examines the ruling classes, with four contributions exploring similar questions: the existence of a transnational capitalist class, consolidation of its political power, whether it acts as a class "for itself", the relationship between productive and finance capital, and the implications for states of transnational capitalism. There is broad agreement within these analyses that transnational capital is embedded in particular territories and continues to rely on the backing of state institutions and power. Claude Serfarti's piece draws out most effectively the implications for those who wish to challenge capitalist rule and is clear about the continuing need to challenge national ruling classes.

In a short essay Alfredo Saad-Filho and Lecio Morais analyse the events of June 2013, in which mass protests erupted throughout the major cities of Brazil in response to transport fare hikes. They discuss the confusion and disorientation created within a movement not given clear direction by the left, leaving it open to co-option by the middle class and even forces of the far-right. This essay would have benefitted from a longer discussion of the lessons for the left. The alignment of the landless peasants' movement and the support most parties of the Brazilian radical left have given to Dilma Rousseff's administration, as well as the attempt by sections of the far left to establish a left alternative to Rousseff's Workers' Party, are buried in the footnotes.

The piece that most directly grapples with the contemporary political strategy is by Andrew Murray, an official in the Unite union. He outlines the problems faced by attempts to build electoral projects to the left of the Labour Party. This leads to a harsh, but at times persuasive, critique of the Left Unity project, focusing on the disconnect between its political aspirations and its limited roots within the working class or any mass workers' movement, and on the relative resilience of Labour at a time when many will vote to get the Tories out.

Murray tends to counterpose to building a left electoral challenge the projects he is involved in: the People's Assembly and attempts to reclaim Labour. His contribution is pessimistic about the state of workers' organisation generally, arguing for a painstaking attempt to rebuild effective union organisation before any left challenge to Labour can be conceived. But he entirely evades the role played by the trade union bureaucracy and its potential to limit working class activity, a serious error given that struggle has historically proved the most effective way of building or rebuilding rank and file union organisation. He also downplays the way that the political aspirations of sections of the class who are increasingly disconnected from Labour could potentially feed into revived struggle.

Considering the preoccupation in *Socialist Register* with analysing neoliberalism and crisis, it is curious that this edition carries so little careful dissection of the overall composition and shape of the working class and its organisations, beyond the more theoretical contributions of Huws and Palmer. This may be a result of the previous edition being themed around strategy, but it leaves the 2014 *Register* feeling light in terms of addressing strategic questions, aside from Murray's very one-sided intervention. Nonetheless, it is welcome that the editors have chosen to focus on the question of class, about which there is such disorientation on the left today.

The contested history of the left and Zionism
Miriam Scharf

Philip Mendes, **Jews and the Left: the Rise and Fall of a Political Alliance** *(Palgrave Macmillan, 2014), £65,* and Paul Kelemen, **The British Left and Zionism: History of a Divorce** *(Manchester University Press, 2012), £15.99*

These two books, one concentrating on Jews and the left internationally and the other on Zionism and the British left, show some convergence in their pre Second World War coverage of left support for Zionism. But the different political perspectives of the authors—Mendes is pro-Zionist and Kelemen is not—lead to very different references, analyses and commentary for the period after the establishment of the state of Israel.

Mendes's premise is that Jews form a community and as such have particular "objective Jewish interests". Mendes's focus is on Jewish involvement in the left and he provides detail of the shift in different countries and political parties from universalist, ie supporting changes that would benefit all exploited classes or groups, to particularist views of Jews.

Jews who retain universalist, more socialist, attitudes after 1948—and Mendes acknowledges many of them—are suspect.

Kelemen, by contrast, begins by pointing out the ethnic exclusiveness of Zionism as a problem. Given that Israel is an ethnically defined state founded on the dispossession of the Palestinians, what he aims to explain to us is not so much the divorce of the left from Zionism but why there was a marriage in the first place.

Kelemen details pre-1939 policies, speeches and documents from the Labour Party, Communist Party and Anglo-Jewry to provide this explanation. He then evidences British government attitudes, especially among Labour MPs, to the postwar situation. Noted throughout is the lack of concern for, or sometimes any reference whatever to the Palestinians. Tracing the shape of Zionist ideology, Kelemen notes the principle of national self-determination as adopted by the Labour Party in 1917. He contrasts Lenin's endorsement of self-determination as a way to undermine imperialism with Harold Wilson's vision of an evolutionary process for non-European peoples under Western tutelage. He shows how the latter view prevailed among Labourites whose Social Darwinist tendencies led them to contend that European Jews would develop Palestine for the "greater good" in a way that Muslim Arabs could not. Providing evidence that the nonconformist heritage of the British labour movement—in which "Israelites" were venerated—fed this view, he shows how the kind of anti-Semitism that characterises the Jews as a different and special people also helped the Zionist project and provided an unchallenged racism against Arabs and Palestinians.

The identification of Zionism with social progress was the political line of the labour Zionist party Poale Zion, which Mendes characterises as "Left Zionist", a party linked to the Zionist labour organisations in Palestine. Both authors document the importance of Poale Zion in promulgating and winning Labour Party support for the idea that Jews settling in Palestine conformed to a new socialist ideal. Mendes cites Kelemen on the British Labour Party from 1936-45, when "successive annual party conferences supported the establishment of a Jewish state". Quotes from Labour leaders, like Herbert Morrison and Richard Crossman, exhibit the exceptionalism with regard to Israel that, for Mendes, is welcomed as understanding the Jewish interest. Similar quotations used by Kelemen demonstrate why and how those with social democratic ideas supported Zionism.

Kelemen shows the case for a Jewish nation as an imperialist ally is crucial to understanding the Realpolitik favouring Zionism. For example, he quotes Ramsay MacDonald in 1929: "It is of greatest importance to us that we should keep American oil interests in good relations with us." For Mendes, there is only "alleged collaboration with Western imperialism", even post-Suez.

Both books look at pre-war Jewish support for left parties, clearly showing that the still largely working class Jewish population were far less interested in going to Palestine than in improving their material conditions where they were. Jews were disproportionately active in the Communist Party, Labour Party and trade unions in the UK; and Mendes shows this was also the case worldwide. Here Mendes's contribution on Bundism, the majority working class and socialist response to anti-Semitism and oppression in Eastern Europe, is useful: "The Bund accused the Zionist movement of legitimitising Polish anti-Semitism and also attacked its negation of the national rights

of the Arab inhabitants of Palestine." The Bund opposed the creation of Israel in 1948, claiming, "It was designed to serve the imperialistic interests of the Western powers, and would only perpetuate the conflict between Jews and Arabs."

Kelemen and Mendes provide detailed research on the Communist Party, in the former case solely the Communist Party of Great Britain: the CP's anti-colonialist opposition to Zionism, its support for the Union of Arab and Jewish Workers in Palestine against the Jewish only Histadrut, and its support of Arab demands to cease Jewish immigration. They also show that during the rise of fascism support for Zionism rose in the Jewish working class. Both report the most important change for all national CPs was when the line from Moscow reversed into support for the Zionists against British imperialism in 1947. Kelemen quotes telling coverage from the CPGB's daily newspaper, indicating their confusion and then submission, so that by August 1948, "the only force the *Daily Worker* was prepared to exonerate from causing Palestinians to abandon their homes was the Israeli army". He shows how other left papers including the *Daily Herald* and the *Tribune* told the same story.

Mendes records the attitude of Communist Parties showing acceptance of the Moscow line that Israel was part of the struggle against British and Anglo-American imperialism. American, French and Canadian CPs write of "a just war of independence against British and US-sponsored imperialism". Though much harder to swallow for the Arab CPs the joint statement issued by the CPs of the Middle East in October 1948 condemns the "Arab invasion of Palestine", dutifully tailing Stalin's line.

In regard to the CP, Mendes's description of Jews' disproportionate prominence in leadership roles in post-war Eastern European governments provides interesting reading, but is more pertinent to how Stalinism used anti-Semitism than to a discussion about Zionism.

Perhaps more relevant to readers now is the discussion by both writers of the left in relation to Israel following the Second World War. After the Holocaust they concur in showing how the idea common across the political spectrum was that Europe's surviving Jews should have a nation. Kelemen shows that, in the Labour Party, the fact that Israel provided an important strategic ally to the US, and therefore the UK, served to counter Soviet influence and Arab nationalism. This made Zionism popular on the right, while the left continued its support for Israel's "social democratic values". He sees this convergence as enabling the popularising of "an image of Israel as a beacon of progress in the Middle East". Mendes notes that the response of the 1944 Labour Party Conference to the Holocaust was to vote for admission of Jews to Palestine "in such numbers as to become a majority" to urge "the 'transfer' of the Arab population to neighbouring countries". He quotes approvingly leftists, among them Harold Laski, Michael Foot and Aneurin Bevan, arguing for the party's traditional Zionist perspectives and praising both the Histadrut and "socialist" Zionist parties and culture.

Then comes the break, described by Kelemen in terms of how some of the left changed their understanding of the nature of the Israeli state to that of an illegal occupier and imperialist ally, and so began the left's divorce from Zionism. Both writers see Israel's 1967 victory and subsequent occupation of the West Bank and Gaza as a watershed. Both identify the rise of the "new left" in the 1960s, their analysis of Israel being influenced by the

emergence of the Palestine Liberation Organisation and the wider world recognition of Palestinians as a national group with national rights.

Kelemen, aware of the accusation of anti-Semitism waiting in the wings, shows objectively how the left was able to break with Zionism and to stand up for Palestinian rights. He relates this to developments among the Palestinian political parties and does good service to the radical left outside the Labour Party mainstream. Kelemen traces the conflict between a pro-Zionist Labour leadership and grassroots activists. This includes the launch of the Palestine Solidarity Campaign in 1969 alongside Harold Wilson's backing of Israel. It also includes the Blair/Brown governments' support for Israel parallel to the proliferation of pro-Palestinian groups during their tenure with dropping levels of support for the Labour Friends of Israel and the Trade Union Friends of Israel. In contrast, Mendes's desire to de-legitimise anti-Zionism leads him to include insignificant esoteric groups and to misrepresent more influential Marxists and Trotskyists.

Mendes says a consequence of the 1967 war was that "support for Israel became the principal determinant of Jewish identity". The left after this is characterised by those who support a two-state solution. He resorts to judgemental and subjective language for other analyses:

"anti-Zionist fundamentalists today wish to eliminate the actual existing nation state of Israel. Israelis and their Jewish supporters are depicted as inherently evil oppressors... Conversely, Palestinians are depicted as intrinsically innocent victims. In place of the fundamental and objective centrality of the state of Israel to contemporary Jewish identity, anti-Zionist fundamentalists...utilise ethnic stereotyping of all Israelis...[and] construct a subjective fantasy world in which Israel is detached from its specifically Jewish roots, and then miraculously destroyed by remote control" (pp125-126).

In Kelemen's account different proposals are examined, for example the debate between Ralph Miliband and Marcel Liebman, with the latter arguing for a one-state solution and exposing Israel as an ally of Western imperialism.

One of the most demanding aspects in writing such an account is the massive number of events that provide the context for the development of ideas on the left. Kelemen has not only included the left's various responses to different government papers and reports on Palestine but has made an impressive effort to show how major events in 1947-8, Suez, the 1967 war, etc affected the different elements of the left. He has excavated much interesting evidence of these responses. To give an example from during the 1982 invasion of Lebanon: By August 1982 only two resolutions of 500 submitted to Labour Party Conference concerned the Middle East; a month later 46 resolutions critical of Israel had been submitted. At the conference a resolution from Norwood Constituency Labour Party called for support for "the establishment of a democratic secular state in Palestine as the long-term solution to the Palestine problem"—it passed.

The younger generation of the British left is now pro-Palestinian and critical of Israeli occupation and bombing. Palestinians have become an acknowledged symbol of the oppressed and for the fight for freedom and justice. Kelemen's book showing the history of how the British left finally reached this position is meticulously well researched and well written. Mendes, although including interesting material, has a familiarly skewed analysis. This he exemplifies in his concluding contrast between

"Western values" and "the culture of the Arab world", pessimistically forecasting that the latter "would be very unlikely to protect the human rights of Israeli Jews".

Love football—hate Fifa
Des Barrow

Dave Zirin, Brazil's Dance with the Devil: The World Cup, the Olympics, and the Fight for Democracy (Haymarket, 2014), £11.99

Dave Zirin is a left wing sports writer from the United States who has written extensively on the Olympics, including a biography of John Carlos. Here he digs beneath the shiny surface of Brazil projected by the ruling Workers' Party (PT) and details how they are using mega sporting events—the 2014 football world cup and 2016 Olympic Games—both to promote an image (of a stable democracy and a powerhouse economy), and as tools with which to further their neoliberal project. Millions of Brazilians marching on soccer stadiums wasn't part of the plan. And the protesters have got more to be angry about than a rise in bus fares. Zirin explores the resistance of the Brazilian people to the spending cuts, environmental destruction, broken promises, historical revision, tooling up of the police and demolition of favelas that first burst onto the streets in spectacular fashion during the Confederations Cup in 2013.

When Lula stepped down after eight years as president in 2011, he did so as the world's most popular living politician, who had cut infant mortality by a staggering 40 percent and increased the minimum wage by 50 percent. The PT had apparently transformed the economy from one which, in 1998, required the largest rescue package in the history of the IMF: 41 billion dollars plus. A mere decade later Lula could boast that Brazil was lending money to the IMF! Brazil overtook the UK to become the world's fifth largest economy in 2011. But the underlying fragility of the economy that Zirin exposes has, since the book was published, developed into recession, and just in time for the FIFA world cup.

Lula's successor, Dilma Rousseff, led the PT to a third successive victory and its greatest number of seats; but as the recession takes hold and disillusionment grows, it looks like the PT might well lose the coming election.

Zirin's hope is to challenge the notion "that hosting these kinds of sporting mega events is something to which countries should aspire". Along the way he demolishes the conventional wisdom about Brazilian development, reminds us why putting our faith in reformist leaders is a mistake and gives voice to "the fighters for social justice, the community organisers, the residents trying to save their homes".

At the heart of the PT's economic plan is a neoliberal agenda whose real beneficiaries have been the same oligarchs who have had Brazil sewn up ever since it was the largest and most brutal slave state in the world. After hiking up interest rates and slashing public spending Lula became known as "the IMF's favourite president". The stock exchange grew at a rate of 523 percent in the first decade. Between 2006 and 2008 the number of millionaires increased by 70 percent, and a highly regressive taxation regime is in place. Becoming the world's leading beef exporter has gone hand in hand with

land grabs and a hostile attitude to the landless peasant movement. Offshore oil exploitation has been a disaster for the environment. While the PT recognises Palestine as an independent state, Brazil's own indigenous people are being marginalised. And the brutal history of slavery is being sidelined. Not only that, but the trade union movement from which Lula came has been co-opted by the PT, and now represents just 17 percent of workers, compared to more than 30 percent under the dictatorship in the 1980s. Many in the social movements have turned their backs on political parties following the disillusionment. Building a new workers party will be harder because of the current one. But the protests are coming at a time when economic growth has slowed to just 0.9 percent.

Enter the sporting mega events: "It cannot be overstated just how invested Brazil's elite are in seeing these games come off without a hitch", Zirin writes. But those below have a different perspective:

"Brazilians are outraged that services like transportation, education and healthcare are inefficiently run or woefully underfunded yet spending for the world cup alone could reach the fifteen-billion-dollar mark—which would make it more expensive than the previous three world cups combined.

"Outraged also by the disgusting waste of money (eg building a 42,000 seater stadium in Natal, a place where the biggest team gets an average crowd of 5,000), or the gutting and rebuilding of the Maracanã, one of the world's most famous football stadiums. Outraged by the bulldozing of the Indigenous Cultural Centre next door, to make way for...a parking lot" (p19).

Zirin shows how, historically, FIFA and especially the International Olympic

Committee (IOC) are completely dedicated to making the largest sums of money they possibly can for themselves and their sponsors, leading to corruption and a moral compass that points to the most compliant and often dictatorial regimes in the world.

He elaborates throughout the book referencing Naomi Klein's *Shock Doctrine*, whereby the requirements of FIFA and the IOC are used to justify measures from taking people's rights to taking people's homes. What Jules Boykoff calls "Celebration Capitalism" ("the public pays and the private profits") allows a 'security architecture' to be put in place and militarisation of the police. Examples from the Olympic Games of the last ten years back up the case (did you know the London Olympics saw the deployment of more troops than the UK ever had on the ground in Afghanistan?).

But it is the story of the favelas in Rio de Janeiro which is at the heart of this account; how the government is using these sporting events to justify the continuing war by police on favela dwellers; how they are using the world cup to force people and communities out, and hand the land over to developers and the rich. And of course the resistance. Vila Autódromo, a favela lined up to be raised in order to make way for an Olympic Car Park, organised, fought back, and prevented the eviction; in the process, they say, they "have grown as individuals and as a community".

Zirin's final segment is entitled "The Nobodies", meaning the ordinary people of Brazil who have created the "culture, play, dance and energy" of the country; people who FIFA and the IOC are happy to see swept away for their corporate money fests. There's an us and them. "It is their World Cup. But it is our world."

Muslims ate my hamster!
David Szuster

Nathan Lean, **The Islamophobia Industry: How the Right Manufactures Fear of Muslims** *(Pluto Press, 2012), £12.50*

Nathan Lean's book is a most welcome riposte to the Muslim scare stories that saturate our media, firstly by uncovering the falsity behind these stories and secondly by exposing the nefarious web of Islamophobic bloggers, businessmen, politicians, journalists, lobbyists and activists who manufacture and sell this paranoid vision of imminent Muslim takeover for their own political and private ends. For example, when Lean investigates the anti-Muslim hysteria surrounding the creation of the Park51 mosque, the so-called "Ground Zero mosque", he finds Islamophobic fear-merchants accusing its imam of promoting a "stealth jihad" (p64). Rather the Park51 mosque was created as a banal YMCA-like community centre that hopes to build ties between people of all backgrounds (p41).

Through a series of exposés of the major players within this "Islamophobia industry" (set mainly in the US) Lean creates a narrative that connects racist internet bloggers via the likes of Fox News, the Christian right and the Committee on Homeland Security to the murderous rampage of the white supremacist Anders Behring Breivik. These exposés are the book's strength as each fear-peddler is exposed for their baseless bigotry and for what part they play within this (for profit) industry. However, there are fundamental weaknesses within this book.

While Lean's book provides a wealth of evidence for the fabrication of fear of

Muslims, he himself lacks the conceptual tools with which to interpret this evidence. Confronted with the ideological apparatus of capitalism that gives Americans both a scapegoat for the societal disintegration caused by capitalism and a bogeyman enemy to legitimise American imperialism, Lean unwittingly dilutes his account of the systematic demonisation of Muslims by not seeing the motive itself as "systematic", to instead trace it to the simple bigotry, greed and caprice of Islamophobic individuals as narrated through their personal histories: "This is about a concerted effort on the part of a small cabal of xenophobes to manufacture fear for personal gain" (p14).

For example, Lean reveals the following connections: that between New York Police Commissioner Ray Kelly and the Zionist-funded film *Obsession* (which he appears in and uses to train recruits) with the film's narrator, Dr M Zuhdi Jasser. Jasser is also the star witness for the Committee on Homeland Security chaired by Congressman Peter King who is also "buddies" with Ray Kelly. This same film *Obsession* was then used as the ideological and evidential basis for the NYPD's Muslim-focused anti-terrorism stings. But Lean interprets these connections simply as a "self-fulfilling prophecy" (p151) as if caused by unconscious self-deception and bigotry rather than the very means by which the ideological apparatus of capitalism operates: an interlocking web of reinforcing connections sustained by the ideological necessities of American capitalist imperialism.

A further weakness is that racism is not given any socio-historical origin or basis but simply appears, in an idealist way, as a competing narrative which must be resisted by a counter-narrative which Lean tries to provide. Also the political-economic context for such competing narratives is replaced repeatedly by opinion poll data which exacerbates the lack of agency Lean gives to ordinary people, who seem to be merely passive receptacles of Islamophobic propaganda (or anti-Islamophobic messages). Lean never discusses the possibility of "anti-Islamophobia from below", namely, the spontaneous resistance to Islamophobia generated through people's daily struggles against the state and capitalists when allied with their Muslim neighbours. Rather the terrain on which Lean battles Islamophobia is the superstructural realm of academia, the media and government policy and so opinion poll data becomes the expression and methodological basis of Lean's "anti-Islamophobia from above". This idealist and individualist methodology then is to blame for a vague ending that urges people to resist Islamophobia (p184) but contains no collective organisational conclusions (building a united front like Unite Against Fascism, for example).

In addition, a glaring omission is any critique of new atheism (discussed elsewhere by Lean in his blogs) and how its reactionary atheism and Islamophobia have hobbled the liberal left's reaction to the rise of the right in Europe and the US, which will hopefully be remedied in subsequent editions of this book.

In conclusion, *The Islamophobia Industry* is an important contribution to the fight against racism and a must-read for anti-fascist activists for the abundance of evidence Lean provides of the systematic demonisation of Muslims. However, one must read it with a critical Marxist eye to reap the full benefit.

A revolutionary impatience

Alex Callinicos

Daniel Bensaïd, **An Impatient Life: A Political Memoir** *(Verso, 2013),* £24.99

Daniel Bensaïd was, as Tariq Ali says in his foreword to this autobiography, "France's leading Marxist public intellectual" until he died at the age of 63 in 2010. For many years he had lived with the prospect of an early death, and so he wrote a bewilderingly rapid succession of books. All are distinguished by Daniel's revolutionary commitment, his intellectual originality and his superb prose style—drenched in the French literary tradition, his writing is distinctive among Marxists for its use of metaphor, its vividness, and its very broad range of reference.

This autobiography, published in France in 2004, is one of many products of this textual flood that deserve to last. In it Daniel recalls his early years in a working class quarter of Toulouse, his role as a leader of the Jeunesse Communiste Révolutionnaire in the great explosion of May-June 1968, and his political work in subsequent decades for the Ligue Communiste Révolutionnaire (which launched the Nouveau Parti Anticapitaliste in 2009) and the Fourth International (FI). Snapshots from his personal life also figure, but this is, as its subtitle states, a political memoir.

Daniel had a fascinating life at the centre of French radical left politics so there are many pleasures in this book. It's hard to select from so rich a treasure trove, but here are a couple. The first is the pen portrait (among many others) of his redoubtable mother, who refused to speak to her son-in-law for ten years because he expressed doubts about the wisdom of guillotining Louis XVI (Daniel himself was punctilious about remembering the great dates of the French Revolution). When facing a difficult encounter she would comfort herself with the observation: "In any case, they won't make a hole in my arse, I've got one already!"

By contrast, Daniel's account of his many visits to Latin America on behalf of the FI is threaded with bitter tragedy. There are comic moments: at a hostile meeting in 1973 with one Argentinian section, led by Nahuel Moreno, "a long table was laid out, piled high with the complete works of Trotsky. Following each of my interventions, half a dozen specialists would plunge feverishly into the magic books to hunt out a killing quote or a useful crib for the next intervention." But the stakes in this debate were high. The other main wing of the FI in Argentina, led by Mario Roberto Santucho, was organising an armed struggle against the state.

Daniel is sympathetic to the revolutionary impatience that motivated Santucho (at a meeting with him in FI leader Ernest Mandel's house in Brussels he had the feeling, amid the doilies and Marxist classics, of being in "a museum of the European workers' movement"). But he documents the disastrous hecatomb of revolutionary militants (Santucho among them) to which the strategy of guerrilla warfare contributed as the "dirty war" in Argentina escalated towards its climax after the 1976 military coup. Moreno and his followers were right in their critique of the efforts of Latin American revolutionaries to emulate Fidel Castro and Che Guevara. This may help explain why the different fragments of Moreno's tendency dominate the far left in Latin America— even in Brazil, where, as Daniel describes in recalling much happier visits in the

1980s, FI activists played an important role in founding and building the Workers Party.

Alongside political memories such as these, Daniel offers a distillation of his theoretical views, which are developed much more fully in other works such as *Marx for Our Times*. He is a master of the lucid formula that sums up a complex theoretical argument. Here's just one of my favourites: "If it is possible to speak of 'Marxism' in the singular, this should rather be viewed as an archipelago of controversies, conjectures, refutations and experiences, whose history it relates by elucidating the mysteries and prodigies of capital." There is so much that is excellent here that the odd lapse—for example, Daniel's lazy inclusion of Tony Cliff in a list of "authoritarian gurus"—is easy to forget.

David Fernbach has produced a fine translation of this autobiography, which in the English edition is accompanied by an occasionally overwhelming wealth of footnotes explaining who the long list of characters are. My only slight quibble is with the title. In the French original it is *Une lente impatience*, literally "a slow impatience". This doesn't exactly trip off the tongue, but "An Impatient Life" doesn't capture it at all. In the book Daniel conveys his meaning when he writes of "an active waiting, an urgent patience, an endurance and a perseverance that are the opposite of passive waiting for a miracle". This was the stance he believed was necessary for revolutionaries in difficult times. When I first read the book I thought Daniel was exaggerating the difficulties. Now I think what he recommends is exactly what we need.

To sleep, perchance to resist?
Mark Dunk

*Jonathan Crary, **24/7: Late Capitalism and the Ends of Sleep** (Verso, 2014), £7.99*

Touted as a short, sharp polemic on the expansion of capital into every waking minute, *24/7* is a curiosity that promises much but delivers little.

The main drive of Jonathan Crary's musings is that modern capitalism is seeking to eradicate sleep as a barrier to accumulation and has created a new subjectivity constantly subsumed within the ever growing morass of media saturation. "There is always something more interesting happening online", he states blithely. However, for all its gusto this grandiose statement cannot keep up with a reality in which, while the Egyptian generals turned off internet access, the masses were still in the streets making history.

Crary advances the argument that a new passive subjectivity has been imposed upon workers through means such as television and the internet. He reminds us of their addictive properties and their individuation of viewers/users. What he does not remind us of is that even the most addicted TV viewer or internet user in the workforce would find it almost impossible to spend as much time engaged in this kind of immersive activity each week as the 40 plus hours they spend in the workplace.

Crary's privileging of "the new" tends to sideline the continuity of how capitalist social relations have always shaped the relationship of workers to the natural world. While he worries about the development of anti-sleep drugs and reduced average sleeping hours* he misses the fundamental continuity of how workers' relationship to nature has always shifted with the ebbs and flows of class struggle. It was because of this continuity that in 1897 Lenin was able to write in his pamphlet *The New Factory Law*:

"'Night' for the common people, who have to toil all their lives for others, and 'night' for the fine folk, who live on the labour of others, are, according to the 'law', two entirely different things."

For Crary the gaslight in Joseph Wright's painting *Arkright's Cotton Mills by Night* is replaced by the mid-20th century glow of television sets from windows. The all too common subtext is that industrial production is a thing from a bygone era. Indeed this must really be considered the main point Crary is making here; any serious attempt to find a modern comparator for Wright's image would surely place the spill of electric light from the windows of modern textile factories as a closer match.

The problem with this is that it glosses over the distinction between production and consumption. The shirt Crary was wearing when he wrote his tome came neither from the past nor from someone's television room. It came from a factory where workers today still have the power to unite and struggle both against their employers and the capitalist system as a whole.

Crary's sleight of hand replaces Rosa Luxemburg's valuable maxim: "Where the chains of capitalism are forged, there they must be broken", with something resembling the slogan and title of the 1980s BBC children's television classic *Why Don't You*

Just Switch Off Your Television Set And Go Out And Do Something Less Boring Instead? Indeed, Crary's position is worse. Rather than "something less boring" he simply advocates going to bed as a radical act in itself. To be clear—the author believes that sleep is the last realm free from capitalism's influence and goes on to fetishise it as the wellspring from which a strategy of emancipation will leap forward. This is nothing more than a secular prayer, a call to shut our eyes and hope for a miracle. This absurd notion can only hold on the basis that our dreams are born not of our experience of the world we live in but are instead imparted from some fantastical plane beyond our knowledge.

The highly impressionistic method that the author employs often makes it an unnecessarily complex task to engage with the text—rather than rooting his critique of contemporary capitalism firmly in the process of production the author instead draws on an eclectic mix of materialism, academic traditions of psychoanalysis, and anecdote, fusing them with abstract conjecture. As a result Crary often seems to be alluding towards ideas but ultimately fails when it comes to explaining them.

At times the author also seems intent to make the facts fit his thesis. In one passage he asserts that capitalism has failed to commodify sleep—dismissing at a stroke the connection between sleep and shelter, not to mention the production for exchange of such outlandish items as beds and mattresses.

This book would be an amusing novelty if indulgent, dead-end narratives like it had not become such a banality on the left. Faced with a world in turmoil and a continuing employers' offensive socialists need to be armed with clear analysis—they will not find it here.

---

* Reduced, we might note, only in comparison to the post Second World War period of the "long boom" during which shorter working hours had been won by workers' struggle.

Workers against the slaughter

Tony Phillips

A W Zurbrugg (ed) **Not Our War: Writings against the First World War** *(Merlin, 2014), £12.95*

Not our War is the perfect antidote to renewed attempts by the spokespersons of the ruling class such as Michael Gove and Jeremy Paxman to rehabilitate the First World War as a war for democracy. The book is an anthology of voices, ranging from those of revolutionary Marxists, anarchists and syndicalists to pacifists and feminists raised against the slaughter both before and during the war.

Predictably, the official coverage of the war's anniversary minimises and distorts where it does not actually write out of history the opposition to the war. A BBC documentary shown earlier this year claimed that the 1916 Easter Rising and the October Revolution were both organised by German military intelligence! The left, while initially isolated and demoralised by the shock of the capitulation of the leaders of socialist parties and trade unions in most belligerent nations in August 1914, grew into a mighty revolutionary tide that eventually ended the war.

The outbreak of the war did not come out of the blue as conventional accounts suggest. This book makes it very clear that there was widespread concern on the left about the rise of militarism and increasing international tensions in the years before 1914. The book includes an extract from the famous resolution of the Stuttgart Congress of the Second International of socialist parties in 1907 that states that it is the duty of socialists to "use the economic and political crisis created by the war to rouse the masses and thereby to hasten the downfall of the capitalist class"(p45).

However, the resolution also hints at confusion over the roots of the impending conflict, referring to the need for international arbitration and disarmament to avert the war. The French socialist leader Jean Jaurès is quoted arguing that democratisation of the army would prevent aggressive war while arguing that a defensive war is justified.

One of the strengths of the book is that it includes the views of colonial peoples. Many leaders of the Second International had, at best, a patronising and, at worst, a racist view of the inhabitants of the colonies. India and Egypt were pillaged to support the war effort. The people of Cairo were brutalised by occupying Australian troops, which fuelled the independence movement after the war. Colonial troops and, in the case of the US Army, black American soldiers were subject to brutal racism by their officers.

The most inspiring section of the book brings together the voices of those who continued to oppose the war once it started. The leaders of the Second International were not the only leaders of the left to support their own ruling class. The syndicalist leaders of the French CGT union and the "father of anarchism" Peter Kropotkin all swung behind the war effort. The book contains a passionate demolition by US anarchists Emma Goldman and Alexander Berkman of Kropotkin's argument that the most important thing was to defeat German militarism.

The collection covers the first strikes and protests against the effects of the war including the Munitions of War Act which militarised industry in Britain and led to the founding of the rank and file Clyde Workers' Committee. This chapter brings out the growing clarity of the initially beleaguered revolutionaries who kept their heads and their principles. The resolution of the left wing of the anti-war conference held in Zimmerwald in 1915 makes it clear that the war was an imperialist conflict for the redivision of the colonial spoils and that the only way to end it was to struggle for socialism.

The resolution of the follow up conference at Kienthal the following year notes prophetically, "There will be further intensification of the struggle against war and imperialism as a consequence of the ruination and suffering brought on by the calamities of this imperialist age" (p 193). Lenin argues that the key task is to turn the imperialist war into a revolutionary war. There are powerful quotations from the writings and speeches of Rosa Luxemburg, Leon Trotsky, John Maclean, James Connolly and Dušan Popovic from the Serbian SPD, the only socialist party to vote against the war in its national assembly from the start.

The revolutionary struggles in Russia and Germany that ended the war are reflected in statements from the sailors of Kronstadt and Kiel. You won't find their names on any monument, but these were among the true heroes of the First World War. The proclamation of the Military Revolutionary Committee of the Petrograd Soviet to the Russian army announcing the overthrow of the Kerensky government by the workers is quoted: "The Petrograd Soviet interprets the programme of the new government as: immediate proposals of a general democratic peace, immediate transfer of the great landed estates to the peasants and the honest convocation of the constituent assembly."

While the book includes some fiery anti-militarist rhetoric, particularly from French syndicalists, militarism is portrayed as something distinct from contemporary capitalism rather than being inherent in the system in the epoch of imperialism. It is a pity that there are no extracts from Rudolf Hilferding's *Finance Capital*, Luxemburg's *The Accumulation of Capital* or even the Liberal John Hobson's *Imperialism*, all published in this period, which contain material that points towards the link between the rise of militarism and the growing international conflicts over sources of raw materials, markets and investment opportunities.

I noticed a couple of mistakes. Karl Liebknecht is quoted as opposing a general strike against war when in fact it was his father, Wilhelm. Maclean's close comrade was called Harry not Henry McShane. However, these are minor quibbles in a book that is a great resource for arguments against those who want to justify the war on its 100th anniversary.

bookmarks

the socialist bookshop 020 7637 1848
1 bloomsbury street london wc1b 3qe
www.bookmarksbookshop.co.uk

read.learn.fight

Britain's leading bookshop for radical books

From climate change to anti-war, from black struggle to histories of uprisings in every part of the world.

Visit our shop or buy online to support bookselling independent of the big chains. We can provide any title currently in print and give advice on a wide range of topics from multicultural children's books to Marxism, economics and philosophy.

Bookmarks provides stalls at trade union conferences and campaign meetings. Let us know if you would like us to supply books for your organisation or event.

Pick of the quarter

The most recent issue of *Socialism and Democracy* celebrates the 150th anniversary of The First International. Marcello Musto recalls the history of the International and Patrick Bond traces the history of and barriers to working class internationalism in South Africa from the apartheid era to today. Tony Daley's article in the same issue addresses the extraordinary attempts made by German-owned T-Mobile USA to harass its call centre workers and prevent them from forming a trade union.

The latest *History Workshop Journal* (issue 78) features a free access article by Charles Forsdick and Christian Høgsbjerg on the Soviet film director Sergei Eisenstein's project to make a film about the Haitian Revolution. The film, set to star Paul Robeson, was never completed, becoming "one of the great unmade films of the 20th century". Forsdick and Høgsbjerg show how the attempt to portray the Haitian Revolution took on a new significance in the context of the shifting power struggles within the Soviet Union of the 1930s as counter-revolution took hold and Eisenstein himself was increasingly subject to censorship.

The same issue also includes an interesting article by Catherine Hall which raises timely and thought-provoking questions about the historiography of slavery on the 70th anniversary of the publication of Eric Williams's classic *Capitalism and Slavery*.

The latest issue of *New Left Review* (II/88) includes some interesting pieces. An interview with Gleb Pavlovsky, ex-adviser to Vladimir Putin, is revealing about the Russian president's ultra-capitalist worldview:

"He understood the coming of capitalism in a Soviet way. We were all taught that capitalism is a kingdom of demagogues, behind whom stands big money, and behind that, a military machine which aspires to control the whole world. It's a very clear, simple picture which I think Putin had in his head—not as an official ideology, but as a form of common sense. His thinking was that in the Soviet Union, we were idiots; we had tried to build a fair society when we should have been making money. If we had made more money than the Western capitalists, we could have just bought them up, or we could have created a weapon which they didn't have. That's all there is to it. It was a game and we lost, because we didn't do several simple things: we didn't create our own class of capitalists, we didn't give the capitalist predators on our side a chance to develop and devour the capitalist predators on theirs."

The same issue carries an important 1961 lecture by Jean-Paul Sartre on Marxism and subjectivity. It includes a critique of Georg Lukács's *History and Class Consciousness* and is introduced by Fredric Jameson.

AC & CR